ENGLISH PRONUNCIATION EXERCISES

for

Japanese Students

HARRIETTE GORDON GRATE

PRENTICE HALL REGENTS, Englewood Cliffs, NJ 07632

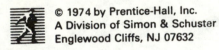 © 1974 by Prentice-Hall, Inc.
A Division of Simon & Schuster
Englewood Cliffs, NJ 07632

Printed in the United States of America

10 9 8 7 6 5 4 3 2

ISBN 0-13-281296-7 01

Prentice-Hall International (UK) Limited, *London*
Prentice-Hall of Australia Pty. Limited, *Sydney*
Prentice-Hall Canada Inc., *Toronto*
Prentice-Hall Hispanoamericana, S.A., *Mexico*
Prentice-Hall of India Private Limited, *New Delhi*
Prentice-Hall of Japan, Inc., *Tokyo*
Simon & Schuster Asia Pte. Ltd., *Singapore*
Editora Prentice-Hall do Brasil, Ltda., *Rio de Janeiro*

TABLE OF CONTENTS

REDUCED FORMS

ADDITIONAL CHART EXERCISES

INTONATION

Introduction

This book provides materials and procedures for intensive practice in English pronunciation, focusing on those sounds which most frequently present difficulty for Japanese students. Common intonation patterns and reduced forms are included. The format for the presentation of vowel and consonant phonemes is a unique combination of chart and sentence exercises. Ample practice material relieves the teacher of the necessity of preparing supplementary exercises. A special feature is a diagnostic test to help identify each student's particular problems.

The book is the product of eight years' experience with Japanese students; the exercises have been extensively tested and have proved highly effective at all levels of study — elementary, intermediate, and advanced. Recordings on cassettes of the exercises are available for use in the classroom, language laboratory, and home. A separate booklet of instructions in Japanese has been prepared by Professor Ikuo Koike of Sophia University.

Consonants, vowels, and reduced forms are dealt with in separate sections. Intonation lessons appear at intervals throughout the text; for convenient reference they are listed as a group at the end of the Table of Contents.

Phonemic symbols are used in lesson heads, sub-heads, and sound production instructions. The symbols are enclosed in brackets; contrasted sounds are separated by a slash: [l/r], [ð/θ], etc. Consonants are represented by IPA symbols; vowel symbols are based on the Trager-Smith system.

Consonants:

[p]	poor, happy, soap
[b]	buy, habit, stub
[k]	key, packer, joke
[g]	go, bigger, egg
[t]	tie, butter, ate
[d]	do, wedding, add
[h]	how, reheat
[hw]	when, awhile
[w]	we, away
[f]	for, taffy, wife
[v]	van, over, save
[s]	so, nicer, miss
[z]	zoo, easy, maze

[ʃ]	show, pushing, ash
[ʒ]	Asian, rouge
[tʃ]	chop, catcher, each
[dʒ]	joy, badger, age
[θ]	thank, method, mouth
[ð]	there, rather, bathe
[l]	low, sailor, heel
[r]	ray, sorry, air
[m]	my, hammer, some
[n]	no, any, on
[ŋ]	singer, long
[y]	yes, reunion

Vowels:

[i]	bit
[e]	bet
[æ]	bat
[ʌ]	but
[ə]	banana
[a]	box
[u]	book
[ɔ]	bought
[iy]	beet
[ey]	bate
[ay]	bite
[oy]	boy
[uw]	boot
[ow]	boat
[aw]	out

Contrast Lessons

In the consonant and vowel sections, the majority of the lessons contrast phonemes which the student at first may find difficult to differentiate. The aim of the contrast is fourfold: (1) to help the student to hear the difference between the sounds; (2) to make him aware that this difference is significant in English — that if we substitute one sound for the other, we change the meaning of an utterance; (3) to teach him to make each of the sounds distinctly; and (4) to enable him to shift easily and accurately from one sound to another.

In some lessons, the phoneme comparison is intended to stress similarities rather than differences: for example, to show that [f] and [v] have the same articulation, or that [t] and [d] between vowels may sound virtually the same. Released initial stops are contrasted with unreleased final stops, pointing up a distinction which does not affect meaning but which is important to good pronunciation.

i

Lesson Format

The standard contrast lesson appears on facing pages. Sound production instructions and profile diagrams appear at the top of the left-hand page. (The speech organs referred to in the instructions are identified in the diagram on page xi). Below the diagrams and instructions is the Contrast Chart; this is an aggregation of minimal or near-minimal pairs, so arranged that one can read across the odd-numbered lines to practice one sound, across the even-numbered lines to practice the other sound, and down to contrast the two sounds. On the opposite page are four groups of sentences: A, B, C, and D. In each group, the sound pattern of the sentences corresponds to a specific chart procedure. Italicized instructions on the sentence page indicate the practice procedures to be followed.

Practice Procedure

Example: Lesson 1: [l/r] in Initial Position (pp. 2-3)

Step 1: Listening. The student listens as the teacher gives examples of the two sounds: several [l]–words, several [r]–words, then a number of [l/r] minimal pairs. (These examples can be taken from the contrast chart: read line 1, then line 2, then vertical pairs across.)

Step 2: Practicing Initial [l]. The student studies the instructions for making [l] and the profile diagram on the left, noting the position of the tongue, lips, and jaws. Following instruction A on page 3, he reads the odd-numbered lines of the chart, repeating each word after the teacher or the voice on the tape. In each line, he practices [l] before a different vowel: line 1 — *lay, laid, lake* . . . ; line 3 — *leaf, leave, lead* . . . ; etc. The words are short and the pace is brisk; in two or three minutes of practice the student has 54 opportunities to achieve and maintain production of the sound. (If additional practice is needed, he can be asked to read the [l]–words in each column.) Upon completing the chart practice, he turns to page 3 and reads the ten sentences in group A, repeating each one after the teacher. Each of these short sentences contains four words beginning with [l]; initial [r] is excluded.

Step 3: Practicing Initial [r]. The practice procedure for [r] parallels that for [l]. The student studies the instructions for making [r] and the profile diagram on the right. Following instruction B on page 3, he reads the even-numbered lines of the chart, repeating each word after the teacher. He then reads the ten sentences in group B, again imitating the teacher's pronunciation. Each of these short sentences contains three or four words beginning with [r]; initial [l] is excluded.

Step 4: Contrasting [l]–*sentences with* [r]–*sentences.* In this exercise, the student begins to practice shifting from [l] to [r] and back again. He is instructed to reread the sentences from groups A and B, but this time to read across the page (A1, B1, etc.) so that an [r]–sentence follows each [l]–sentence. As he is already familiar with the material, the student may be allowed to read by himself, with the teacher intervening only to correct errors. (This exercise may, if desired, be preceded by chart practice: have the student read the chart lines in consecutive order, thus alternating [l]–lines with [r]–lines.)

Step 5: Contrasting [l]–*words with* [r]–*words.* The student next contrasts [l] with [r] by reading a large number of minimal pairs. Following instruction C, he reads vertical pairs across the chart (A1–2: *lay–ray*; B1–2: *laid–raid*; etc.), repeating each pair after the teacher. As the exercise proceeds, the teacher gradually increases the speed of the shift. The student then reads the ten sentences in Group C, again imitating the teacher's pronunciation. Each of these short sentences contains two minimal or near-minimal pairs.

Step 6: Minimal pair review and longer [l/r] *sentences.* Following instruction D, the student reads down each column of the chart, practicing [l] and [r] before a different vowel in each pair. He may be able to perform the exercise unaided, with occasional correction from the teacher; or he may be asked to imitate the teacher's pronunciation in one column and then read the next column by himself. Finally, he reads the ten sentences in group D, repeating each one after the teacher. These are longer sentences in which [l]–words alternate with [r]–words.

Shorter Contrast Lessons

Where less extensive practice is required, a complete contrast lesson may appear on a single page. The practice procedure is in most cases the same as that outlined above; in a few cases it is abbreviated. At the back of the book are additional consonant contrast lessons consisting of chart exercises only.

Multiple-contrast Lessons

Vowels, like consonants, are presented in contrast pairs. With two exceptions, each vowel is contrasted with several other vowels; these overlapping contrasts are summarized in multiple-contrast review lessons. Each review consists of a chart and ten sentences. The chart is composed of minimal or near-minimal sets (*ought–out–Ott–oat*, etc.).

Non-contrast Lessons

Where a sound presents difficulty only in certain phonetic environments, it is helpful to make the sound first in an "easy" environment, then to repeat it in the difficult one. This approach is taken in those lessons which deal with a single target sound. The four types of procedure used are described below.

Momentum Exercises

Method: The student's ability to make the target consonant in final position is used to facilitate production of the consonant in initial position.

Applications: The student is likely to confuse the consonants [s] and [ʃ] before the vowels [i] and [iy]. As these consonants are not normally confused when they are in final position, we can use final [s] to facilitate production of initial [si] and [siy] (*less sick*; *Miss Seeley*), and final [ʃ] to aid in the production of initial [ʃi] and [ʃiy] (*rush Schick*; *wish she*). Similarly, [w] before [u] may be difficult, but final [uw] is not; hence we can use final [uw] to help in the production of initial [wu] (*who would*).

Reinforcement Exercises

Method: The student's ability to make the target consonant before most vowels is used to facilitate production of the consonant before certain "problem" vowels.

Applications: As noted above, the student is likely to confuse [s] with [ʃ] before the vowels [i] and [iy]; he is also likely to drop [w] before the vowel [u], pronouncing *would* [wud] as [ud]). As these consonants present no difficulty before other vowels, correct production can be promoted by preceding each "problem-vowel" word with a similar "easy-vowel" word (*sop–sip, so–see*; *shop–ship, show–she*; *will–wool, wade–wood*).

Buildup Exercises

Method: The student's ability to make the target consonant in initial position is used to facilitate production of the consonant in initial clusters.

Applications: Even after mastering [l] and [r] in initial position, the student is likely to confuse the two sounds when they occur in initial consonant clusters. Correct pronunciation is facilitated by preceding each [l]–cluster word with a similar initial–[l] word (*led–bled, lam–clam*) and each [r]–cluster word with a similar initial–[r] word (*wrench–French, raid–grade*). The student is also likely to drop [w] when it is part of a consonant cluster. Since [w] poses no difficulty in initial position (except before [u]), retention of the sound in clusters is promoted by preceding each [w]–cluster word with a similar initial–[w] word (*win–twin, wade–swayed*).

Step-down Exercises

Method: The student's ability to make the target consonant in medial position is used to facilitate production of the consonant in final position.

Applications: The student normally has no difficulty with medial [n], but he is likely to substitute an indistinct nasal sound for final [n]. Similarly, even after mastering the distinction between [ʒ] and [dʒ] in medial position, he may substitute [ʒ] (or [tʃ]) for [dʒ] in final position. Correct production of the final consonant is facilitated by preceding each final–[n] word with a similar medial–[n] word (*penny–pen, gunner–gun*), and each final–[dʒ] word with a similar medial–[dʒ] word (*budget–budge, rigid–ridge*).

Intonation Lessons.

Twelve lessons provide intensive practice in important intonation patterns. The lessons are sequentially developed and should be studied in the order of their appearance.

Pattern Markings. A contour line with pitch numbers appears above each group of practice sentences. In the sentences themselves, the primary stress of each phrase is marked ′. Where the practice sentences contain more than one phrase, the contour line is broken between phrases, and a comma or a slash indicates the phrase division in each sentence.

Pattern Numbers. Intonation patterns are referred to by the numbers of the pitch sequence: *the 231 pattern,* etc. The symbol ⌣ is added to indicate a rise at the end of the phrase: *23⌣,* etc. For sentences with more than one phrase, the phrase division is indicated by a slash: *232⌣/231,* etc. Parentheses inserted in the pattern number indicate that the enclosed pitch occurs in some, but not all, of the practice sentences: *23⌣(2)3⌣/231.*

My deep appreciation to Robert A. Grate of English for the Japanese Businessman for preparing the profile diagrams, sound production instructions, and intonation exercises.

iv

Diagnostic Test

To the Teacher: This test is designed to identify those sounds which the student needs to practice. It can also serve as an indicator of his progress during the course. Each student should be tested individually. It is suggested that you exchange books with him so that you can mark the problem sounds in his copy. Ask him to read vertical pairs across (or single lines where there is no contrast). Since this is a test, not practice, do not provide a model for him to imitate. Where remedial practice is required, put a check mark in the space provided. The last column indicates the lesson to be practiced for each sound or contrast pair. During the course, as the student masters each sound in turn, he can be instructed to circle the appropriate check mark.

Consonants					(✔)	Lesson Number
[l/r]: initial	lay ray	lush rush	leap reap	load road	_____	1
[l/r]: medial	belly berry	stealing steering	pilot pirate	tally tarry	_____	5
[l/r]: final	pool poor	fail fair	tile tire	owl our	_____	6
[l/r]: clusters	bleed breed	clam cram	glow grow	flock frock	_____	2, 3, 4
[k]: final (unaspirated)	shack	ache	book	sock	_____	7
[g]: final (unreleased)	egg	bag	pig	dog	_____	8
[p]: final (unreleased)	keep	soap	top	up	_____	9
[b]: final (unreleased)	tub	cab	ebb	fib	_____	10
[t]: final (unreleased)	note	eight	might	got	_____	11

Consonants					(✔)	Lesson Number
[d] : final (unreleased)	shed	made	odd	sad	____	12
Unreleased stops before consonants	necktie tugboat	napkin rubdown	football redcoat	lockjaw dragnet	____	13
[kit/kt] : final	packet pact	bucket bucked	ticket ticked	pocket pocked	____	105
[t/d] : suffixes	backed bagged	mopped mobbed	raced raised	searched surged	____	51
[t/d] : flap	biting biding	mutter mudder	heated heeded	coat it code it	____	14
flap / [r]	catty carry	medic Merrick	Betty berry	paddy parry	____	15
[d/r] : unstressed prefixes	detain retain	deject reject	devise revise	demote remote	____	16
[h/f] : initial	who'd food	halt fault	her fur	horse force	____	20
[hw/f] : initial	whit fit	whether feather	whine fine	wheat feet	____	21
[f/v] : initial	fan van	fear veer	few view	fine vine	____	22
[f/v] : final	leaf leave	half have	waif wave	proof prove	____	23
[b/v] : initial	best vest	boat vote	buy vie	bays vase	____	24
[b/v] : medial	fiber fiver	saber savor	curbing curving	gabble gavel	____	25
[b/v] : final	jibe jive	dub dove	Gibb give	ebb Ev	____	26
[v/w] : initial	vent went	vein wane	vault Walt	vise wise	____	99
[w/hw] : initial	witch which	wet whet	were whir	wine whine	____	98
[wu]	wood	wool	woman	wolf	____	18

Consonants					(✔)	Lesson Number
[w] : clusters	dwell	swan	quake	twin	_____	19
[si/ʃi]	sip ship	sill shill	sin shin	simmer shimmer	_____	28, 29, 30
[siy/ʃiy]	see she	seat sheet	seep sheep	seen sheen	_____	31, 32, 33
[hi/ʃi]	hip ship	him shim	hill shill	hint shin	_____	100
[hiy/ʃiy]	he she	heap sheep	heat sheet	heed she'd	_____	100
[ʃ/ʒ] : medial	mesher measure	Asher azure	vicious vision	Haitian Asian	_____	103
[z/ʒ] : medial	fusing fusion	visit vision	using usual	closing closure	_____	104
[ʒ/dʒ] : medial	lesion legion	Asian aging	version virgin	visual vigil	_____	43
[tʃ/dʒ] : initial	chest jest	choke joke	chain Jane	chump jump	_____	106
[tʃ/dʒ] : final	etch edge	march Marge	catch cadge	perch purge	_____	107
[t/tʃ] : initial	tin chin	tease cheese	too chew	tier cheer	_____	47
[d/dʒ] : initial	din gin	deep jeep	deuce juice	dear jeer	_____	46
[d/z] : initial	dip zip	dean Zena	do zoo	dear zero	_____	48
[ð/z]	then Zen	than zander	withered wizard	scythe size	_____	39
[ð/d]	they day	those doze	heather header	bathe bayed	_____	40
[ð/θ]	thy thigh	that thatch	either ether	teethe teeth	_____	38
[ʃ/θ] : initial	Shaw thaw	shirred third	shy thigh	shorn thorn	_____	102

Consonants						Lesson Number
[t/θ] : initial	tug thug	tank thank	tie thigh	toad Thoden	_____	101
[s/θ] : initial	sigh thigh	saw thaw	sink think	sunder thunder	_____	35
[s/θ] : final	mass math	tense tenth	face faith	niece neath	_____	36
[s] + [θ]	worse things Worth sings	Bess thought Beth sought	Smith's thanks sixth sank		_____	37
[s/z] : final	dose doze	peace peas	ice eyes	face faze	_____	111
[s/z] : suffixes	safes saves	picks pigs	oats odes	bets beds	_____	49
[s] : final clusters	gifts	acts	costs	asks	_____	112
[iz] : suffix	sizes	guesses	dishes	matches	_____	50
[n/m] : final	then them	bean beam	gain game	dine dime	_____	108
[n/ŋ] : final	fan fang	win wing	stun stung	kin king	_____	53
[g/ŋ] : medial	bagging banging	swigging swinging	gagster gangster	digger dinghy	_____	54
[g/ŋ] : final	wig wing	lug lung	sag sang	hug hung	_____	109
[g/ŋg] : medial	hugger hunger	figure finger	bigger bingo	juggle jungle	_____	55
[ŋ/ŋg] : medial	flinger finger	tangy tangle	youngish younger	dinghy dingle	_____	110

Vowels					(✔)	Lesson Number
[iy/i]	eat it	bead bid	keen kin	peek pick	_____	57
[i/e]	itch etch	chick check	miss mess	bid bed	_____	58
[ey/e]	age edge	stain sten	wait wet	chase chess	_____	61
[ey/æ]	aim am	fate fat	pace pass	main man	_____	62
[æ/e]	and end	pack peck	ham hem	sat set	_____	63
[æ/a]	add odd	hat hot	jab job	band bond	_____	66
[æ/ʌ]	ankle uncle	mad mud	back buck	staff stuff	_____	67
[ʌ/a]	utter otter	duck dock	nut not	sub sob	_____	68
[ʌ/e]	hum hem	muss mess	chuck check	bug beg	_____	69
[ow/a]	own on	hope hop	goat got	soak sock	_____	72
[a/aw]	otter outer	fond found	shot shout	pond pound	_____	73
[ow/aw]	hoe how	no now	tone town	coach couch	_____	74
[ow/ɔ]	so saw	coast cost	boat bought	woke walk	_____	75
[ɔ/a]	hawk hock	dawn Don	caught cot	yawn yon	_____	76
[ɔ/ʌ]	song sung	long lung	chalk chuck	fawn fun	_____	79
[ʌ/u]	tuck took	buck book	stud stood	shudder should	_____	80

Vowels					(✔)	Lesson Number
[ɔ/or]	Shaw shore	sauce source	fought fort	pause pores	_____	83
[ɔ/ər]	saw sir	walk work	toss terse	cost cursed	_____	84
[ər/or]	herd hoard	turn torn	shirt short	worm warm	_____	35
[a/ar]	hot heart	dock dark	shop sharp	God guard	_____	88
[ar/ər]	far fur	barn burn	hard heard	cart curt	_____	89

The Organs of Speech

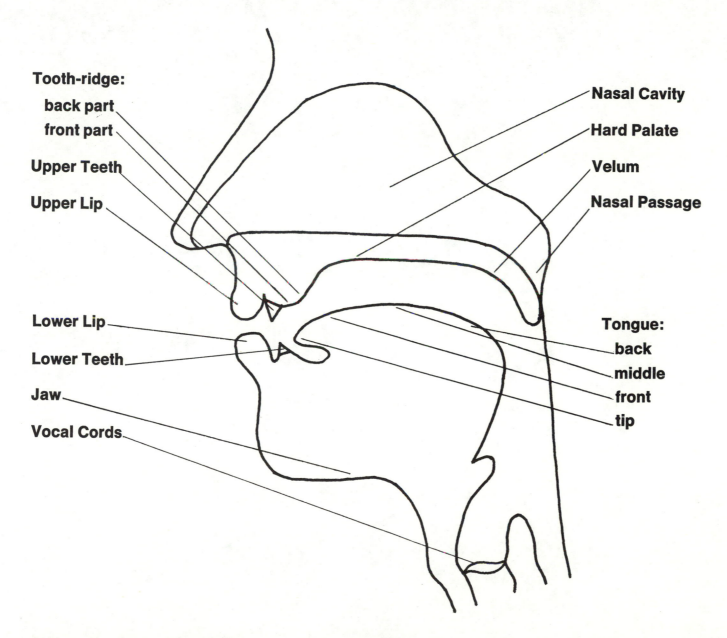

Tooth-ridge:
back part
front part
Upper Teeth
Upper Lip
Lower Lip
Lower Teeth
Jaw
Vocal Cords

Nasal Cavity
Hard Palate
Velum
Nasal Passage
Tongue:
back
middle
front
tip

Voiced sounds are produced with the vocal cords nearly closed and vibrating. Voiceless sounds are made with the vocal cords open. In the profile diagrams, a vibrating line (⌇⌇) indicates that the sound is voiced; dashes (——) indicate that it is voiceless.

Where production of the sound involves movement of the tongue, lips, or jaw, the starting position is shown by a solid line, the direction of movement by an arrow, and the final position by a broken line.

CONSONANTS

LESSON 1
[l/r] *in Initial Position*

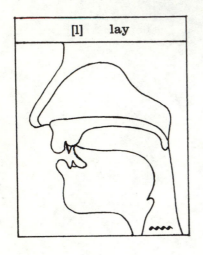

To make [l], touch the tooth-ridge with the tip of the tongue, and let the voiced air stream pass over the turned-down sides of the tongue.

To make [r], curl the tip of the tongue up and back so that it points toward the hard palate without touching it; round the lips very slightly. Let the voiced air stream pass between tongue tip and palate.

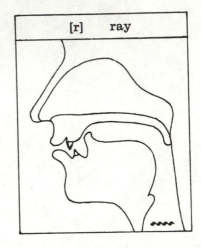

Contrast Chart

	A	B	C	D	E	F
1.	lay	laid	lake	lain	lace	late
2.	ray	raid	rake	rain	race	rate
3.	leap	lease	lead	leak	leaf	leach
4.	reap	Reece	read	reek	reef	reach
5.	life	lime	line	lice	light	lies
6.	rife	rhyme	Rhine	rice	right	rise
7.	low	lone	lobe	loam	load	lope
8.	roe	roan	robe	roam	road	rope
9.	loom	loot	lose	loosed	loon	lewd
10.	room	root	ruse	roost	rune	rude
11.	lash	lag	lamb	lap	lack	land
12.	rash	rag	ram	rap	rack	Rand
13.	lend	led	lest	let	left	lex
14.	rend	red	rest	ret	reft	rex
15.	lit	lick	lip	lid	list	limb
16.	writ	Rick	rip	rid	wrist	rim
17.	lug	lust	Lunt	lush	lump	luck
18.	rug	rust	runt	rush	rump	ruck

Contrast Exercises

A. *In the CHART on the opposite page, read the odd-numbered lines across (1, 3, 5, etc.). Then read the SENTENCES below.*

1. Linton's late for his language lesson.
2. The lame lion lay on the ledge.
3. Leah lost the love letter.
4. Let the lad lead his own life.
5. Can't Lenny light the lamp later?
6. I liked Latin a lot less.
7. Lucy loves lemon and lime sodas.
8. Who was Lloyd's last leading lady?
9. He laughed at the legend of the Lost Lagoon.
10. Luke limps on his left leg.

B. *In the CHART on the opposite page, read the even-numbered lines across (2, 4, 6, etc.). Then read the SENTENCES below.*

1. It's the wrong rhythm for a romantic song.
2. Rodney wrenched his right wrist.
3. Take the ramp to reach Ridge Road.
4. Rex was ready to raise the roof.
5. The rangers rushed to the rescue.
6. Reggie ran the risk of wrecking it.
7. The rain rusted Ryan's rake.
8. Reuben reads the *Rochester Register*.
9. There's no rhyme or reason to Randy's reaction.
10. Rhoda ruined the rib roast.

Now read SENTENCES alternately from A and B above (A1,B1; A2,B2; A3,B3; etc.).

C. *In the CHART on the opposite page, read vertical pairs across (A1–2, B1–2, C1–2, etc.). Then read the SENTENCES below.*

1. Raft laughed at Ray's laziness.
2. At least Reece is less restive.
3. Rider lied about Lee's reasons.
4. I lent the rent to Roger's lodger.
5. Ross lost the lady's radio.
6. Riker likes to write light verse.
7. Leeds reads a lot of rot.
8. The rookie looked in Rocky's locker.
9. Lake raked the wrong lawn.
10. Reeve's leaving the rest to Lester.

D. *In the CHART on the opposite page, read down each column. Then read the SENTENCES below.*

1. Let's do a remake of "The Long Red Line."
2. The Richmond Larks racked up eleven runs.
3. Ralph stayed in London for the rest of his leave.
4. I'd rather get Libby's recipe for lamb and rice.
5. The lawyer recommended litigation to recover our losses.
6. At last report, the lieutenant was ready to leave the regiment.
7. Remington's landlord repaired the leaky roof.
8. The long ride left Rita a little ragged.
9. Lydia's roommate is listening to records in the lounge.
10. The lamb roamed the low rocks looking for roots.

LESSON 2
[l] *in Initial Clusters*

When pronouncing a consonant cluster ending in [l] (like the [spl] of *split* or the [gl] of *glow*), be sure that the tongue actually touches the tooth-ridge to form [l]. Also, take care not to insert a vowel before [l]: *blade* is [bleyd], not [bəleyd]. To avoid this, begin to move the tongue tip toward the tooth-ridge while making the preceding sound.

Buildup Exercises

Read each section below as follows: In the CHART, read vertical pairs across (A1–2, B1–2, etc.), forming the [l] of the second word like the initial [l] of the first; then read line 2. Next read the SENTENCES.

		A	B	C	D	E	F
The [bl] Cluster:	1.	lade	lead	light	lock	land	luster
	2.	blade	bleed	blight	block	bland	bluster

a) Lane Blaine is at Lake Blake.
b) It's a low blow to the local blokes.
c) The blond's blouse is blue and black.
d) Is that blood on Bligh's blotter?

		A	B	C	D	E	F
The [kl] Cluster:	1.	lamb	left	lick	loud	lot	leave
	2.	clam	cleft	click	cloud	clot	cleave

a) It's Lana Clancy's last class.
b) Lyon's client is Lady Clayton.
c) Clint claims he climbed the cliff.
d) One clue was the clock in the clothes closet.

		A	B	C	D	E	F
The [fl] Cluster:	1.	lie	lee	low	lute	lap	led
	2.	fly	flee	flow	flute	flap	fled

a) That's Linda Flynn's little flivver.
b) At least Fleeson sees the law's flaws.
c) Flint flipped the flimsy flask.
d) The flock floundered in the flash flood.

		A	B	C	D	E	F
The [gl] Cluster:	1.	loss	laze	loam	land	lean	listen
	2.	gloss	glaze	gloam	gland	glean	glisten

a) Lance glanced at the last glass.
b) Lend Glenda those lovely gloves.
c) A glowworm glimmered in the gloomy glade.
d) There's a glob of glue on Glidden's globe.

4

	A	B	C	D	E	F
The [pl] **Cluster:** 1.	ledge	luck	loom	lank	lace	lop
2.	pledge	pluck	plume	plank	place	plop

a) Liza applied at the Lansing plant.

b) "Lee, please," Lena pleaded.

c) The planter plans to plow the plot.

d) The Plummers sent plastic plates and platters.

	A	B	C	D	E	F
The [sl] **Cluster:** 1.	lab	led	low	lot	lug	link
2.	slab	sled	slow	slot	slug	slink

a) Later Slater would lie slyly about it.

b) It lashed and slashed at Lou's sloop.

c) Slade slept the sleep of the just.

d) We slipped and slid down the slope.

	A	B	C	D	E	F
The [spl] **Cluster:** 1.	litter	line	lint	lash	lend	latter
2.	splitter	spline	splint	splash	splendor	splatter

a) I saw the last splashdown.

b) He lay splayed out.

c) They splurged on a splendid split-level home.

d) Splaine spliced the splintered spars.

Review Exercises

	A	B	C	D	E
1.	blade	bleat	Bligh'd	blat	blip
2.	Clay'd	cleat	Clyde	clatter	clip
3.	flayed	fleet	fly	flat	flip
4.	glade	glee	glide	glad	glib
5.	played	pleat	plied	platter	Plymouth
6.	Slade	sleet	slide	slat	slip
7.	splayed	spleen	splice	splat	split

A. *In the CHART above, read across each line. Then read the SENTENCES below.*

1. Block was blinded by the blast.
2. Claudia clasped the clinging cloak.
3. I flayed the flounder and flipped the flap-jacks.
4. We got a glimpse of Glen's glider.
5. The plaza is a pleasant place to play.
6. Sloane slipped a slug in the slot.
7. The Splandings' ball had more splash than splendor.

B. *In the CHART above, read down each column. Then read the SENTENCES below.*

1. Fletcher's gladiolas are in splendid bloom.
2. Please clean Glynn's black flannel slacks.
3. Bliss flew the plane clear to Glasgow.
4. I'd like a platter of bluefish and clams with a glass of wine.
5. Gladys plans to display the sleds.
6. Our class play was Slocum's "Glass Splinter."
7. Blanding bought the plants for the Slaterville Flower Club.

LESSON 3

[r] *in Initial Clusters*

When making [r] at the end of a consonant cluster (as in the [spr] of *sprint*), be sure that the tip of the tongue does *not* touch anything. Also, take care not to insert a vowel before [r]: *braid* is [breyd], not [bəreyd]. To avoid this, begin to round the lips, and —where possible—to curl the tongue into [r] position, while making the preceding sound.

Buildup Exercises

Read each section below as follows: In the CHART, read vertical pairs across (A1–2, B1–2, etc.), forming the [r] of the second word like the initial [r] of the first; then read line 2. Next read the SENTENCES.

		A	B	C	D	E	F
The [br] **Cluster:**	1.	raid	rat	rest	rude	rock	rouse
	2.	braid	brat	breast	brood	brock	browse

a) Rider's bride writes bright rhymes.

b) Ridgeway's in Bridgeport renting Brent's home.

c) She's bringing brown bread for breakfast.

d) My brother brought it to a broker in the Bronx.

The [kr] **Cluster:**	1.	rack	rain	reed	rhyme	rose	ram
	2.	crack	crane	creed	crime	crows	cram

a) The rowdy crowd made Ross cross.

b) Ray's crazy about Raft's craft.

c) I found some crushed crumpets and cracker crumbs.

d) Crawford's crew created this crisis.

The [dr] **Cluster:**	1.	roan	rain	red	ram	rouse	raw
	2.	drone	drain	dread	dram	drowse	draw

a) Rudy drew a ragged dragon.

b) Riker's driving Riggs to drink.

c) Drummond's "Dragon Dreams" won the drama award.

d) Miss Drayton's dress is drip-dry.

	A	B	C	D	E	F
The [fr] Cluster: 1.	ride	reek	rate	round	wrench	rap
2.	fried	freak	freight	frowned	French	frappe

a) Rose froze the rest of the fresh meat.
b) Radin's afraid of riding on Fridays.
c) Fran's frock is frayed in front.
d) The frogman frightened Frieda's friend.

	A	B	C	D	E	F
The [gr] Cluster: 1.	rid	ripe	ram	wrist	rove	rump
2.	grid	gripe	gram	grist	grove	grump

a) Ray Grady reads Greek.
b) Roses grow round the grounds.
c) Griffin grew green grapes.
d) Graham greeted his great-grandmother.

	A	B	C	D	E	F
The [pr] Cluster: 1.	rank	rod	rune	rate	ride	robe
2.	prank	prod	prune	prate	pride	probe

a) Rader praised Roger's project.
b) Romney promised he'd rent it to Prentice.
c) It proves the President practices what he preaches.
d) The Princeton Press printed the professor's private papers.

	A	B	C	D	E	F
The [tr] Cluster: 1.	rate	ripe	ramp	rend	rim	rot
2.	trait	tripe	tramp	trend	trim	trot

a) The rest of the treasure's in a rusty trunk.
b) With wry triumph, he told Ruth the truth.
c) They transferred to a troop train at Trieste.
d) Troy tried to trace the trio.

	A	B	C	D	E	F
The [skr] Cluster: 1.	ream	rough	ram	reach	route	rim
2.	scream	scruff	scram	screech	scrutiny	scrim

a) Don't just rub it — scrub it!
b) He ripped the script out of my hands.
c) Scribner screwed the screen on.
d) They scrimped and scraped and scratched for money.

	A	B	C	D	E	F
The [spr] Cluster: 1.	rain	right	rung	writ	rue	rout
2.	sprain	sprite	sprung	sprit	sprue	sprout

a) I bought a red spread today.
b) His recent spree cost a fortune.
c) Spratt is as spry as a springbuck.
d) Sprockett sprayed the spruce.

	A	B	C	D	E	F
The [str] Cluster: 1.	robe	rate	ripe	rum	rove	reek
2.	strobe	straight	stripe	strum	strove	streak

a) Raymond strayed into Reed Street.

b) Rip it, strip it, wrap it, and strap it.

c) Striker strode straight home.

d) Strand's strategy struck me as strange.

	A	B	C	D	E	F
The [θr] Cluster: 1.	row	rust	roan	rum	rive	race
2.	throw	thrust	throne	thrum	thrive	Thrace

a) Rhett threatened to ruin Throop.

b) Ruby's through with the red thread.

c) Three thrushes thrashed about.

d) Throckmorton's throat was throbbing with pain.

	A	B	C	D	E	F
The [ʃr] Cluster: 1.	Rhine	rift	rub	rend	rove	rink
2.	shrine	shrift	shrub	shrend	shrove	shrink

a) Even men of rank shrank back.

b) If you're so rugged, shrug it off.

c) Shriver shredded the shrimp.

d) Schraft was shrewd to shroud it in mystery.

Review Exercises

	A	B	C	D	E
1.	bray	Breen	bride	brew	brittle
2.	cray	Cree	cried	crew	critter
3.	dray	dream	dried	drew	drip
4.	fray	free	fried	fruit	fritter
5.	gray	green	grind	grew	grit
6.	pray	preen	pride	Pru	pretty
7.	tray	tree	tried	true	trip
8.	scrape	screen	scribe	screw	scrip
9.	spray	spree	spry	spruce	sprig
10.	stray	stream	stride	strew	strip
11.	Thrace	three	thrice	threw	thrift
12.	Shrader	shriek	shrike	shrew	shrimp

A. *In the CHART above, read across each line. Then read the SENTENCES below.*

1. Bridget's brother broke her braces.
2. A crazed creature crept out of the crater.
3. Dryden drew the drawing-room drapes.
4. Frank was in Fresno on Friday.
5. Grant has a good grasp of Greek grammar.
6. Prepare to practice proper pronunciation.
7. The truck was trapped in Trenton traffic.
8. Scrap the "Scranton Scrapper" script.
9. Sprague sprang off the springboard.
10. The stress and strain may stretch his strength.
11. Thripp threaded through the throng.
12. Schrag got short shrift in Shreveport.

B. *In the CHART above, read down each column. Then read the SENTENCES below.*

1. Scriven's brother crossed the prairie by train.
2. The professor brought three drawings from Crete.
3. Spruitt dreamed of strange shrieking creatures.
4. They traced Shroder to 33 Spreen Street in Granite City.
5. Scripps agreed to try out for the Broadway run of "A Friday in Spring."
6. The troops dragged the frightened prisoner through the streets.
7. Cranston's prize was a free trip to Great Britain.
8. My friend dropped his scrapbook in the crowded grocery store.
9. Granny drives a pretty shrewd bargain.
10. Scrimshaw threatened to use strike-breakers to spray the crop.

9

[l/r] *in Initial Clusters*

Contrast Exercises

	A	B	C	D	E	F
1.	Blake	bleed	bloke	blew	bland	blonds
2.	brake	breed	broke	brew	brand	bronze
3.	clay	cleat	cloak	clue	clam	clock
4.	cray	Crete	croak	crew	cram	crock
5.	flay	flees	flow	flute	flap	flock
6.	fray	freeze	fro	fruit	frappe	frock
7.	glade	glean	gloat	glue	gland	glottal
8.	grade	green	groat	grew	grand	grotto
9.	plate	pleased	plosive	plume	plank	plod
10.	prate	priest	prose	prune	prank	prod
11.	splay	spleen	splice	split	splat	splotch
12.	spray	spree	spry	sprit	sprat	sprocket

A. *In the CHART above, read the odd-numbered lines across (1, 3, 5, etc.). Then read the SENTENCES below.*

1. The blizzard blew the blankets away.
2. The blue blood blushed at his blunder.

3. Claude's clad in clean clothes.
4. The Clinton Clinic is close to the Cloisters.
5. Floyd's flying to Flint on Flight 207.
6. The fleet flew the flag at half-mast.
7. They've lived in Glendale, Gloucester, and Glen Cove.
8. In the gloom, Glynn's glass gleamed.
9. Plover's play has a plodding plot.
10. Plimpton planned a pleasant day in Plymouth.
11. Splashing and spluttering, he vented his spleen.
12. He was a splendid sight, all splattered and splotched with paint.

B. *In the CHART above, read the even-numbered lines across (2, 4, 6, etc.). Then read the SENTENCES below.*

1. Brenda brushed out her brown braids.
2. Brian's brother is with the British Broadcasting Company.
3. Chris craves crisp crackers.
4. The crane crushed a crate of cranberries.
5. Frye's friend is from France.
6. The frightened frog froze on the frond.
7. Grandpa was gratified that Grace had graduated.
8. Grass is growing on grandma's grave.
9. The pro praised his proud apprentice.
10. I presume the prize was presented to Prewitt.
11. Sprigs sprout in the spring.
12. Sprag has a spread in Spruce County.

Now read SENTENCES alternately from A and B above (A1,B1; A2,B2; A3,B3; etc.).

C. *In the CHART on the opposite page, read vertical pairs across (A1–2, B1–2, C1–2, etc.). Then read the SENTENCES below.*

1. Did Blake break the black brackets?
2. There's a blue bruise on Blau's brow.
3. Kramer claims the rate of crime is climbing.
4. "Clay's crazy!" Clyde cried.
5. Fred fled from the flood.
6. Frick flicked the flea free.
7. Gleason agrees my grandma's glamorous.
8. The glad grad was a gloomy groom.
9. Miss Prentiss gets plenty of practice on plackets.
10. The players prayed the play'd be praised.
11. The springboard splintered, and Spratt fell *splat*.
12. Splaine sprained his back, and the sprinter got a splinter in his foot.

D. *In the CHART on the opposite page, read down each column. Then read the SENTENCES below.*

1. Please press my creased clothes and brush my black coat.
2. Spry splurged on a flight from Glasgow to Greenland.
3. A clean crisp breeze blew the frigate to Florida.
4. Preston's plot became crystal clear to Greenglass.
5. Greta glowed when Platte presented the fresh flowers.
6. Prescott planned the class cruise for Glasburg's graduates.
7. She bought green gloves, a brown blouse, and a crimson cloak.
8. Proctor's Place is on Broadway, a block from Flushing Avenue.
9. Bloom brought a splendid spread back from Flanders.
10. Last spring the *Splainville Chronicle* closed down.

LESSON 5

[l/r] *in Medial Position*

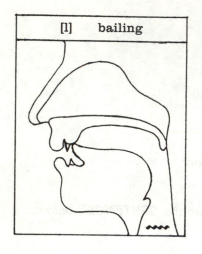

[l]   bailing

To make [l], touch the tooth-ridge with the tip of the tongue, and let the voiced air stream pass over the turned-down sides of the tongue.

To make [r], curl the tip of the tongue up and back so that it points toward the hard palate without touching it; round the lips very slightly. Let the voiced air stream pass between tongue tip and palate.

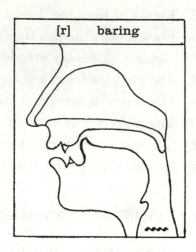

[r]   baring

Contrast Chart

	A	B	C	D	E
1.	bailing	tailing	scaling	failing	wailing
2.	baring	tearing	scaring	faring	wearing
3.	kneeling	peeling	stealing	ceiling	spieling
4.	nearing	peering	steering	searing	spearing
5.	calling	walling	bawling	stalling	galling
6.	coring	warring	boring	storing	goring
7.	galley	Bali	pally	Calley	tally
8.	Gary	Barry	parry	carry	tarry
9.	ballast	calendar	malice	balance	palace
10.	barrister	Karen	Maris	barren	Paris
11.	fallow	hallow	callow	palate	ballot
12.	Farrow	harrow	carrot	parrot	Barrett
13.	pilot	Silas	vilest	wily	Milo
14.	pirate	Cyrus	virus	wiry	Myra
15.	allay	belated	elect	Eileen	cologne
16.	array	berated	erect	Irene	Corona
17.	allegation	delegation	modulation	adulation	appellation
18.	arrogation	derogation	moderation	adjuration	aberration

12

Contrast Exercises

A. *In the CHART on the opposite page, read the odd-numbered lines across (1, 3, 5, etc.). Then read the SENTENCES below.*

1. Kelly's a highly polished fellow.
2. He's willing to allocate millions to it.
3. Allan's gaily sailing along.
4. They finally beat the Illinois bowling team.
5. Billy's always wheeling and dealing.
6. She does a daily column in the Columbia College paper.
7. Della's allowance is eleven cents.
8. The invalid's family is penniless.
9. Stella's a talented cellist.
10. Dillon's feeling awfully mellow.

B. *In the CHART on the opposite page, read the even-numbered lines across (2, 4, 6, etc.). Then read the SENTENCES below.*

1. The sheriff arrested him in Tarrytown.
2. Barry's very sorry he's married.
3. The barrister hurried to correct the error.
4. Mary's weary of worrying.
5. My parrot eats curried carrots.
6. The grand jury is inquiring into his operations.
7. Murray has an arrogant bearing.
8. Morris arranged the charity event.
9. His parents arrive in Merrick tomorrow.
10. He gave an accurate summary of its history.

Now read SENTENCES alternately from A and B above (A1,B1; A2,B2; A3,B3; etc.).

C. *In the CHART on the opposite page, read vertical pairs across (A1–2, B1–2, C1–2, etc.). Then read the SENTENCES below.*

1. Perry's pelican arrived alive.
2. Hello, Herrick. It's Cory calling.
3. Helen inherited Mrs. Daley's dairy.
4. The director was selected for his appealing appearance.
5. Paula's pouring Shelly some sherry.
6. Deering's had dealings with the Paris police.
7. He was telling Terry about feeling inferior.
8. Ellen's very jealous of Jerry.
9. Tomorrow Molly can collect the corrections.
10. Miss Seeley's serious about marrying O'Malley.

D. *In the CHART on the opposite page, read down each column. Then read the SENTENCES below.*

1. Alice arrived alone around eleven.
2. His current alibi is very silly.
3. Eric's selling herring in a delicatessen on Barrow Street.
4. She's touring Colombia, Peru, Bolivia, and Paraguay.
5. Harry was eventually arrested in Alabama for a serious crime.
6. He's feeling terrible about failing arithmetic.
7. Dora followed the story-teller around.
8. My experiments with pollutants aroused Fallon's curiosity.
9. Phyllis is preparing a gallon of cherry jelly.
10. They're scheduling the foreign policy conference for July.

LESSON 6
[l/r] *in Final Position*

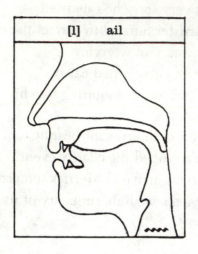

[l]   ail

For final [l], the back of the tongue is usually rather high. Otherwise, make [l] and [r] as practiced in the preceding lessons. Note: After the vowels [ey iy ay oy aw], the unstressed vowel [ə] is often inserted before final [l]: *ale* [eyəl], *eel* [iyəl], *aisle* [ayəl], *oil* [oyəl], *owl* [awəl]. After [ay] and [aw], [ə] is often inserted before final [r]: *tire* [tayər], *hour* [awər].

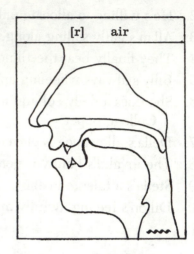

[r]   air

Contrast Chart

	A	B	C	D	E	F
1.	ail	dale	pale	mail	bail	hail
2.	air	dare	pair	mare	bare	hair
3.	veal	meal	steal	kneel	deal	teal
4.	veer	mere	steer	near	dear	tear
5.	dial	wile	tile	pile	file	mile
6.	dire	wire	tire	pyre	fire	mire
7.	mole	hole	goal	sole	stole	bowl
8.	mower	hoer	goer	sower	stower	Boer
9.	tool	pool	bool	shool	spool	jewel
10.	tour	poor	boor	sure	spoor	jure
11.	ball	call	shawl	tall	mall	wall
12.	bore	core	shore	tore	more	war
13.	foil	boil	moil	coil	toil	soil
14.	foyer	Boyer	Moyer	coyer	toyer	sawyer
15.	owl	towel	scowl	bowel	cowl	dowel
16.	our	tower	scour	bower	cower	Dower
17.	stale	fail	tale	snail	wail	scale
18.	stare	fair	tare	snare	wear	scare

14

Contrast Exercises

A. *In the CHART on the opposite page, read the odd-numbered lines across (1, 3, 5, etc.). Then read the SENTENCES below.*

1. It will entail a whole new schedule.
2. They'll all play football and baseball.
3. He took an awful spill in the school hall.
4. She'll still have the beautiful doll.
5. The full-scale model will be useful.
6. He'll need a special tool to install it.
7. Tell Al we'll sell it.
8. I'll have a small bowl of oatmeal.
9. Next fall he'll file an appeal.
10. We'll all stay until nightfall.

B. *In the CHART on the opposite page, read the even-numbered lines across (2, 4, 6, etc.). Then read the SENTENCES below.*

1. I'm sure they're somewhere near here.
2. Four pair are in the dryer now.
3. Here are some more to compare it with.
4. Where were you before the downpour?
5. He's in the cigar store over there.
6. I hear your car is for hire.
7. Mr. Dyer tore his hair.
8. They were on tour for a year.
9. Is that your souvenir from Singapore?
10. Score another for her team.

Now read SENTENCES alternately from A and B above (A1,B1; A2,B2; A3,B3; etc.).

C. *In the CHART on the opposite page, read vertical pairs across (A1–2, B1–2, C1–2, etc.). Then read the SENTENCES below.*

1. Nevil will never find all the ore.
2. I fear they feel Cecile's sincere.
3. Eagle is eager to help poor Poole.
4. Didn't Paul pour Beale a beer?
5. He'll be here to honor O'Connell.
6. Doesn't Kale care that the affair may fail?
7. Peale can't appear before fall.
8. They'll be there to give Shale his share.
9. Powell has power over all of them.
10. I'll hire Neil as engineer.

D. *In the CHART on the opposite page, read down each column. Then read the SENTENCES below.*

1. You can wear casual attire at the Hotel Mayfair.
2. She'll star in the Hale and O'Hare production of "Steel Pier."
3. All the doctor's skill and care was of no avail.
4. He'll prepare a final paper on Will Shakespeare.
5. I'm well aware you feel unsure of his voter appeal.
6. Jill wore a beautiful cashmere stole.
7. The Premier's goodwill tour will end in Baltimore.
8. Will Boyer call another council of war?
9. An offender can still get a fair trial here.
10. Neither Yale nor Cornell can compare to our school.

15

LESSON 7

The Stop [k] *in Initial and Final Positions*

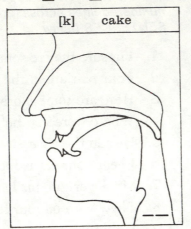

[k]   cake

To make initial [k], stop the flow of air through the mouth by touching the velum with the back of the tongue; then release the stop with a voiceless puff of air (aspiration).

For final [k], make a voiceless contact of tongue with velum; then either release without aspiration, or do not release at all—end the sound before breaking the contact.

Contrast Exercises

	A	B	C	D	E
1.	cagey	kale	Casey	came	kayo
2.	Jake	lake	sake	make	ache
3.	kitchen	Kinney	kith	killer	kissing
4.	chick	knick	thick	lick	sick
5.	collie	copper	common	car	Connor
6.	lock	pock	mock	rock	knock
7.	castle	cameo	callous	canny	cashing
8.	sack	Mack	lack	knack	shack
9.	coachman	cozy	cousin	coming	color
10.	choke	soak	suck	muck	luck

A. *In the CHART above, read lines 1, 3, 5, 7, and 9. Then read the SENTENCES below.*

B. *In the CHART above, read each two-line group as follows: vertical pairs across (A1–2, B1–2, etc.), then the second line. Then read the SENTENCES below.*

1. Connie's cousin comes from Kansas.
2. Carry the camera carefully.
3. Cathy's career was a colorful one.
4. I'll have a cup of coffee and a corn muffin.
5. Kiley's commission came through.
6. We can call on Kay, can't we?
7. Kenner made a killing in California.
8. Leave the couch cushions in the car.
9. Who's caring for Cora's kids?
10. Karen is a copycat.

1. Ike and Mike look alike.
2. Take the check to the bank.
3. Mark was in shock after the wreck.
4. With luck, she'll have work this week.
5. Thank Nick for my sake.
6. I think she took them for a walk.
7. Take the book back now.
8. My pink silk blouse shrank.
9. Why should Jack risk his neck?
10. Make me a thick milk shake.

Now read SENTENCES alternately from A and B above (A1,B1; A2,B2; A3,B3; etc.).

LESSON 8

The Stop [g] *in Initial and Final Positions*

To make initial [g], stop the flow of air through the mouth by touching the velum with the back of the tongue; then release the stop with a voiced explosion.

For final [g], make a voiced contact of tongue with velum; do not release—end the sound before breaking the contact. (This unreleased stop is usual at the end of a sentence, or when the following word begins with a consonant; before a word starting with a vowel, release the [g] with voice but without explosion.)

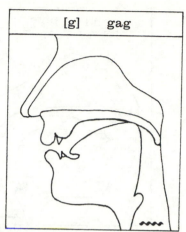

[g]   gag

Contrast Exercises

	A	B	C	D	E
1.	gamma	gashing	gaffer	gallery	Gary
2.	mag	shag	fag	lag	rag
3.	gossamer	gosling	golly	goffer	golfer
4.	smog	log	slog	fog	flog
5.	gully	gummy	gusher	guzzle	Gussie
6.	lug	mug	shrug	slug	hug
7.	going	goring	Gorman	gay	gave
8.	Hoag	rogue	morgue	Hague	vague
9.	guess	Geller	Gavin	gassy	goofy
10.	egg	leg	vag	sag	fugue

A. *In the CHART above, read lines 1, 3, 5, 7, and 9. Then read the SENTENCES below.*

1. The last gallon of gas is gone.
2. Is Gary going to Ghana?
3. "Guns and Gold" was a ghastly film.
4. Gail has gowns galore.
5. The Governor gave the game away.
6. You're a good guy, Gus.
7. I guess the girl is guilty.
8. Gordon gets my goat sometimes.
9. I dream about ghosts, goblins, and ghouls.
10. Gilbert was our guest in Galveston.

B. *In the CHART above, read each two-line group as follows: vertical pairs across (A1–2, B1–2, etc.), then the second line. Then read the SENTENCES below.*

1. The shag rug is in vogue now.
2. Our league has its own flag.
3. Is Berg really such a big humbug?
4. The travelogue was made in Prague.
5. Doug has an Irish mug and a brogue.
6. This frog was once a polliwog.
7. Peg made a vague reply.
8. This is smog, not fog.
9. Meg wrote the dialogue for "The Rogue."
10. I've often seen the tail wag the dog.

Now read SENTENCES alternately from A and B above (A1,B1; A2,B2; A3,B3; etc.).

LESSON 9
The Stop [p] *in Initial and Final Positions*

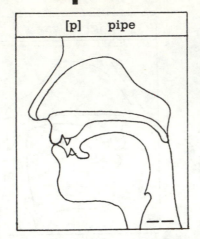

[p]   pipe

To make initial [p], stop the flow of air from the mouth by touching the lips together; then release the stop with a voiceless puff of air (aspiration).

For final [p], make a voiceless closure of the lips; do not release—end the sound before opening the lips. (This unreleased stop is usual at the end of a sentence, or when the following word begins with a consonant; before a word starting with a vowel, release the [p] without aspiration.)

Contrast Exercises

	A	B	C	D	E
1.	peeling	penal	peaceful	peevish	peachy
2.	leap	neap	sleep	veep	cheap
3.	pansy	passer	patching	palace	Pamela
4.	nap	sap	chap	lap	map
5.	posy	Poe	pony	poem	polling
6.	soap	hope	nope	mope	lope
7.	posture	Polly	pommel	possum	posh
8.	chop	lop	mop	sop	shop
9.	pillar	pitcher	pigeon	pithy	pin
10.	lip	chip	gyp	hip	nip

A. *In the CHART above, read lines 1, 3, 5, 7, and 9. Then read the SENTENCES below.*

1. Here, Paula, have a piece of peach pie.
2. I'll pay for the pen and pencil.
3. From Panama, Paine went to Peru.
4. Please pass the peas.
5. The pills are in Pamela's purse.
6. He painted a picture of his parents.
7. Powell's pitching pennies.
8. She's in the parlor playing the piano.
9. Paige is pulling his punches.
10. I'm in no position to purchase the pearls.

B. *In the CHART above, read each two-line group as follows: vertical pairs across (A1–2, B1–2, etc.), then the second line. Then read the SENTENCES below.*

1. I'll have shrimp, soup, and a lamb chop.
2. Bishop Thorpe brought the map.
3. Is this horoscope on the up and up?
4. Birds chirp and cheep; dogs yip and yap.
5. You'll slip on such a steep slope.
6. Our group made a trip to the Cape.
7. Have Philip stop off in Antwerp.
8. Now sweep up the shop.
9. I hope this will help you sleep.
10. See him skip, hop, and leap in the air!

Now read SENTENCES alternately from A and B above (A1,B1; A2,B2; A3,B3; etc.).

LESSON 10

The Stop [b] *in Initial and Final Positions*

To make initial [b], stop the flow of air from the mouth by touching the lips together; then release the stop with a voiced explosion.

For final [b], make a voiced closure of the lips; do not release—end the sound before opening the lips. (This unreleased final stop is usual at the end of a sentence, or when the following word begins with a consonant; before a word starting with a vowel, release the [b] with voice but with little or no explosion.)

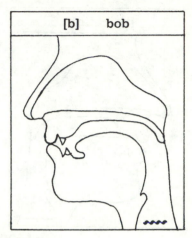

[b]   bob

Contrast Exercises

	A	B	C	D	E
1.	badger	balance	banner	baffle	Basil
2.	jab	lab	nab	flab	slab
3.	bunch	bunny	budge	bustle	buffalo
4.	chub	nub	hub	sub	flub
5.	Beulah	bureau	Bessie	berry	boring
6.	lube	rube	ebb	reb	orb
7.	bombing	Boswell	botching	bonny	bother
8.	mob	sob	job	knob	throb
9.	bilgy	Biff	biller	busy	Binnie
10.	jib	fib	rib	sib	nib

A. *In the CHART above, read lines 1, 3, 5, 7, and 9. Then read the SENTENCES below.*

1. Why not buy the boy a balloon?
2. Billy's as busy as busy can be.
3. This biology book is so boring!
4. Ben's always been bashful.
5. My boss was born in Buffalo.
6. They say Bailey belongs on the bench.
7. I believe he's been in Boston before.
8. The boys have Benson over a barrel.
9. Baseball is big business.
10. Byron will be in Belgium by then.

B. *In the CHART above, read each two-line group as follows: vertical pairs across (A1–2, B1–2, etc.), then the second line. Then read the SENTENCES below.*

1. Ask McNab to describe the place.
2. "The Webb Job" was a drab film.
3. Why do they rib Gerb so?
4. I'm afraid they'll scrub the Aqualab project.
5. Jacob was in that mob scene.
6. What did Loeb prescribe?
7. The squab and the crab were superb.
8. McCabe made a grab for the club.
9. He's a Serb, not an Arab.
10. That may rub Jebb the wrong way.

Now read SENTENCES alternately from A and B above (A1,B1; A2,B2; A3,B3; etc.).

19

LESSON 11

The Stop [t] *in Initial and Final Positions*

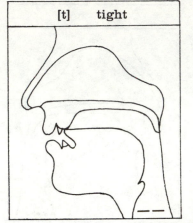

[t]   tight

To make initial [t], stop the flow of air through the mouth by touching the tooth-ridge with the tip of the tongue; then release the stop with a voiceless puff of air (aspiration).

For final [t], make a voiceless contact of tongue with tooth-ridge; do not release—end the sound before breaking the contact. (This unreleased final stop is usual at the end of a sentence, or when the following word begins with a consonant.)

Contrast Exercises

	A	B	C	D	E
1.	tarry	taffy	tassle	tam	tanner
2.	rat	fat	slat	mat	gnat
3.	tiller	Timmons	tinny	tiffany	tizzy
4.	lit	mitt	knit	fit	sit
5.	timer	tiling	tiring	Tyson	typhus
6.	might	light	right	site	fight
7.	teacher	teener	teeming	tailor	tamer
8.	cheat	neat	meat	late	mate
9.	town	tower	towel	tonsil	Toliver
10.	knout	rout	lout	knot	lot

A. *In the CHART above, read lines 1, 3, 5, 7, and 9. Then read the SENTENCES below.*

1. Tyler's telephoning his tailor now.
2. He's in the Town Tavern, tying one on.
3. Tim is too touchy.
4. This time he has a tiger by the tail.
5. I know Terry touch-types.
6. "Ten Tales of Terror" is nine too many.
7. Turner's on the Texas team.
8. The tug is towing the tanker in.
9. Tom usually turns in before ten.
10. There's a terrible tie-up near the terminal.

B. *In the CHART above, read each two-line group as follows: vertical pairs across (A1–2, B1–2, etc.), then the second line. Then read the SENTENCES below.*

1. That might not be so smart.
2. I thought Pat was all set.
3. They met me at the airport.
4. Let Kate sit near me.
5. Cut that nonsense out!
6. She just wrote them a note.
7. Jarrett bought one sweat shirt.
8. I hate being out so late.
9. It fit quite nicely.
10. Harriet cut the visit short.

Now read SENTENCES alternately from A and B above (A1,B1; A2,B2; A3,B3; etc.).

20

LESSON 12
The Stop [d] *in Initial and Final Positions*

To make initial [d], stop the flow of air through the mouth by touching the tooth-ridge with the tip of the tongue; then release the stop with a voiced explosion.

For final [d], make a voiced contact of tongue with tooth-ridge; do not release—end the sound before breaking the contact. (This unreleased final stop is usual at the end of a sentence, or when the following word begins with a consonant.)

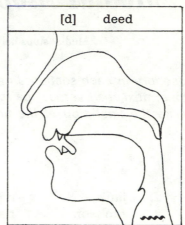

[d]   deed

Contrast Exercises

	A	B	C	D	E
1.	dealer	demon	dean	Deering	diesel
2.	lead	mead	need	read	seed
3.	diver	dialing	dicer	dining	dire
4.	vied	lied	side	snide	ride
5.	donor	doughy	doling	dosing	dome
6.	node	ode	load	sewed	mode
7.	Dewey	Duchin	dooming	dueling	dunes
8.	wooed	chewed	mood	lewd	nude
9.	deafen	Denver	daffy	dashing	dally
10.	fed	Ned	fad	shad	lad

A. *In the CHART above, read lines 1, 3, 5, 7, and 9. Then read the SENTENCES below.*

1. Don delivers *The Daily Dispatch.*
2. The difference, dear, is a dollar.
3. When was Dave due in Dallas?
4. There's no denying the damage he's done.
5. Dora differs with him on a dozen things.
6. I'll be down in Delaware this December.
7. Daniel's dozing in the dining room.
8. Even a day's delay is dangerous.
9. Do you always do the dishes this way?
10. We saw a dazzling display of Dana's designs.

B. *In the CHART above, read each two-line group as follows: vertical pairs across (A1–2, B1–2, etc.), then the second line. Then read the SENTENCES below.*

1. I heard they'd sold the old place.
2. Rod was in a bad mood.
3. She'd never had red suede shoes.
4. Clyde showed them the road.
5. Even a bird would need more food.
6. Have some homemade lemonade, Fred.
7. She said she'd send word soon.
8. Enid proved they'd been there.
9. I'm glad she finally made the grade.
10. Floyd called the child back.

Now read SENTENCES alternately from A and B above (A1,B1; A2,B2; A3,B3; etc.).

21

LESSON 13

Medial Stops before Consonants

Medial stops before a consonant are usually unreleased.

Follow this procedure in each section: In each two-line group of the CHART, read the first line with unreleased final stops; next read vertical pairs across (A1–2, B1–2, etc.), pronouncing the medial stop of the second world like the final stop of the first; then read the second line. Finally, read the SENTENCES.

		A	**B**	**C**	**D**	**E**
The stop [k]:	1.	jack	hack	lock	rock	knock
	2.	Jackson	hackney	lockjaw	rock-bound	knockdown
	3.	hick	Dick	Rick	meek	beak
	4.	Hickman	dictum	rickshaw	meekness	Beekman
	5.	buck	huck	neck	hawk	folk
	6.	buckboard	huckster	necktie	hawkshaw	folktale

a) I'd rather park near Parkside Avenue.
b) Vic sent the eviction notice.

c) The doctor's practice is in Jackson Heights.
d) Macdougal's sickness made him inactive.

		A	**B**	**C**	**D**	**E**
The stop [g]:	1.	fig	zig	jig	dig	pig
	2.	figment	zigzag	jigsaw	dignity	pigmy
	3.	hag	mag	flag	bag	drag
	4.	Agnes	magpie	flagman	bagpipe	dragnet
	5.	leg	egg	drug	jug	tug
	6.	legman	eggshell	drugstore	jugful	tugboat

a) Save that rag for the ragman.
b) Peg put up the pegboard.

c) Cagney's flagship is the *Sigma*.
d) Rigby wrote "The Ogden Enigma."

		A	**B**	**C**	**D**	**E**
The stop [p]:	1.	amp	chap	nap	lap	rap
	2.	Sampson	Chapman	napkin	lapdog	rapture
	3.	lip	hip	rip	whip	tip
	4.	elliptic	hypnosis	ripsaw	whipcord	tiptop
	5.	hope	soap	rope	up	cup
	6.	hopeful	soapbox	ropeway	upstairs	cupcake

a) They all hop when Hopkins gives the word.
b) They're going to strip Shipman of his stripes.

c) That cheapskate buys only shopworn goods.
d) Captain Hapgood won the sweepstakes.

	A	B	C	D	E
The stop [b]:					
1.	bob	mob	hob	lob	cob
2.	bobtail	mobster	hobnail	lobster	cobweb
3.	hub	rub	club	grub	snub
4.	hubcap	rubdown	clubmoss	grubstake	snub-nosed
5.	fib	rib	cab	slab	dab
6.	fibster	ribwort	cabdriver	slabwood	dabchick

a) Don't rib Scribner anymore.

b) The web tightened around Webster.

c) Dobson's object was obvious to everyone.

d) Abner Tubman is a subway worker.

	A	B	C	D	E
The stop [t]:					
1.	wit	fit	lit	quit	whit
2.	witless	fitness	litmus	quitclaim	Whitman
3.	fate	weight	foot	hot	Mott
4.	fateful	weightless	football	hotdog	motley
5.	mat	cat	right	sight	fright
6.	Matson	catcall	rightly	sightseer	frightful

a) He ate gratefully.

b) They might whitewash it.

c) Atkins witnessed Patman's fall.

d) Lately Bentley's been having nightmares.

	A	B	C	D	E
The stop [d]:					
1.	head	red	thread	odd	cod
2.	headphone	redcoat	threadbare	oddball	codfish
3.	amid	kid	side	road	load
4.	midtown	kidney	sidecar	roadhouse	lodestone
5.	lord	sword	need	ad	sad
6.	lordship	swordplay	needless	adverse	sadness

a) She read Medgar's note.

b) Then I rued my rudeness.

c) Rodney's admission will cause endless problems.

d) "Madcap Adventure" is Sidney's new movie.

LESSON 14

The Flap [t/d] *between Vowels*

1) When [t] and [d] occur between vowels—either before an unstressed vowel in the same word (*bitter, ladder*), or at the end of a word before a vowel in the same phrase (*put on, mad at*)—they are usually pronounced as "flaps." The tongue tip strikes the tooth-ridge and moves quickly away, barely interrupting the air stream. There is no aspiration and no explosion. 2) Unlike the stop [t], the flap [t] is voiced, and sounds very much like flap [d]. In word-pairs like *matter-madder*, the *tt* and *dd* are often pronounced exactly the same; the vowel, however, is usually longer before *d* than before *t*. 3) The flap sound is also used for [t] and [d] between a vowel and syllabic [l] (*battle, riddle*). In this case the tongue tip does not move away from the ridge; instead, the sides of the tongue immediately turn down to form [l]. 4) Note that before a *stressed* vowel in the same word, the stop [t], not the flap [t], is used (*attempt, return*).

Comparison Exercises

	A	B	C	D	E	F
1.	bitter	latter	shutter	metal	title	hurtle
2.	bidder	ladder	shudder	meddle	tidal	hurdle
3.	seated	fated	coated	putting	knotting	biting
4.	ceded	faded	coded	pudding	nodding	biding
5.	pat it	set it	lettuce	wrote off	het up	let on
6.	pad it	said it	led us	rode off	head up	led on

A. *In the CHART above, read lines 1, 3, and 5. Then read the SENTENCES below.*

1. Ritter's sitting pretty now.
2. "Bottoms up!" is Cotter's motto.
3. Whiting's writing an exciting novel.
4. Kate'd waited to be invited.
5. We got out at eight o'clock.

B. *In the CHART above, read lines 2, 4, and 6. Then read the SENTENCES below.*

1. Is Teddy going steady already?
2. Ida's Hideaway is on Rider Avenue.
3. Edith was reading "The Leader."
4. She decided she needed a beaded skirt.
5. He'd aid Ed if he could.

Now read SENTENCES alternately from A and B above (A1,B1; A2,B2; A3,B3; etc.).

C. *In the CHART above, read vertical pairs across (A1–2, B1–2, etc.). Then read the SENTENCES below.*

1. Later the lady became Tudor's tutor.
2. Eddie's getting better bedding soon.
3. Kitty's kidding with the meter reader.
4. Peter conceded that Lydia was prettier.
5. Matt is mad as mad can be.

D. *In the CHART above, read down each column. Then read the SENTENCES below.*

1. They're meeting to consider a settlement.
2. Rita's had a lot of freedom.
3. Ada recited it again.
4. The middle part was a little muddled.
5. Jody hated to be chided about it.

24

LESSON 15

Medial Flap/Medial [r]

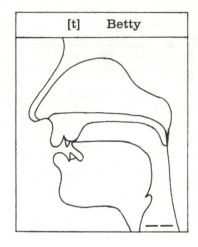

[t]   Betty

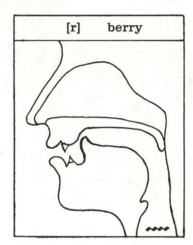

[r]   berry

To make the voiced flap sound for medial [t] and [d], strike the tooth-ridge with the tip of the tongue.

To make medial [r], curl the tip of the tongue up and back, without allowing it to touch anything. (Note: British speakers, but not Americans, often use a flap sound for medial [r].)

Contrast Exercises

	A	B	C	D	E
1.	audible	nautical	bawdy	water	lauding
2.	oracle	Nora	boring	warring	Loring
3.	Scotty	solder	jotting	moderate	spotting
4.	scarring	sorrow	jarring	morrow	sparring
5.	Paddy	fatter	ladder	gadding	natty
6.	parry	Farrow	Larry	Garroway	narrow

A. *In the CHART above, read lines 1, 3, and 5. Then read the SENTENCES below.*

1. Betty's letters are getting better.
2. Addison's caddy's a golf fanatic.
3. Otto's got an exotic bottle collection.
4. Freddie's already heading home.
5. Lauter's daughter is awfully haughty.

B. *In the CHART above, read lines 2, 4, and 6. Then read the SENTENCES below.*

1. The sheriff's in terrible peril.
2. Larry's an arrogant character.
3. Doris will be horribly sorry.
4. Berries and cherries are perishable.
5. There's an aura of moralism about Cora.

Now read SENTENCES alternately from A and B above (A1,B1; A2,B2; A3,B3; etc.).

C. *In the CHART above, read vertical pairs across (A1–2, B1–2, etc.). Then read the SENTENCES below.*

1. Berigan's betting on a medical miracle.
2. Teddy's terrible behavior shattered Sharon.
3. In these matters Maris is as petty as Perry.
4. His daughter Dora married Madison.
5. Darin's daddy is as modern as tomorrow.

D. *In the CHART above, read down each column. Then read the SENTENCES below.*

1. It was very considerate of Cutter to carry it.
2. Edison apparently found it upsetting.
3. Harry's waiting in the auditorium.
4. Patty borrowed my orange sweater.
5. I got a terrible headache from your stereo.

LESSON 16

Initial [d/r] in Unstressed Prefixes

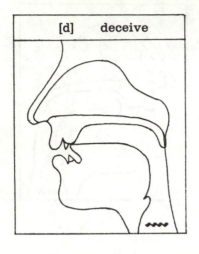

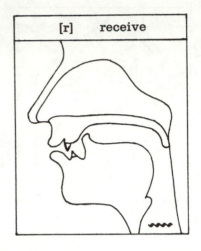

Be careful to pronounce [d] and [r] distinctly before unstressed vowels, particularly in the prefixes *de-* and *re-*. For [d], the tongue tip touches the tooth-ridge; for [r], the tongue is curled back and the tongue tip touches nothing.

(Note that *de-* and *re-* may be pronounced [diy/riy], [di/ri], or [də/rə].)

Contrast Chart

	A	B	C	D
1.	deceit	deplete	deceive	decedent
2.	receipt	replete	receive	recede
3.	detain	delate	declaim	defray
4.	retain	relate	reclaim	refrain
5.	demise	decline	delight	devise
6.	remise	recline	relied	revise
7.	deject	deceptive	depress	deflect
8.	reject	receptive	repress	reflect
9.	desist	division	decision	delinquent
10.	resist	revision	recision	relinquish
11.	divert	defer	deter	decurrent
12.	revert	refer	return	recurrent
13.	decant	demand	devalue	denounce
14.	recant	remand	revalue	renounce
15.	deform	decorum	demote	depose
16.	reform	record	remote	repose
17.	deposit	devolve	deduction	detention
18.	reposit	revolve	reduction	retention

Contrast Exercises

A. *In the CHART on the opposite page, read the odd-numbered lines across (1, 3, 5, etc.). Then read the SENTENCES below.*

1. She defiantly defended the defector.
2. The demotion demoralized Denise.
3. I denounced his deliberate deception.
4. Delaney was delighted with the deluxe accommodations.
5. They're debating the desirability of decentralizing.
6. Devine was defeated in Detroit.
7. The detective demanded a description.
8. DeWitt was deferred last December.
9. The defense was determined to delay the trial.
10. He declined to declare them as dependents.

B. *In the CHART on the opposite page, read the even-numbered lines across (2, 4, 6, etc.). Then read the SENTENCES below.*

1. They refused to refund the retainer.
2. The recruit's response was restrained.
3. Rebecca refrained from reciting her reasons.
4. The reviewer remembered repeating the story.
5. Refreshments for the reception are in the refrigerator.
6. Even the revised report was rejected.
7. He regretted referring to their relationship.
8. The receptionist recalled receiving it.
9. We were reluctant to rely on the results of the poll.
10. It was marked "Return Receipt Requested."

Now read SENTENCES alternately from A and B above (A1,B1; A2,B2; A3,B3; etc.).

C. *In the CHART on the opposite page, read vertical pairs across (A1–2, B1–2, C1–2, etc.). Then read the SENTENCES below.*

1. The designer resigned today.
2. To retract would detract from your image.
3. She delayed relaying the message.
4. The reporter was deported yesterday.
5. I deduced he'd reduced the amount.
6. They resolved to dissolve the corporation.
7. He deserves a reserved seat.
8. The respondent was despondent.
9. She decided to reside nearby.
10. It's hard to define "refinement."

D. *In the CHART on the opposite page, read down each column. Then read the SENTENCES below.*

1. DeMille regretted delaying the rehearsal.
2. The Republicans demanded a retraction of his demeaning remarks.
3. He denied retaining a detective to retrieve the device.
4. We're returning to Des Moines to resume his defense.
5. The degree of recovery will depend on his resilience.
6. She deserves a reward for decoding the reply.
7. Though deploring her reaction, we deliberately remained detached.
8. They described him as respectable, dependable, and responsible.
9. The department store refused to deliver it without the required deposit.
10. DeVoe is reforming, despite his resistance to change.

LESSON 17

Intonation: Statement Pattern

Statements and commands, and questions that start with a question word, normally have 231 intonation. The voice begins on pitch 2, rises to pitch 3 at the stress, then falls to pitch 1 and remains there until the end of the phrase. Only the syllable with primary stress is said on pitch 3. If one or more syllables follow

the stress, the voice *steps* down to pitch 1: *I knów that.*  *I knów it is.* If the last syllable takes the stress,

the voice *glides* down: *I knów.*

Statements and Commands

A. Compare step-down and glide-down endings in the paired statements below.

1. I háve them.   I háve.
2. She ásked me.   She ásked.
3. It's cólder.   It's cóld.
4. He dídn't.   He díd.
5. I'll gó there.   I'll gó.

6. You should cáll her.   You should cáll.
7. He can stánd it.   He can stánd.
8. She forgót to.   She forgót.
9. They might héar us.   They might héar.
10. It was dárker.   It was dárk.

B. Read the following statements, keeping your voice on pitch 2 until you reach the stress. Read down (1-10), then across (1-6, 2-7, etc.).

1. I'm glad to méet you.
2. I'll see you láter.
3. This is my cóusin.
4. She's studying Énglish.
5. We weren't very húngry.

6. We ran out of gás.
7. I don't understánd.
8. He's gone to the stóre.
9. The film was too lóng.
10. It's hard to expláin.

C. Direct commands and requests have the same intonation as statements. (Read down, then across.)

1. Let me hélp you.
2. Stop at the córner.
3. Pick up some pórk chops.
4. Please speak more slówly.
5. Put it on the táble.

6. Please have a séat.
7. Let's take the bús.
8. Please tell me móre.
9. Let me take your cóat.
10. Make yourself at hóme.

D. In the longer sentences below, be sure to hold your voice on pitch 2 before the stress.

1. The trouble must be in the fán.
2. I wonder where I left my kéys.
3. The message may have been deláyed.
4. I'm afraid our dinner's gotten cóld.
5. The children just got back from schóol.

28

E. Everything after the stressed syllable is said on pitch 1. In the following sentences, several syllables follow the stress. (Read down, then across.)

1. They're living in Báltimore.
2. I think it's ridículous.
3. You don't know the hálf of it.
4. He seems to be sérious.
5. Please handle it cárefully.
6. I wanted to téll him about it.
7. She honestly pítied the fellow.
8. He hasn't been féeling well lately.
9. I doubt that he's héard of the language.
10. We're having them óver tomorrow.

Question-word Questions

A. Read the following brief conversations, using 231 intonation for both questions and answers.

1. Where's the súitcase?
2. What's for bréakfast?
3. Who's the áuthor?
4. When's the cóncert?
5. Where's he góing?

In the cár.
Ham and éggs.
Henry Smíth.
On the fífth.
To Japán.

6. When will he knów?
7. Where have you béen?
8. Which one is yóurs?
9. How much did it cóst?
10. What time does it stárt?

By tomórrow.
Out wálking.
The réd one.
A dóllar.
At séven.

B. Read these progressively longer sentences, keeping your voice on pitch 2 before the stress. (Read down, then across.)

1. How áre you?
2. What's the mátter?
3. When did it háppen?
4. Why didn't you sáy so?
5. How long has he been wáiting?
6. Who was your favorite téacher?
7. How much would it cost to repáir it?
8. When does the next plane leave for Chicágo?
9. What time do we have to be at the státion?
10. Where would you like us to put the piáno?

11. What's néw?
12. Who was thát?
13. How do you dó?
14. Which way did he gó?
15. How often do you pláy?
16. When do you plan to retúrn?
17. How soon is he picking us úp?
18. Where do I get the bus to New Yórk?
19. How large an apartment do you requíre?
20. Why does it take him so long to get úp?

C. In the sentences below, keep your voice on pitch 1 after the stress. (Read down, then across.)

1. What tíme is it?
2. How óld is he now?
3. Who tóld him about it?
4. Why méntion the subject?
5. What dífference does it make?
6. Why don't you márry him?
7. What kind of wórk does he do?
8. How long did he stáy at the place?
9. What model cár was she driving?
10. Why didn't you ásk them about her?

29

LESSON 18
[w] *before* [u]

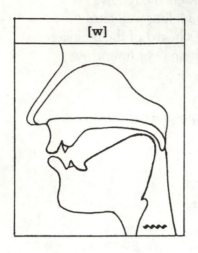 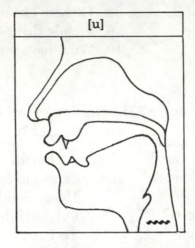

To make [wu], begin in [w] position, with the lips tightly rounded and the back of the tongue high in the mouth; then open the lips slightly to make [u]. Be sure to voice the [w] before gliding into the [u] sound: *wood* is [wud], not [ud].

Momentum Exercises

In the CHART below, read across each line, then down the final column. In each two-word phrase, hold the tight [w] lip position between the two words.

1.	new‿wood	through‿wood	Lou‿Wood	→WOOD
2.	few‿would	two‿would	Sue‿would	→WOULD
3.	true‿woman	new‿woman	shoe‿woman	→WOMAN
4.	new‿wool	glue‿wool	through‿wool	→WOOL
5.	zoo‿wolf	true‿wolf	Drew‿Wolff	→WOLF
6.	two‿wolves	few‿wolves	true‿wolves	→WOLVES

Read the SENTENCES below, again holding the tight [w] lip position between the marked words.

1. To glue‿wood, use WOOD glue.
2. I need blue‿wool; is that WOOL blue?
3. You‿would, WOULDN'T you?
4. Lou‿Wolff can't come; a WOLF caught Lou.
5. To screw‿wood, use WOOD screws.
6. I bought a new‿woofer. Is this WOOFER new?
7. Two‿would do it; WOULD you buy two?
8. Moths chew‿wool, and this WOOL's been chewed.
9. Hugh‿would; WOULD you?
10. She's a new‿woman, that WOMAN I knew.

Reinforcement Exercises

	A	B	C	D	E
1.	wall	wad	women	wordy	wife
2.	wool	would	woman	woody	woof
3.	widen	Walt	Woden	welling	weed
4.	wooden	wolf	wouldn't	woolen	wood
5.	worlds	Willy	wafer	wedded	Wister
6.	wolves	woolly	woofer	wooded	Wooster

A. *In the CHART above, read down each column. Then read the SENTENCES below. (In each word-pair, the initial [w] should sound the same in the second word as in the first.)*

1. Wendell Woodruff wanted woolen socks.
2. No one would wait for the woman.
3. Wary woodsmen watch for wild wolves.
4. Wanda wouldn't wear wool.
5. One woman was waiting in Woodlawn.
6. The worn woolen waistcoat was Woodson's.
7. Winnie's wolfhound went "Woof!"
8. For once, Woodrow wasn't woolgathering.
9. Wasn't Wolfgang's wife a wonderful woman?
10. The weary woodsman walked woodenly homeward.

B. *In the CHART above, read each two-line group as follows: vertical pairs across (A1–2, B1–2, etc.), then the second line of the group. Then read the SENTENCES below.*

1. A wise woman wouldn't walk in the woods. If a woman walked in the woods, wandering wolves would get her.

2. Woody the woodsman built a wooden woodshed. If Woody the woodsman hadn't used wood, the woodshed wouldn't be wooden.

3. The woman woodcutter is too busy to woolgather. If the woman woodcutter weren't too busy to woolgather, would the woman woodcutter woolgather?

4. Woolley wouldn't give a wooden nickel for the woodenware the woman wanted, and the woman wouldn't give a wooden nickel for the wood block Woolley wanted.

5. The woman wouldn't wash woodwork because the woodcutter wouldn't cut wood. If the woodcutter would cut wood, would the woman wash woodwork?

LESSON 19

[w] *in Clusters*

After making the initial sound (or sounds) of the cluster, round the lips tightly to
form [w] before gliding into the vowel.

Buildup Exercises

*Read each section below as follows: In the CHART, read line 1, then vertical pairs across (A1–2, B1–2,
etc.), forming the [w] of the second word like the initial [w] of the first. Then read line 2. Next read the
SENTENCES.*

		A	B	C	D	E
The [dw] Cluster:	1.	win	well	wane	welling	war
	2.	dwindle	dwell	Duane	dwelling	dwarf

a) I'll wire O'Dwyer today.

b) His winnings are dwindling.

c) Don't dwell on it, Dwight.

d) Just buy Duane a sandwich.

		A	B	C	D	E
The [gw] Cluster:	1.	wen	win	Wanda	wend	wampum
	2.	Gwen	Guin	iguana	Gwen'd	Guam

a) Watt's in Guatemala.

b) I wish they'd extinguish the fire.

c) The Guarani language is spoken in Paraguay.

d) Gwynn is a distinguished linguist.

		A	B	C	D	E
The [kw] Cluster:	1.	wick	weary	widow	wake	winter
	2.	quick	query	quid	quake	quint

a) Wyatt quietly wired to inquire about it.

b) Will's tranquility may win Quinn's trust.

c) McQuade's in quite a quandary.

d) Quentin's quips are frequently quoted.

		A	B	C	D	E
The [sw] Cluster:	1.	wipe	wade	wish	way	wing
	2.	swipe	suede	swish	sway	swing

a) Warden swore Wynn'd swindled him.

b) Wade persuaded Watkins to swap.

c) Sweeney swiftly swallowed it.

d) Swenson the Swede swears in Swahili.

	A	B	C	D	E
The [skw] Cluster: 1.	winch	wall	were	will	worm
2.	squinch	squall	squirrel	squill	squirm

a) Wanda squandered it in Waring Square.

b) He's William Asquith West, Esquire.

c) The squire squeezed the squatters out.

d) The squeaks, squawks, and squeals were unbearable.

	A	B	C	D	E
The [tw] Cluster: 1.	wig	weak	win	world	witch
2.	twig	tweak	twin	twirled	twitch

a) Wendell's twenty; Weiss is twice that.

b) The wine is for Twining.

c) Twain has twelve tweed suits.

d) He's betwixt and between.

Review Exercises

	A	B	C	D
1.	dwell	dwindle	Dwan	Dwight
2.	Guelph	Gwynn	guava	Guayaquil
3.	quell	Quinn	quad	quinine
4.	swell	swindle	swaddle	swine
5.	squelch	squint	squab	squire
6.	twelve	twinge	twaddle	twine

A. *In the CHART above, read across each line. Then read the SENTENCES below.*

1. Dwyer's mansion dwarfs my humble dwelling.
2. The plane left LaGuardia for Managua, Nicaragua.
3. They were quick to question my qualifications.
4. Swing and sway with the Swann Band.
5. Squibb grows squash in Squaw Valley.
6. The Twill boys are like Tweedledee and Tweedledum.

B. *In the CHART above, read down each column. Then read the SENTENCES below.*

1. Dworkin quit the swimming squad.
2. His twin is quite a linguist.
3. "Squalor" appeared in the *Sweetbriar Quarterly*.
4. Duane swears in twelve languages.
5. He got the Swinburne quotation all twisted.
6. Gwen dissuaded them from dwelling on the consequences.

LESSON 20
[h/f] *in Initial Position*

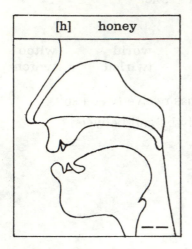

[h]   honey

To make [h], blow a voiceless stream of air from the mouth, with the lips and tongue shaped to form the following vowel. Do not allow the lower lip to touch the upper teeth.

To make [f], touch the tips of the upper teeth with the lower lip, and force out a voiceless stream of air.

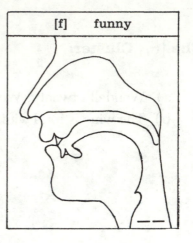

[f]   funny

Contrast Chart

	A	B	C	D	E
1.	hew	Hume	hued	Hugo	Hughes
2.	few	fume	feud	fugue	fuse
3.	who	who'll	who'd	whose	hooch
4.	phoo	fool	food	foozle	Fuji
5.	hood	hook	hooded	hooker	hoodless
6.	foot	full	footed	fuller	footless
7.	hunk	honey	humble	huddle	hung
8.	funk	funny	fumble	fuddle	fungus
9.	hall	hawk	halt	haunt	haughty
10.	fall	Falk	fault	faun	fought
11.	hoe	home	hole	hone	hold
12.	foe	foam	foal	phone	fold
13.	hoar	horse	hoard	hormone	Horton
14.	four	force	Ford	Forman	fort
15.	her	heard	hurl	hurtle	Hearn
16.	fir	furred	furl	fertile	fern
17.	high	height	hind	hire	heist
18.	fie	fight	find	fire	feisty

34

Contrast Exercises

A. *In the CHART on the opposite page, read the odd-numbered lines across (1, 3, 5, etc.). Then read the SENTENCES below.*

1. Hood's been hooked on Haydn since childhood.
2. Hordes of Horne's cohorts were there.
3. Who's in "Who's Who"? Hoover, that's who!
4. Herman heard her rehearsing.
5. Hundreds of hungry husbands are hustling home.
6. Hyman's hiking on Highland Heights.
7. The Hooker Hood Company's in Red Hook.
8. The homecoming's at Hogan's Hotel.
9. Hewlett's humor was a huge success.
10. The hawker was halted on Hawthorne Street.

B. *In the CHART on the opposite page, read the even-numbered lines across (2, 4, 6, etc.). Then read the SENTENCES below.*

1. In football annals, Fuller's a mere footnote.
2. Forman was forced to forfeit four games.
3. It would be foolish to fool with the food supply.
4. Ferguson's first furlough was deferred.
5. Their function is to funnel the funds to Futterman.
6. Fyke finally fired the file clerk.
7. The *Fulton Fulcrum* ran the full story.
8. Fogel's folks are photogenic.
9. Few of them went to the refugee's funeral.
10. Foster fought against falling asleep.

Now read SENTENCES alternately from A and B above (A1,B1; A2,B2; A3,B3; etc.).

C. *In the CHART on the opposite page, read vertical pairs across (A1–2, B1–2, C1–2, etc.). Then read the SENTENCES below.*

1. "It's a hoax, folks," Hume fumed.
2. Ferdinand heard Hood's footsteps.
3. The hormone formula made Horton a fortune.
4. Hawkins fought Hugh's feuds for him.
5. Who's been fooling with the hi-fi?
6. Hooper's foolish to hold Foley responsible.
7. Those four horses were formerly Horner's.
8. Hearst was the first to see Halsey falter.
9. I have a funny hunch Foote's been hood-winked.
10. Hiring and firing are Hunter's functions.

D. *In the CHART on the opposite page, read down each column. Then read the SENTENCES below.*

1. Fortmann and Hubbard are in the Football Hall of Fame.
2. Remember Hubert Fumble in "The Case of the Phony Houdini"?
3. Hooke'll win a fortune if he's holding a full house.
4. Her husband founded the Houston Foster Home Fund.
5. Hoodman played fullback for Herkimer Falls High.
6. He still haunts the firehouse on 101st Street.
7. Fido hides food behind the furnace.
8. Hootenannies are fun for the whole family.
9. Hawes made a few hurried phone calls to his fellow directors.
10. "Hangman's Fury" is a horse opera featuring Tom Foolery and his horse Feathers.

LESSON 21
[hw/f] *in Initial Position*

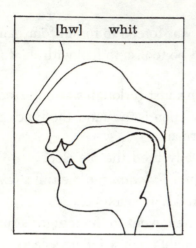

To make [hw], blow a voiceless stream of air from the mouth, with the lips tightly rounded in [w] position; then glide into the following vowel. Do not allow the lower lip to touch the upper teeth.

To make [f], touch the tips of the upper teeth with the lower lip, and force out a voiceless stream of air.

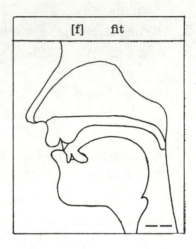

Contrast Chart

	A	B	C	D
1.	whit	whish	Whig	whistle
2.	fit	fish	fig	fissile
3.	whey	whale	whelk	wherry
4.	fey	fail	fell	ferry
5.	whee	wheat	wheel	wheeze
6.	fee	feet	feel	fees
7.	why	whine	white	while
8.	fie	fine	fight	file
9.	which	whips	whist	whinny
10.	Fitch	Phipps	fist	finny
11.	when	whether	whence	whelps
12.	fen	feather	fence	Phelps
13.	whir	whirl	whirtle	whirred
14.	fir	furl	fertile	furred
15.	wheeled	wheedle	whacked	wham
16.	field	feed	fact	famine
17.	whisk	whiz	whim	whittle
18.	Fisk	fizz	fimble	fiddle

36

Contrast Exercises

A. *In the CHART on the opposite page, read the odd-numbered lines across (1, 3, 5, etc.). Then read the SENTENCES below.*

1. What makes whirlwinds and whirlpools?
2. He's a whiz at whittling whales and such.
3. Why is Whitehead whipping them up?
4. Which wheelbarrow is which?
5. Where is Wheatley's white suit?
6. What animal whinnies and whickers?
7. Which whistle-stop is this, Whipple?
8. When did your whiskers turn white?
9. Whitcomb doesn't know what's what.
10. I don't understand all the wherefores and whereases.

B. *In the CHART on the opposite page, read the even-numbered lines across (2, 4, 6, etc.). Then read the SENTENCES below.*

1. Phyllis forged it just for fun.
2. I'll finish my finals before the first.
3. Fabian's famous in the fashion field.
4. Father forgot to fill in the forms.
5. Fenmore fixed it for fair.
6. They forced the fence to split fifty-fifty.
7. Farrell's a familiar figure in Philadelphia.
8. The fish food is forty-four cents.
9. Fisher finally found the fan.
10. "False Faces" is a full-length feature.

Now read SENTENCES alternately from A and B above (A1,B1; A2,B2; A3,B3; etc.).

C. *In the CHART on the opposite page, read vertical pairs across (A1–2, B1–2, C1–2, etc.). Then read the SENTENCES below.*

1. While I filed papers, Whinton finished the mail.
2. Wheeler feels Whaley failed.
3. I figured on Whigg's buying a whiskey fizz.
4. When is the Fenton-Whiting fight?
5. "They've whisked Fisk away," Fitz whispered.
6. Wheaton's fee seemed fair to Wharing.
7. Why fire the Whelton fellow?
8. Ask Fitch which wheel Felix wants.
9. When'll Fennell reach Fort Wharton?
10. Wherry's ferry is at Wharf 14.

D. *In the CHART on the opposite page, read down each column. Then read the SENTENCES below.*

1. Finch thought "White Fire" was a whale of a film.
2. You'll find the Whitakers listed in the Wheeling phone book.
3. Whitney faced a whipping for telling a whopper.
4. They feasted on the whitefish Whiley'd fixed for dinner.
5. Whitman's folks have the wherewithal to finance his whims.
6. We followed Whelan to the foot of Whiteface Mountain.
7. Wheelock found a whippoorwill in the forest.
8. I think the famous Wheel of Fortune is out of whack.
9. Faye whispered a few whimsical comments.
10. The white filly whinnied at the first whiff of fodder.

LESSON 22

[f/v] *in Initial Position*

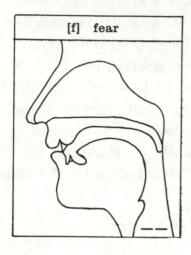

[f]   fear

To make [f] and [v], touch the tips of the upper teeth with the lower lip and force out a stream of air—voiceless for [f], voiced for [v]. Be sure that the upper and lower lips are not in contact.

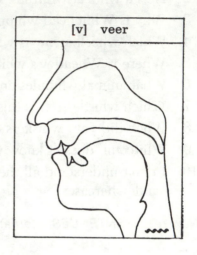

[v]   veer

Contrast Chart

	A	B	C	D	E
1.	feign	phase	fake	fairy	fail
2.	vein	vase	vacant	vary	veil
3.	fear	feel	feral	fiend	feet
4.	veer	veal	virile	venal	veto
5.	fie	fine	file	fight	final
6.	vie	vine	vile	vital	vinyl
7.	foal	focal	photo	fogey	foamer
8.	vole	vocal	vote	vogue	vomer
9.	fat	fast	fan	facile	fact
10.	vat	vast	van	vassal	vacuum
11.	fend	fetter	fetch	felt	fester
12.	vend	vet	vetch	veldt	vest
13.	fist	fidget	fig	fizz	fin
14.	vista	vigil	vigor	visit	vintage
15.	fern	fur	firm	firth	fertile
16.	vernal	verge	vermin	vertex	vertical
17.	fox	folly	fodder	follicle	farmer
18.	vox	volley	vodka	volatile	varmint

38

Contrast Exercises

A. In the CHART on the opposite page, read the odd-numbered lines across (1, 3, 5, etc.). Then read the SENTENCES below.

1. Finney's all for physical fitness.
2. Find the factory foreman, fast!
3. Farley's foot felt funny.
4. Forty firemen fought the fire.
5. The Ford Foundation furnished the funds.
6. Fetch the Fox file for me.
7. Faye faced the family's fury.
8. The farmer forgot to feed the foal.
9. Ferber's fee is fifty-four dollars.
10. First phone for food.

B. In the CHART on the opposite page, read the even-numbered lines across (2, 4, 6, etc.). Then read the SENTENCES below.

1. He's vicious, vain, and very violent.
2. In my view, Vance is the villain.
3. On my vacation I'll visit Vienna.
4. Valerie has varicose veins.
5. My home is on "V" Street in Vine Valley.
6. Vanning's read Virgil and Voltaire.
7. I got the vermilion vase in Victoria.
8. The vocalist is Vicky Vaughn.
9. Valkyrie Vanadium is a vast enterprise.
10. We can't vaccinate him against viper's venom.

Now read SENTENCES alternately from A and B above (A1,B1; A2,B2; A3,B3; etc.).

C. In the CHART on the opposite page, read vertical pairs across (A1–2, B1–2, C1–2, etc.). Then read the SENTENCES below.

1. Vinson finished the first verse.
2. Feeney's vehicle is vastly faster.
3. Violet filed the following volumes.
4. A few viewers felt vexed.
5. Vilma filmed "The Vampire Family."
6. Veale feels the ferry's very dangerous.
7. The villagers filled Fernando's veranda.
8. Farnum varnished Vern's furniture.
9. Vining finally fixed the Victrola.
10. Vale'd failed to pay the visa fees.

D. In the CHART on the opposite page, read down each column. Then read the SENTENCES below.

1. Victors fear the vengeance of their vanquished foes.
2. Fernet is a veteran of the fighting at Verdun.
3. She vanished last fall with Van Dyke's funds.
4. My fiancé's very fond of venison, fish and vodka.
5. Varley finally visited his folks in Virginia.
6. The Vassar faculty valued the physicist's views.
7. Fanny made vanilla fudge for the vicar of Fenwick.
8. The original version of the final verse was very funny.
9. It was the famous violinist's first visit to Fiji.
10. Vera forgot to get vitamins, figs, and vinegar.

LESSON 23

[f/v] *in Final Position*

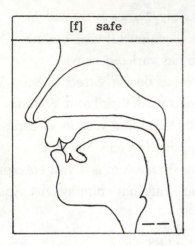

[f] safe

To make [f] and [v], touch the tips of the upper teeth with the lower lip and force out a stream of air—voiceless for [f], voiced for [v]. Be careful not to touch the lips together, and not to add a vowel to final [v]: *give* is [giv], not [givə].

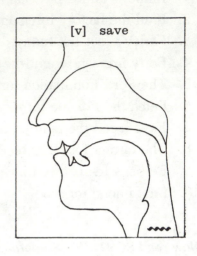

[v] save

Contrast Chart

	A	B	C	D
1.	safe	waif	Lafe	strafe
2.	save	wave	lave	stave
3.	grief	thief	reef	sheaf
4.	grieve	thieve	reeve	sheave
5.	fife	life	strife	rife
6.	five	alive	strive	arrive
7.	luff	buff	guff	stuff
8.	love	above	glove	shove
9.	Schiff	stiff	cliff	Griff
10.	shiv	sieve	live	give
11.	half	calf	staff	scarf
12.	have	calve	salve	carve
13.	eff	ref	shelf	delf
14.	Ev	rev	shelve	delve
15.	proof	roof	oaf	loaf
16.	prove	groove	cove	clove
17.	serf	turf	quaff	off
18.	serve	Irv	suave	mauve

40

Contrast Exercises

A. *In the CHART on the opposite page, read the odd-numbered lines across (1, 3, 5, etc.). Then read the SENTENCES below.*

1. Tell the chef this beef is tough.
2. MacDuff has grief enough.
3. "Life is brief," read the epitaph.
4. Rudolph himself came off well.
5. **I bought a scarf, kerchief, and muff.**
6. No rough stuff, Cliff.
7. Half the staff remained aloof.
8. The sheriff has proof Murph did it.
9. They couldn't laugh off the tariff.
10. Ralph was playing golf in Flagstaff.

B. *In the CHART on the opposite page, read the even-numbered lines across (2, 4, 6, etc.). Then read the SENTENCES below.*

1. Doesn't Dave deserve a leave?
2. I'll have him pave the drive.
3. Eve didn't preserve the negative.
4. They've thrown Olive a curve.
5. I've got to leave Ev here.
6. Give Steve a shave.
7. You can't reserve all five of them.
8. We've gotten Marv a reprieve.
9. He gave each relative an expensive present.
10. Can you prove the move will serve our interests?

Now read SENTENCES alternately from A and B above (A1,B1; A2,B2; A3,B3; etc.).

C. *In the CHART on the opposite page, read vertical pairs across (A1–2, B1–2, C1–2, etc.). Then read the SENTENCES below.*

1. You can't slough love off.
2. Why does Rafe rave so?
3. They'll approve the roof repairs.
4. I think Dev is deaf.
5. He failed to achieve his chief goal.
6. Doesn't the razor chafe when you shave?
7. Leave the leaf on the table.
8. Duff is a dove on foreign policy.
9. He's single, but I've a wife.
10. A massive mastiff guarded the door.

D. *In the CHART on the opposite page, read down each column. Then read the SENTENCES below.*

1. Clive himself is a native of Cardiff.
2. It's safe to assume the executive staff will approve.
3. Jeff gave a brief, rather imaginative description of life in Tel Aviv.
4. I'll remove the paragraph that's so offensive to Schiff.
5. Though Joseph was very persuasive, he wasn't persuasive enough.
6. You'll leave yourself no alternative but to bluff your way out.
7. Randolph should arrive at half past five.
8. Have the sheriff remove the handcuff.
9. Griff's punitive response was really self-destructive.
10. For a tough operative, he's oddly sensitive to a rebuff.

LESSON 24

[b/v] *in Initial Position*

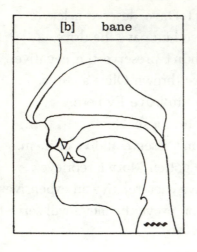

[b]	bane

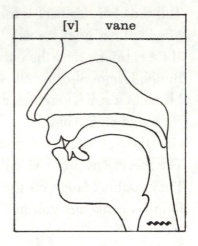

[v]	vane

To make initial [b], stop the flow of air from the mouth by touching the lips together; then release the stop with a voiced explosion.

To make [v], touch the tips of the upper teeth with the lower lip and force out a voiced stream of air. Be sure that the upper and lower lips are not in contact.

Contrast Chart

	A	B	C	D	E
1.	bane	bays	bail	bacon	bagel
2.	vane	vase	veil	vacant	vague
3.	beer	beep	bees	Beal	bean
4.	veer	veep	visa	veal	venal
5.	buy	bile	bind	bite	bide
6.	vie	vile	vined	vital	vied
7.	bowl	boat	bogey	bore	bolt
8.	vole	vote	vogue	vortex	volt
9.	bat	bast	ballad	balance	banish
10.	vat	vast	valid	valance	vanish
11.	belt	bend	best	bencher	bellum
12.	veldt	vend	vest	venture	vellum
13.	bicker	billon	busy	bid	biscuit
14.	vicar	villain	visage	video	viscous
15.	burgeon	burst	Burman	Bert	burden
16.	virgin	versed	vermin	vertex	verdant
17.	box	bomb	Balt	bowel	Bulgar
18.	vox	vomit	vault	vowel	vulgar

42

Contrast Exercises

A. *In the CHART on the opposite page, read the odd-numbered lines across (1, 3, 5, etc.). Then read the SENTENCES below.*

1. Both bats belong to Byron.
2. His boasting was boring beyond belief.
3. The Burton boy behaved badly.
4. He's the best bookbinder in Boston.
5. Bill's boots are at the bottom of the box.
6. The Better Business Bureau's behind it.
7. Bess bought a bunch of bananas.
8. Bit by bit, Bert backed off.
9. Betsy's boyfriend became a banker.
10. The ball bounced between the buildings.

B. *In the CHART on the opposite page, read the even-numbered lines across (2, 4, 6, etc.). Then read the SENTENCES below.*

1. Vogel's valet vanished in Valencia.
2. Violet vests are not in vogue.
3. Vollmer verified the victim's version.
4. Veterans very rarely volunteer.
5. Varley claims the Vikings visited Vermont.
6. The vandals smashed a valuable violin.
7. Veronica's virtuous, if rather vague.
8. The Vice-Consul voided her visa.
9. Victoria has vim, vigor, and vitality.
10. The verdict vindicated Vincent's honor.

Now read SENTENCES alternately from A and B above (A1,B1; A2,B2; A3,B3; etc.).

C. *In the CHART on the opposite page, read vertical pairs across (A1–2, B1–2, C1–2, etc.). Then read the SENTENCES below.*

1. Banning's vanity requires bigger victories.
2. The vet bet that Vinnie'd been there.
3. Berry's very interested in his visitor's business.
4. The case was *Berson versus the Banner Van Company.*
5. Vernon's burning Varga's barn!
6. Bowker vowed to beat the veto.
7. They're building a villa near Billington Village.
8. V. B. Voss is our boss.
9. The boy's voice is big and vigorous.
10. Viller billed us for the vinyl bindings.

D. *In the CHART on the opposite page, read down each column. Then read the SENTENCES below.*

1. Victor battered the vicious bully, who vowed to batter Victor back.
2. "Beyond Venus," Barney Verdon's new musical, opened in Virginia Beach.
3. The voters are becoming very bitter about violence in the big cities.
4. Barry's visitor borrowed my volley ball.
5. The Ventura Better Vacuum Bag Company is on the verge of bankruptcy.
6. Vince bought the vodka; I'll buy the vermouth.
7. He keeps his bonds in the Varick Street branch of the Vickers Bank.
8. Verna's bored with her view of the beach.
9. There's very little basis for Valentine's bitterness.
10. Vance left because of their vile backbiting.

LESSON 25
[b/v] *in Medial Position*

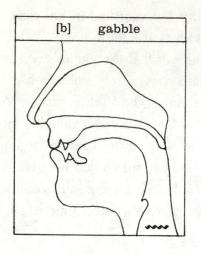

[b]   gabble

To make medial [b], stop the flow of air from the mouth by touching the lips together; then release the voiced air stream—but less explosively than for initial [b].

To make [v], touch the tips of the upper teeth with the lower lip and force out a voiced stream of air. Be sure that the upper and lower lips are not in contact.

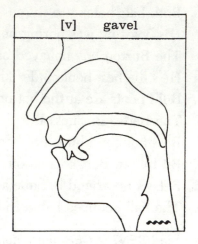

[v]   gavel

Contrast Chart

	A	B	C	D	E
1.	gabble	rabble	grabble	jabber	cabin
2.	gavel	ravel	gravel	javelin	cavern
3.	ribber	Libby	quibble	dribble	Sibyl
4.	river	liver	quiver	drivel	civil
5.	saber	Faber	oboe	rober	Doberman
6.	savor	favor	over	rover	Dover
7.	jibing	ibis	fiber	libel	tribal
8.	jiving	ivy	fiver	liven	rival
9.	urban	curbing	Herbert	derby	gerbil
10.	Irving	curving	pervert	dervish	Jervis
11.	Cabot	habit	rabbit	cabbage	scabby
12.	Cavett	have it	ravish	savage	scavenge
13.	nibble	ribbon	kibitz	tribute	liberty
14.	Niven	riven	civets	trivia	livery
15.	lubber	treble	debit	chubby	Hubbell
16.	lover	Trevor	devil	shovel	hovel
17.	abort	abide	abuse	abashed	about
18.	cavort	divide	reviews	avast	avouch

Contrast Exercises

A. *In the CHART on the opposite page, read the odd-numbered lines across (1, 3, 5, etc.). Then read the SENTENCES below.*

1. Collecting labels is Robert's hobby.
2. How about a rebate on the webbing?
3. Abby's ribbon is in the cabinet.
4. My neighbor's shabby habits annoy me.
5. Maybe it's Debbie's baby.
6. The debate was about Labor's role.
7. Bobby's rabbit has rabies.
8. The rebels disbanded in the Gobi desert.
9. I'm dubious about Tobin's ability.
10. He plays the oboe in a Quebec cabaret.

B. *In the CHART on the opposite page, read the even-numbered lines across (2, 4, 6, etc.). Then read the SENTENCES below.*

1. He developed an aversion to avocados.
2. I advised him to avoid investing in it.
3. David's in seventh heaven.
4. It covers every eventuality.
5. Trevor provided the caviar.
6. She's arriving at Riverhead this evening.
7. Steven's never gone to Savannah.
8. I'm convinced we can prevent cavities.
9. He did Everett several favors.
10. The Governor attacked the civil service system.

Now read SENTENCES alternately from A and B above (A1,B1; A2,B2; A3,B3; etc.).

C. *In the CHART on the opposite page, read vertical pairs across (A1–2, B1–2, C1–2, etc.). Then read the SENTENCES below.*

1. The rebels reveled in their victory.
2. Gibbon's given me a present.
3. The abbot's an avid chess player.
4. Old Mr. Rayburn's raving again.
5. She covered the cupboard with wallpaper.
6. That's my favorite fable.
7. Maybe Mavis left it here.
8. They're serving Serbian food.
9. Libby is livid over it.
10. We bought a marvelous marble statue.

D. *In the CHART on the opposite page, read down each column. Then read the SENTENCES below.*

1. It's evidently his habit to overlook his subordinates' oversights.
2. Toby's Tavern is on Abigail Avenue in Hubbardsville.
3. "Over the Abyss" is a novel about the Revolutionary War.
4. Sabina discovered it in an abandoned hovel near Mobile.
5. There are even laborsaving devices that nobody uses.
6. Cabot brought us several fabulous souvenirs from Tibet.
7. The movie is about the overthrow of a liberal government.
8. Neville's robot is giving me the heebie-jeebies.
9. They'll eventually abolish seven airborne divisions.
10. Evans rebuffed every one of the lobbyist's overtures.

LESSON 26
[b/v] *in Final Position*

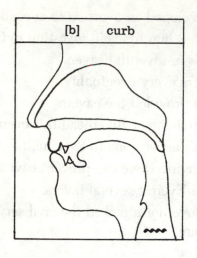

[b]	curb

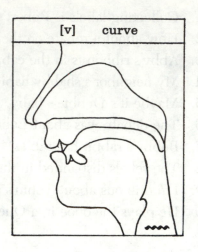

[v]	curve

To make final [b], stop the flow of air from the mouth by touching the lips together. The contact must be voiced. Do not release—end the sound with the lips closed. (If the following word begins with a vowel, release the stop with voice but with little or no explosion.)

To make [v], touch the tips of the upper teeth with the lower lip and force out a voiced stream of air. Be careful not to touch the lips together, and not to add a vowel to final [v]: *give* is [giv], not [givə].

Contrast Chart

	A	B	C	D
1.	Herb	curb	Serb	slurb
2.	Irv	curve	serve	swerve
3.	jibe	scribe	tribe	ascribe
4.	jive	strive	drive	arrive
5.	sib	Gibb	glib	jib
6.	sieve	give	live	shiv
7.	glub	shrub	dub	club
8.	glove	shove	dove	love
9.	rob	slob	swab	sob
10.	Rahv	Slav	suave	solve
11.	strobe	robe	globe	probe
12.	strove	rove	grove	drove
13.	cab	scab	jab	daub
14.	calve	salve	have	mauve
15.	grebe	plebe	reb	ebb
16.	grieve	peeve	rev	Ev
17.	hub	deb	cube	rube
18.	of	Dev	you've	prove

46

Contrast Exercises

A. *In the CHART on the opposite page, read the odd-numbered lines across (1, 3, 5, etc.). Then read the SENTENCES below.*

1. Inscribe "Bob" on the cube.
2. There's a cobweb on the doorknob.
3. Come on, Herb, let's grab a cab.
4. I don't subscribe to the *Trib*.
5. They got Loeb a lab job.
6. The scribe wore drab garb.
7. Jacob had crab and corn on the cob.
8. There was a mob at the Scarab Club.
9. Webb, you didn't scrub the tub.
10. That snob wouldn't hobnob with a nabob.

B. *In the CHART on the opposite page, read the even-numbered lines across (2, 4, 6, etc.). Then read the SENTENCES below.*

1. We drove in at five to five.
2. Reeve gave him the old heave-ho.
3. She'd love to live in Glen Cove.
4. Move over and give Cleve some room.
5. Please have him serve before we starve.
6. Why save one mauve glove?
7. They gave Merv rave notices.
8. It's an instinctive drive to stay alive.
9. He's gone to grieve at the grave of his love.
10. Eve can't forgive his offensive remarks.

Now read SENTENCES alternately from A and B above (A1,B1; A2,B2; A3,B3; etc.).

C. *In the CHART on the opposite page, read vertical pairs across (A1–2, B1–2, C1–2, etc.). Then read the SENTENCES below.*

1. He gave Gabe a hard time.
2. It didn't perturb Irv a bit.
3. Don't give a glib reply.
4. That robe belongs to Grove.
5. McCabe found a cave in the hills.
6. Ask Deb to delve a little further.
7. Abe can't stave it off forever.
8. No tribe could thrive in this place.
9. It seems okay, but will Doob approve?
10. Where does Caleb live?

D. *In the CHART on the opposite page, read down each column. Then read the SENTENCES below.*

1. There's no alternative, Mr. Taub — we'll have to remove the rib.
2. Jeb strove to curb his aggressive impulses.
3. Don't disturb Steve. I'll prescribe a sedative for him.
4. Lieb has an executive job with a progressive company.
5. I'm positive Bob gave you the stub.
6. Mr. Farb is the representative of the Carib Stove Company.
7. In his suave way, Cobb wove a web of lies.
8. I don't believe McNab has the nerve to ad-lib the speech.
9. Hobb used to live in the Arab enclave.
10. The dove and the squab are too expensive. How about shishkebab?

47

LESSON 27

Intonation: Question Pattern

Questions which call for a "Yes" or "No" answer are normally asked with 23⌐ intonation. The voice begins on pitch 2, rises to pitch 3 at the stress, and remains on pitch 3 until the final syllable, when it rises a little further. This final rise occurs even when the last syllable itself has the stress: the voice jumps to pitch 3 and then glides higher on the vowel.

A. Practice the following short questions. Read down (1-15), then across (1-6-11, 2-7-12, etc.).

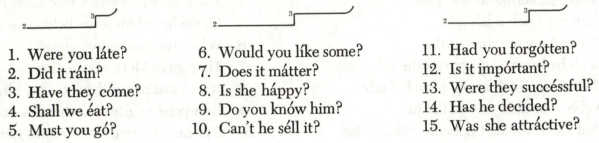

1. Were you láte?
2. Did it ráin?
3. Have they cóme?
4. Shall we éat?
5. Must you gó?

6. Would you líke some?
7. Does it mátter?
8. Is she háppy?
9. Do you knów him?
10. Can't he séll it?

11. Had you forgótten?
12. Is it impórtant?
13. Were they succéssful?
14. Has he decíded?
15. Was she attráctive?

B. "Yes" and "No" may be given several different intonations. Here are three common patterns:

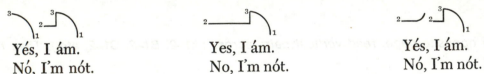

Yés, I ám.
Nó, I'm nót.

Yes, I ám.
No, I'm nót.

Yés, I ám.
Nó, I'm nót.

C. In each of the following sections, read the five questions, then the five answers. Then read across each line (question and answer). When reading the questions, keep your voice on pitch 2 before the stress.

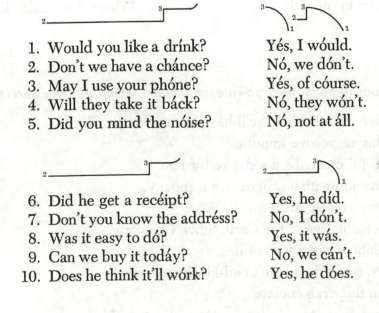

1. Would you like a drínk?
2. Don't we have a chánce?
3. May I use your phóne?
4. Will they take it báck?
5. Did you mind the nóise?

Yés, I wóuld.
Nó, we dón't.
Yés, of cóurse.
Nó, they wón't.
Nó, not at áll.

6. Did he get a recéipt?
7. Don't you know the addréss?
8. Was it easy to dó?
9. Can we buy it todáy?
10. Does he think it'll wórk?

Yes, he díd.
No, I dón't.
Yes, it wás.
No, we cán't.
Yes, he dóes.

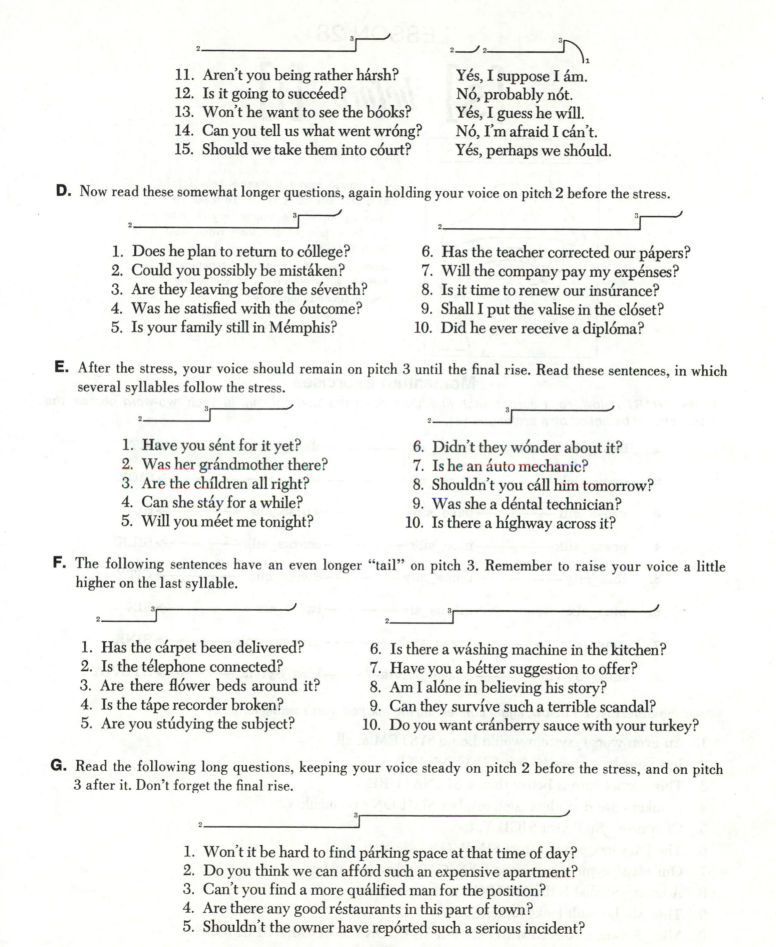

11. Aren't you being rather hársh?   Yés, I suppose I ám.
12. Is it going to succéed?   Nó, probably nót.
13. Won't he want to see the bóoks?   Yés, I guess he wíll.
14. Can you tell us what went wróng?   Nó, I'm afraid I cán't.
15. Should we take them into cóurt?   Yés, perhaps we shóuld.

D. Now read these somewhat longer questions, again holding your voice on pitch 2 before the stress.

1. Does he plan to return to cóllege?
2. Could you possibly be mistáken?
3. Are they leaving before the séventh?
4. Was he satisfied with the óutcome?
5. Is your family still in Mémphis?

6. Has the teacher corrected our pápers?
7. Will the company pay my expénses?
8. Is it time to renew our insúrance?
9. Shall I put the valise in the clóset?
10. Did he ever receive a diplóma?

E. After the stress, your voice should remain on pitch 3 until the final rise. Read these sentences, in which several syllables follow the stress.

1. Have you sént for it yet?
2. Was her grándmother there?
3. Are the chíldren all right?
4. Can she stáy for a while?
5. Will you méet me tonight?

6. Didn't they wónder about it?
7. Is he an áuto mechanic?
8. Shouldn't you cáll him tomorrow?
9. Was she a déntal technician?
10. Is there a híghway across it?

F. The following sentences have an even longer "tail" on pitch 3. Remember to raise your voice a little higher on the last syllable.

1. Has the cárpet been delivered?
2. Is the télephone connected?
3. Are there flówer beds around it?
4. Is the tápe recorder broken?
5. Are you stúdying the subject?

6. Is there a wáshing machine in the kitchen?
7. Have you a bétter suggestion to offer?
8. Am I alóne in believing his story?
9. Can they survíve such a terrible scandal?
10. Do you want cránberry sauce with your turkey?

G. Read the following long questions, keeping your voice steady on pitch 2 before the stress, and on pitch 3 after it. Don't forget the final rise.

1. Won't it be hard to find párking space at that time of day?
2. Do you think we can affórd such an expensive apartment?
3. Can't you find a more quálified man for the position?
4. Are there any good réstaurants in this part of town?
5. Shouldn't the owner have repórted such a serious incident?

49

LESSON 28

[s] *before* [i]

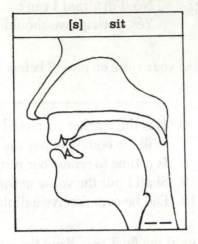

[s] should sound the same before [i] as before any other vowel. To make [s], place the tip of the tongue very close to the front part of the tooth-ridge, just behind (but not touching) the upper teeth. Groove the front of the tongue and force a voiceless stream of air between tongue tip and tooth-ridge.

Momentum Exercises

In the CHART below, read across each line, then down the final column. In each two-word phrase, the words should be linked by a prolonged [s].

1.	Bess͜ sit	Joyce͜ sit	class͜ sit	→ SIT
2.	once͜ sick	nurse͜ sick	less͜ sick	→ SICK
3.	gross͜ sin	base͜ sin	worse͜ sin	→ SIN
4.	press͜ silk	nice͜ silk	coarse͜ silk	→ SILK
5.	this͜ city	tense͜ city	Swiss͜ city	→ CITY
6.	plus͜ six	minus͜ six	twice͜ six	→ SIX
7.	glass͜ sink	brass͜ sink	grease͜ sink	→ SINK
8.	miss͜ Sylvia	chase͜ Sylvia	kiss͜ Sylvia	→ SYLVIA

Read the SENTENCES below, again connecting the marked words with a long [s].

1. An even worse͜ system would be no SYSTEM at all.
2. Jess͜ sins less͜ since he left CINCINNATI.
3. This͜ signet sure is better than a SIGNATURE.
4. Monkeys are doubtless͜ simians, but SIMEON's no monkey.
5. Of course, Sis'll visit SICILY, too.
6. The job's less͜ simple than SIMPSON indicated.
7. Our class͜ cynic won't be so CYNICAL when he's older.
8. A brass͜ cymbal is the SYMBOL of our company.
9. This͜ sill he built looks rather SILLY.
10. Miss͜ Simms misses SIMMONS, but SIMMONS misses Mrs. SIMMONS.

Reinforcement Exercises

	A	B	C	D	E
1.	sat	sun	sex	soft	sop
2.	sit	sin	six	sift	sip
3.	sell	salve	song	suckle	sense
4.	sill	sieve	sing	sickle	since
5.	sauna	sellable	summer	sank	sundry
6.	cinema	syllable	simmer	sink	syndrome

A. *In the CHART above, read down each column. Then read the SENTENCES below. (In each word-pair, the initial [s] should sound the same in the second word as in the first.)*

1. I suppose Simmons has the same symptoms.
2. It sounds silly to say he's sinister.
3. Sarah insisted on specifics.
4. They're sending Sills to Central City.
5. I've smoked six or seven cigarettes already.
6. Sam Cinders is such a cynic.
7. Save your sympathy for someone sick.
8. In September Cindy is sailing for Singapore.
9. There are no such facilities in southern Mississippi.
10. I wonder what Sally's sister subsists on.

B. *In the CHART above, read each two-line group as follows: vertical pairs across (A1–2, B1–2, etc.), then the second line of the group. Then read the SENTENCES below.*

1. Simeon's decision simplified the situation.
2. "Cinderella" is playing at Cinema 16.
3. A cygnet is the symbol of Sycamore City.
4. Priscilla hasn't been lucid since the accident.
5. I'm sick of Cynthia's simpering.
6. The synagogue is situated at 660 Sixth Avenue.
7. Sid's kid sister is sitting up now.
8. They're considering Simms for the Silver Star.
9. Is there a Citizens' Assistance Office in the vicinity?
10. Sibley's "Sixteenth Symphony" is similar to his "Sixth."

LESSON 29

[ʃ] *before* [i]

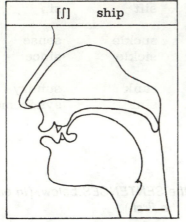

[ʃ]   ship

[ʃ] should sound the same before [i] as before any other vowel. To make [ʃ], curve the front of the tongue high in the mouth, groove it, and bring it very close to the back part of the tooth-ridge. Keep the tongue tip turned down, and round the lips slightly. Force a voiceless stream of air between the tongue and the back of the tooth-ridge.

Momentum Exercises

In the CHART below, read across each line, then down the final column. In each two-word phrase, the words should be linked by a prolonged [ʃ].

1.	Danish ship	Finnish ship	Turkish ship	→ SHIP
2.	hush Schick	rush Schick	push Schick	→ SCHICK
3.	brash shill	boyish shill	knavish shill	→ SHILL
4.	brownish shingle	grayish shingle	whitish shingle	→ SHINGLE
5.	smash schist	crush schist	polish schist	→ SCHIST
6.	flesh shiver	Nash shiver	Hersh shiver	→ SHIVER
7.	British shilling	Scottish shilling	Irish shilling	→ SHILLING
8.	cash shift	rash shift	fresh shift	→ SHIFT

Read the SENTENCES below, again connecting the marked words with a long [ʃ].

1. Let Walsh shift to day work, and I'll SHIFT to nights.
2. That's a rush shipment — SHIP it today.
3. I wish Schiller wouldn't SHILLY-shally.
4. Their battle cry was: "Crush chicanery in CHICAGO!"
5. When you finish shingling the house, you can start SHINGLING the garage.
6. He's a loutish, shiftless fellow with SHIFTY eyes.
7. The Flatbush Shipbuilding Company builds toy SHIPS.
8. Was General Nash chivalrous, or had CHIVALRY died by then?
9. You'd better cash Schilling's check; we haven't a SHILLING in cash.
10. I hate to be harsh, Schiff, but you'll have to SHIFT for yourself.

52

Reinforcement Exercises

	A	B	C	D	E
1.	Shep	shove	shall	shock	Schafer
2.	ship	shiv	shill	Schick	Schiffer
3.	shun	sham	shopper	shaver	shelling
4.	shin	shim	shipper	shiver	shilling
5.	shaft	shekel	shovel	Schuler	shanty
6.	shift	Schickel	chivalry	Schiller	shindig

A. *In the CHART above, read down each column. Then read the SENTENCES below. (In each word-pair, the initial [ʃ] should sound the same in the second word as in the first.)*

1. We're shy a shingle on the Schenley shipment.
2. Everyone at the Shane shindig was watching Shirley shimmy.
3. "Shape up or ship out!" is Shay's favorite shibboleth.
4. I'd like to buy Shelley a shift, but I'm short a shilling.
5. It should've been shipped to Shaw in Chicago.
6. Meanwhile, the Shafers were shivering in a shanty near Shilton.
7. I'm sure Shiller's showmanship will pay off.
8. When they shut down the shipyard they should've shifted the men to another.
9. It's a shame the shipmaster won't show them the ship.
10. The Sherman Ship and Shore Company is in the Shiffman Building.

B. *In the CHART above, read each two-line group as follows: vertical pairs across (A1–2, B1–2, etc.), then the second line of the group. Then read the SENTENCES below.*

1. They had shishkebab at the Shinbone Inn in Chicago.
2. Dr. Schickler treated the midshipman for shingles.
3. It's refreshing to meet such a dashing, chivalrous fellow.
4. Cushing got the last shipment of fishing gear.
5. For a couple of shillings, Schimmel would shill for the Devil.
6. Bushing bruised his shins shinnying up the tree.
7. The ship appeared to shift in the shimmering light.
8. Why is Schick rushing off to Washington?
9. "A Makeshift Courtship" is an astonishing picture.
10. Shiff is finishing the Michigan report.

53

[s/ʃ] *before* [i]

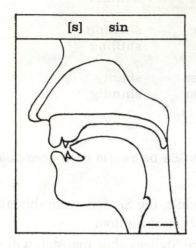

[s]	sin

Both [s] and [ʃ] are made by grooving the front of the tongue and forcing a voiceless stream of air through the narrow space between the tongue and part of the tooth-ridge.

To make [s], place the tip of the tongue very close to the front of the ridge, just behind (but not touching) the upper teeth.

To make [ʃ], curve the front of the tongue high and bring it very close to the back of the ridge, with the tongue tip turned down. Round the lips slightly.

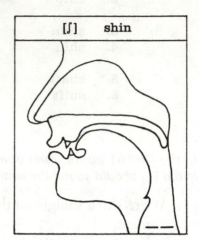

[ʃ]	shin

Contrast Chart

	A	B	C	D
1.	sin	sip	sift	Simms
2.	shin	ship	shift	shims
3.	cyst	sill	sieve	six
4.	schist	shill	shiv	Schick's
5.	simmer	sifter	Cindy	silica
6.	shimmer	shifter	shindy	shilling
7.	civil	simian	Sibyl	syndic
8.	chivalry	shimmy	shibboleth	shindig
9.	sickle	Sinbad	sipping	sibilant
10.	Schickel	shin pad	shipping	shibilant
11.	gassing	classing	massing	sassing
12.	gashing	clashing	mashing	sashing
13.	mussing	bussing	cussing	fussing
14.	mushing	blushing	crushing	flushing
15.	leasing	messing	hissing	Lessing
16.	leashing	meshing	fishing	fleshing
17.	furnacing	trellising	pumicing	menacing
18.	furnishing	relishing	punishing	vanishing

54

Contrast Exercises

A. *In the CHART on the opposite page, read the odd-numbered lines across (1, 3, 5, etc.). Then read the SENTENCES below.*

1. Sylvester has symptoms of silicosis.
2. I simply insist on civility.
3. Singleton's with the Pacific Cylinder Company.
4. That sit-in was in Cincinnati.
5. Simpson's assistant was sizzling mad.
6. A syllabary consists of symbols for syllables.
7. Sibyl has since reconsidered.
8. The Sinclair sisters have similar signatures.
9. The City Cynics are a hot singing group.
10. Lucinda is a citizen of Singapore.

B. *In the CHART on the opposite page, read the even-numbered lines across (2, 4, 6, etc.). Then read the SENTENCES below.*

1. Pershing won a Michigan scholarship.
2. The shift boss fired the shipping clerk.
3. Cushing's makeshift structure came crashing down.
4. The Schiffs first met at a shipboard shindig.
5. Shiffman and Shinner formed a partnership.
6. Tell Shillito there's no chicanery aboard my ship!
7. I have a shipment of shingles for Mr. Shild.
8. I dropped a shilling in the wishing well.
9. Mrs. Shindler bought a chiffon shift.
10. My old shipmate Schiller was shipwrecked.

Now read SENTENCES alternately from A and B above (A1,B1; A2,B2; A3,B3; etc.).

C. *In the CHART on the opposite page, read vertical pairs across (A1–2, B1–2, C1–2, etc.). Then read the SENTENCES below.*

1. Isn't it silly to shilly-shally now?
2. I know Shick's been sick for a long time.
3. With the strike on, not a single shingle moved.
4. The *Michigan* signaled for help.
5. Can't you be more specific, Schiffer?
6. It's simply Shimmel's way of saying no.
7. The shippers precipitated the trouble.
8. She sings in a Flushing cafe.
9. This is a case of Shindler's Syndrome.
10. My sister's shishkebab is delicious.

D. *In the CHART on the opposite page, read down each column. Then read the SENTENCES below.*

1. It's astonishing how consistently Shifrin is singled out for criticism.
2. Sylvia's furnishings are refreshingly simple.
3. One of Shipman's sisters is in Chicago; the other's in San Francisco.
4. The City Council's hushing up Shickel's complicity.
5. I bought the silk shift at Chiffon City.
6. Shilman insisted on finishing his analysis.
7. The Cushing Syndicate owns sixty ships.
8. Schilling does publicity for the Washington Cygnets.
9. It's silly for Shickman to persist in punishing himself.
10. Hasn't Shilton considered washing his hands of the situation?

LESSON 31
[s] *before* [iy] *and* [ir]

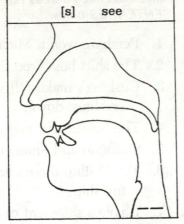

[s] | see

[s] should sound the same before [iy] and [ir] as before any other vowel. To make [s], place the tip of the tongue very close to the front part of the tooth-ridge, just behind (but not touching) the upper teeth. Groove the front of the tongue and force a voiceless stream of air between tongue tip and tooth-ridge.

Momentum Exercises

In the CHART below, read across each line, then down the final column. In each two-word phrase, the words should be linked by a prolonged [s].

1. geese‿see ————— moose‿see ————— mice‿see ————→ SEE
2. house‿seat ————— bus‿seat ————— choice‿seat ————→ SEAT
3. Brice‿seeks ————— Ross‿seeks ————— Gus‿seeks ————→ SEEKS
4. class‿seal ————— place‿seal ————— force‿seal ————→ SEAL
5. chase‿scene ————— trance‿scene ————— tense‿scene ————→ SCENE
6. dress‿seam ————— blouse‿seam ————— press‿seam ————→ SEAM
7. rice‿seed ————— grass‿seed ————— moss‿seed ————→ SEED
8. close‿secret ————— less‿secret ————— once‿secret ————→ SECRET

Read the SENTENCES below, again connecting the marked words with a long [s].

1. No, it isn't a bottomless‿sea; I SEE the bottom now.
2. The grass‿seeder's under the CEDAR tree.
3. Skip the dance‿scene; I've SEEN it already.
4. He saw a face‿seamed with age; it SEEMED a kind face.
5. I prefer this‿sea air to a SIERRA vacation.
6. When Vince‿sees red, you'd better SEIZE Vince.
7. Harris‿C. Quinn is heir to the SEQUIN fortune.
8. Has Tess‿seen your car, Mr. SENIOR?
9. The penthouse‿ceiling leaks; we're SEALING it tomorrow.
10. Let Cass‿see Esther before her SIESTA.

56

Reinforcement Exercises

	A	B	C	D	E
1.	so	side	soar	same	sonic
2.	see	cede	seer	seem	scenic
3.	site	soon	sacred	soap	sage
4.	seat	scene	secret	seep	siege
5.	Susan	soak	saber	size	soupy
6.	season	seek	seaboard	seize	sepia

A. *In the CHART above, read down each column. Then read the SENTENCES below. (In each word-pair, the initial [s] should sound the same in the second word as in the first.)*

1. Sally seems so serious.
2. Sailors see the seven seas.
3. Is such a secret safe with Seymour?
4. Saul was seen in a suburb of Seattle.
5. They sent the Seabees to the South Seas.
6. I'm sorry Segal came sightseeing with us.
7. The second scene was certainly a searing one.
8. Sue seasoned some seaweed.
9. They said Sieger would save the seats.
10. You'll soon see why Sam ceased to care.

B. *In the CHART above, read each two-line group as follows: vertical pairs across (A1–2, B1–2, etc.), then the second line of the group. Then read the SENTENCES below.*

1. Mr. Seabury, Senior is deceased.
2. Without the serum, Dr. Seaver can't proceed.
3. I've seen the seedy side of Seagate.
4. They were at Caesar's Casino in Cedar Rapids.
5. Seaman did the scenery for "Besieged."
6. They've seized Simak's secret papers.
7. It seems Siebert was well received.
8. The emcee beseeched them to be seated.
9. Betsy likes her seafood seasoned.
10. I see Percy's succeeded, as usual.

[ʃ] before [iy] and [ir]

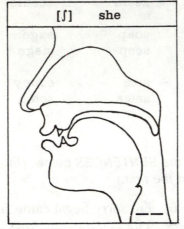

[ʃ] should sound the same before [iy] and [ir] as before any other vowel. To make [ʃ], curve the front of the tongue high in the mouth, groove it, and bring it very close to the back part of the tooth-ridge. Keep the tongue tip turned down, and round the lips slightly. Force a voiceless stream of air between the tongue and the back of the tooth-ridge.

Momentum Exercises

In the CHART below, read across each line, then down the final column. In each two-word phrase, the words should be linked by a prolonged [ʃ].

1. wish she ——— gosh, she ——— hush, she ——→ SHE
2. mesh sheath ——— wash sheath ——— fresh sheath ——→ SHEATH
3. reddish sheen ——— bluish sheen ——— greenish sheen ——→ SHEEN
4. brush sheep ——— push sheep ——— lash sheep ——→ SHEEP
5. Irish Sheehan ——— bookish Sheehan ——— foolish Sheehan ——→ SHEEHAN
6. rash sheik ——— brash sheik ——— boyish sheik ——→ SHEIK
7. boorish Sheed ——— loutish Sheed ——— waspish Sheed ——→ SHEED
8. flash shield ——— splash shield ——— crash shield ——→ SHIELD

Read the SENTENCES below, again connecting the marked words with a long [ʃ].

1. There are fresh sheets on the beds and extra SHEETS in the closet.
2. Jane has the kind of rakish chic that appeals to the SHEIK in me.
3. I wish she'd leave SHEED alone.
4. They publish sheer trash, and it's making SHEERIN rich.
5. I'd like a greenish sheath, but any SHEATH will do.
6. For cash, she knew SHEEHAN would do it.
7. They'll punish Sheila for SHIELDING him.
8. John used to blush sheepishly and make SHEEP's eyes at her.
9. We'll finish sheaving the grain today; the SHEAVING goes very quickly.
10. Give that thickish sheaf to SCHIEFFER.

Reinforcement Exercises

	A	B	C	D	E
1.	show	shine	shade	chef	shoot
2.	she	sheen	she'd	sheaf	sheet
3.	shock	shelled	sure	shape	shove
4.	sheik	shield	sheer	sheep	sheave
5.	shoo-in	shabby	shutting	chauffeur	Shiloh
6.	Sheehan	Sheba	sheeting	Schieffer	Sheila

A. *In the CHART above, read down each column. Then read the SENTENCES below. (In each word-pair, the initial [ʃ] should sound the same in the second word as in the first.)*

1. In short, she should shear it.
2. Show Sheila Shelley's sheepskin.
3. Should she go or shouldn't she?
4. Yes, we have Shasta Sheer Shower Sheets.
5. Sheriff Sheed was shot by a sheepherder.
6. Shouldn't she sharpen the shears?
7. Shawn's sheaf was short a sheet.
8. "Shame of Sheba" is showing in Sheepshead Bay.
9. It's a short, sheer, shiny sheath.
10. I'm sure she wasn't shy or sheepish about it.

B. *In the CHART above, read each two-line group as follows: vertical pairs across (A1–2, B1–2, etc.), then the second line of the group. Then read the SENTENCES below.*

1. She'd shield Sheehan if Sheehan would shield her.
2. Shearing garnisheed the machinist's salary.
3. She's terribly wishy-washy, isn't she?
4. Shealy looked sheepishly at the broken windshield.
5. She told Horatio to get pistachio.
6. Schieff is a cashier in Hershey.
7. She appreciated the sheik's cooperation.
8. Shields is negotiating for new machinery.
9. She got where she is by being ingratiating.
10. Schieber's sheep look emaciated.

[s/ʃ] *before* [iy] *and* [ir]

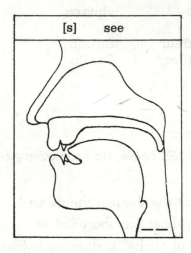

[s]   see

Both [s] and [ʃ] are made by grooving the front of the tongue and forcing a voiceless stream of air through the narrow space between the tongue and part of the tooth-ridge.

To make [s], place the tip of the tongue very close to the front of the ridge, just behind (but not touching) the upper teeth.

To make [ʃ], curve the front of the tongue high and bring it very close to the back of the ridge, with the tongue tip turned down. Round the lips slightly.

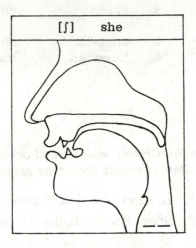

[ʃ]   she

Contrast Chart

	A	B	C	D
1.	see	seek	seethe	seal
2.	she	chic	sheathe	Sheila
3.	seen	seed	sere	seize
4.	sheen	she'd	sheer	she's
5.	seep	seat	sealed	Seaver
6.	sheep	sheet	shield	sheave
7.	Sieber	Siefer	seesaw	secant
8.	Sheba	sheaf	she saw	she can't
9.	seaside	seaboard	sea devil	seagoing
10.	she sighed	she bored	she-devil	she going
11.	brassy	gassy	lassie	Massey
12.	brashy	gashy	flashy	mashie
13.	Gussie	fussy	mussy	Percy
14.	gushy	brushy	mushy	Hershey
15.	messy	Plessey	missy	prissy
16.	meshy	fleshy	fishy	squishy
17.	pussy	Marcie	fancy	classy
18.	pushy	marshy	banshee	ashy

Contrast Exercises

A. In the CHART on the opposite page, read the odd-numbered lines across (1, 3, 5, etc.). Then read the SENTENCES below.

1. Francine has season seats at the opera.
2. Are they seriously seeking a cease-fire?
3. Nancy's too conceited to concede.
4. What seamstress would put sequins on a seersucker suit?
5. At least Elsie has seen the Colosseum.
6. The Seamen's Fund receives half the proceeds.
7. Lucille's sightseeing in Muncie.
8. I liked the last scene of Seale's "Seadog."
9. Jessie seems to have exceeded the limit.
10. Haven't you seen Patsy's seesaw?

B. In the CHART on the opposite page, read the even-numbered lines across (2, 4, 6, etc.). Then read the SENTENCES below.

1. She has Schieber's sheaf of notes.
2. Her sheath is chic, but too sheer.
3. She got her sheepskin from Shields College.
4. Sheen bought the mashie in Sheepshead Bay.
5. Yesterday she borrowed Shealy's shears.
6. How fast can we depreciate the sheet metal machinery?
7. Isn't she Sheila Shearer of Sheeptown?
8. Sheen's negotiating out of sheer desperation.
9. Shiefer officiated at the initiation.
10. She can't differentiate between one species and another.

Now read SENTENCES alternately from A and B above (A1,B1; A2,B2; A3,B3; etc.).

C. In the CHART on the opposite page, read vertical pairs across (A1–2, B1–2, C1–2, etc.). Then read the SENTENCES below.

1. If she can't see Cantor, she means to see Meany.
2. Shields concealed the sheik's secret papers.
3. She may see May while she's at the Seattle Fair.
4. Won't she bring Siebring to the Sheed proceedings?
5. To see if she could get the facts, she brooked Seabrook's displeasure.
6. Sears is a cashier at Sheehan's Casino.
7. Can't Schieff see that she's a seasoned reporter?
8. When she made "The Seamaid," she gave Seagrave a part.
9. Everyone could see she was serious about Shearing.
10. She'd meant to see many places, and she'd succeeded.

D. In the CHART on the opposite page, read down each column. Then read the SENTENCES below.

1. She was seized before she could leave Tennessee.
2. The preceding day she'd taken a taxi to Hershey.
3. Seeley cashiered his senior machinist.
4. She had one big scene in Marshey's "Sea Queen."
5. Lucy has a cushy job with the Seaton Sheet Company.
6. She didn't seem to appreciate the scenery.
7. When will she cease trying to shield Maxine?
8. She'd seen the sheath in a Quincy shop.
9. Could the tearsheets conceivably substantiate Cecile's charges?
10. Sheila seems to have taken a fancy to Horatio.

LESSON 34

Intonation: Direct Address

A name, title, or other expression used in direct address is spoken as a separate phrase before or after the main phrase of a sentence. The direct address phrase may be given several different intonations. In the frequently used 2‿ pattern, the voice begins on pitch 2, rising at the end to a level a little lower than pitch 3. If the direct address phrase has only one syllable (*Jóhn*), or if the final syllable is stressed

(*Mr. McCóy*), the voice usually *glides* up: *Jóhn. Mr. McCóy*. If the final syllable is unstressed, the voice

often *steps* up: *Mrs. Jáckson*. In these exercises, both types will be marked as follows: 2‾‾‾‾‾

A. In the following sentences, the pattern 2‿ direct address phrase precedes a main phrase with statement intonation.

1. Mr. Rálston, this is Mr. Átkins.
2. Fáther, how's your héadache?
3. Jáckson, contról yourself.
4. Your Hónor, I'm ínnocent!
5. Dóctor, what's wróng with me?

6. Mr. Córsi, I'm John Gráy.
7. Chíldren, it's time for béd.
8. María, we've had a wonderful tíme.
9. Ófficer, I need your hélp.
10. Hárris, you've done it agáin!

B. Here the pattern 2‿ phrase precedes a main phrase with question intonation.

1. Jím, are you coming alóng?
2. Wáiter, may I have the chéck?
3. Stéve, is anything wróng?
4. Kíds, could you make less nóise?
5. Ánn, are you getting húngry?

6. Proféssor, is this statement trúe?
7. Árthur, won't you stay for dínner?
8. Hóney, have you seen my glásses?
9. Mrs. Jónes, would you like some cóffee?
10. Géneral, are you making prógress?

C. The direct address phrase may come at the end of the sentence. When the main phrase has statement intonation, the voice falls to pitch 2, rather than to pitch 1, before a pattern 2‿ direct address phrase.

1. Good mórning, Mr. Máson.
2. Glad to méet you, Mr. O'Néill.
3. Please be séated, géntlemen.
4. Excúse me, Mrs. Hárris.
5. How áre you, Jánet?

6. How do you dó, Mr. Óaks?
7. Helló, young féllow.
8. Hí, Tóm.
9. Let's gó, mén!
10. What's úp, Cárol?

D. In the following sentences, the direct address phrase follows a main phrase with question intonation. The voice first rises to pitch 3 in the main phrase, which ends not with a rise but with a slight "slowing down" of the voice, often in the form of a lengthened final syllable. The direct address phrase is spoken on pitch 3, with a rise at the end. Note that this phrase has its own primary stress; make your voice louder on the marked syllable.

1. Can you lend me a dóllar, Míke?
2. Shall we get stárted, fólks?
3. Do you like the víew, Miss Ámes?
4. May I ask a quéstion, Mr. Cháirman?
5. Did you wash your hánds, Bóbby?

6. Have you told Dád about it, Jóe?
7. Can we relý on that, Mr. Thómpson?
8. Is it impórtant to you, Máry?
9. Was the méal satisfactory, Mádam?
10. May I quóte you on that, Mr. Président?

E. *Direct address with falling intonation*: When it precedes the main phrase, the direct address phrase often has a 31 or 231 pattern. This intonation may express alarm or concern. It is also used when greeting an acquaintance or when trying to get someone's attention.

1. Vícky, it's good to sée you!
2. Móther, what's the mátter?
3. Bílly, where wére you?
4. Hárry, it's past eléven!
5. Jónathan, how áre you?

6. Mrs. Thómas, are you all ríght?
7. Rebécca, didn't you héar me?
8. Mr. Bénson, won't you jóin us?
9. Diána, aren't you réady yet?
10. Miss Rodríguez, can I hélp you?

LESSON 35

[s/θ] *in Initial Position*

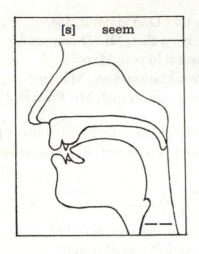

[s] seem

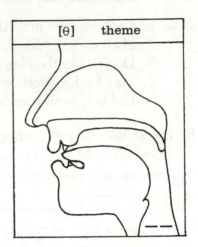

[θ] theme

To make [s], place the tip of the tongue very close to the front part of the tooth-ridge, just behind (but not touching) the upper teeth. Groove the front of the tongue and force a voiceless stream of air between tongue tip and tooth-ridge.

To make [θ], touch the tips of the upper teeth with the tip of the flattened tongue and force out a voiceless stream of air.

Contrast Chart

	A	B	C	D	E
1.	see	seeder	seam	Seaver	Seattle
2.	thief	Theda	theme	thievery	theatric
3.	sigh	Simon	sire	size	strive
4.	thigh	thiamine	thyroid	thighs	thrive
5.	sacker	sally	satchel	swag	sash
6.	Thackeray	thallic	thatch	thwack	thrash
7.	sill	sick	sin	symbol	sink
8.	thill	thick	thin	thimble	think
9.	surd	sirs	Serbia	certain	sermon
10.	third	Thursday	Thurber	thirty	Thurman
11.	summer	sunder	sump	suds	slug
12.	thumber	thunder	thump	thuds	thug
13.	set	said	seven	send	sell
14.	threat	thread	theft	thenyl	Thelma
15.	saw	sought	Saul	sore	swore
16.	thaw	thought	thrall	Thor	thwart
17.	sane	sway	sate	sole	soda
18.	thane	Thwaite	theta	thole	Thoden

64

Contrast Exercises

A. In the CHART on the opposite page, read the odd-numbered lines across (1, 3, 5, etc.). Then read the SENTENCES below.

1. Save Sally some salad.
2. In September Sears had a sale on satin.
3. Sullivan said it so simply.
4. Soon we'll set sail for San Salvador.
5. Sanders seems to have second sight.
6. An old sailor sang some salty songs.
7. For Salk's sake, he'll suffer in silence.
8. It's a sorry selection of summer suits.
9. We're serving sirloin steak for supper.
10. "Secret Search" is a superior soap opera.

B. In the CHART on the opposite page, read the even-numbered lines across (2, 4, 6, etc.). Then read the SENTENCES below.

1. Thorns and thistles thrive in thickets.
2. The theater's at 13 Thresher Avenue.
3. Thimble and Thread is a thrift shop.
4. Theodore got thirstier and thirstier.
5. My theme is "Theologians and Theology."
6. Thea's read a thousand thrillers.
7. His theory's been thoroughly thrashed out.
8. He's been loyal through thick and thin.
9. Thatcher had a thoroughbred named Thunder.
10. His plans were thwarted, thanks to Thurber.

Now read SENTENCES alternately from A and B above (A1,B1; A2,B2; A3,B3; etc.).

C. In the CHART on the opposite page, read vertical pairs across (A1–2, B1–2, C1–2, etc.). Then read the SENTENCES below.

1. You can thank Sanky for your theater seats.
2. Thaller is smaller and thinner than Cinders.
3. I thought I saw your therapist, Sarah.
4. Singleton thinks there were several thefts.
5. I'd say Thayer sold Thoden out.
6. If Thad were sad, he wouldn't sing a thing.
7. Thelma seldom goes to see Theo.
8. Your third sermon had a more seemly theme.
9. Sue threw him some thumbtacks.
10. I'm certain Thurston was at the service on Thursday.

D. In the CHART on the opposite page, read down each column. Then read the SENTENCES below.

1. Thorne spent thirty cents for thread.
2. My secretary has a throbbing headache and a sore throat.
3. Summers got through at seven-thirty on Saturday.
4. I suppose you think Senator Thurman has gone soft.
5. Thorpe sent him three separate threatening letters.
6. Did someone throw something at Selma?
7. Sam Thorndike lives at 63 Sayers Avenue.
8. Her daughter is thirteen and still sucks her thumb.
9. Thea was surprised at his thoughtful and sensitive reply.
10. One scientist is on the threshold of a sensational theoretical advance.

LESSON 36

[s/θ] *in Final Position*

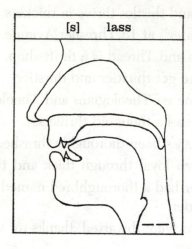

[s] lass

To make [s], place the tip of the tongue very close to the front part of the tooth-ridge, just behind (but not touching) the upper teeth. Groove the front of the tongue and force a voiceless stream of air between tongue tip and tooth-ridge.

To make [θ], touch the tips of the upper teeth with the tip of the flattened tongue and force out a voiceless stream of air.

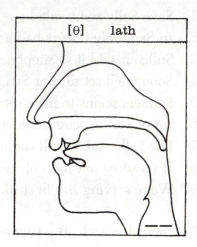

[θ] lath

Contrast Chart

	A	B	C	D
1.	lass	bass	mass	pass
2.	lath	bath	math	path
3.	moss	Ross	loss	cross
4.	moth	wroth	cloth	froth
5.	Roos	moose	obtuse	caboose
6.	Ruth	vermouth	tooth	booth
7.	purse	nurse	disburse	immerse
8.	Perth	unearth	birth	mirth
9.	Bess	dress	else	tense
10.	Beth	death	health	tenth
11.	gross	verbose	dose	close
12.	growth	both	oath	loath
13.	Reese	niece	Venus	crease
14.	wreath	neath	zenith	bequeath
15.	kiss	Pris	prince	race
16.	kith	pith	plinth	wraith
17.	ass	crass	toss	boss
18.	hath	wrath	troth	broth

66

Contrast Exercises

A. *In the CHART on the opposite page, read the odd-numbered lines across (1, 3, 5, etc.). Then read the SENTENCES below.*

1. The Swiss miss is a classy lass.
2. This house would be nice for us.
3. Joyce couldn't parse this sentence.
4. How'd you trace us to this address?
5. Curtis held a press conference.
6. Congress may pass the Morse amendment.
7. Brace versus Brace is a famous case.
8. Don't embarrass Miss Brice.
9. It's useless to discuss peace terms.
10. Try once more to convince Jess it's not hopeless.

B. *In the CHART on the opposite page, read the even-numbered lines across (2, 4, 6, etc.). Then read the SENTENCES below.*

1. Kenneth had health, wealth, and youth.
2. "Death of a Telepath" is the fifth tale.
3. Keith has length and width, but no depth.
4. The truth is, Beth is uncouth.
5. We both left on the eleventh of the month.
6. In the aftermath, his wrath became mirth.
7. It took mammoth effort to unearth the monolith.
8. The mouth of the Firth of Forth is north of here.
9. The eighth roll of cloth is worth a tenth of the ninth.
10. Judith appeared in "Macbeth" and "Twelfth Night."

Now read SENTENCES alternately from A and B above (A1,B1; A2,B2; A3,B3; etc.).

C. *In the CHART on the opposite page, read vertical pairs across (A1–2, B1–2, C1–2, etc.). Then read the SENTENCES below.*

1. Can't Faith face the facts?
2. The traffic is worse on Worth Avenue.
3. Cross Roth off the list.
4. He's of no use to the youth movement.
5. That would be beneath Bernice.
6. I'm afraid that's just a myth, Miss.
7. At the grass roots, McGrath is rather weak.
8. They don't enforce a fourth of them.
9. Hortense was tenth in line.
10. There's no truth in the truce reports.

D. *In the CHART on the opposite page, read down each column. Then read the SENTENCES below.*

1. The price of that sheath is twice its worth.
2. Of course Ruth can pass math!
3. The North may face a dearth of rice.
4. Miss Garth is powerless to bequeath it to anyone.
5. I'll get my bonus on the fourteenth of this month.
6. There's no proof, unless Booth steps forth as a witness.
7. Yes, Plymouth was his place of birth.
8. I guess Meredith will practice in Elizabeth, New Jersey.
9. I'm not exactly toothless — I wear false teeth.
10. Keith had boundless faith in the police.

LESSON 37

[s] *and* [θ] *in Combination*

[s] and [θ] often occur close together: in final clusters (*tenTHS*), at the end of one word and the beginning of the next (*leSS THin*), separated by a vowel (*SouTH*), etc. This lesson provides practice in shifting between [s] position (tongue just behind—but not touching—the upper teeth) and [θ] position (tongue touching the tips of the upper teeth).

Buildup Exercises

Read each section as follows: In the CHART, read vertical pairs across (A1–2, B1–2, etc.), then the second line. Then read the SENTENCES.

		A	B	C	D
[sθ]:	1.	loose	Reece	worse	voice
	2.	loose thatch	Reece Theater	worse things	voice thick

a) Grace always takes three aspirins.
b) Can't you trace my niece through the school?
c) Bess thinks it's threaded wrong.
d) Miss Thoden had to race through it.

		A	B	C	D
[θs]:	1.	math	moth	girth	tenth
	2.	math's	moth's	girth's	tenths

a) The truth is, Ruth's glad.
b) Ask Meredith if the wreath's all right.
c) Mr. Garth sent Beth south for the winter.
d) He lives on North Seventh Street.

		A	B	C	D
[θsθ]:	1.	cloth's	youth's	path's	tooth's
	2.	cloth's thin	youth's through	path's thorny	tooth's throbbing

a) Roth says Faith's thirty years old.
b) McGrath's about three-fourths through.
c) The Worths think Keith's theory is right.
d) The myths Theo told affected Ruth's thinking.

Contrast Exercises

Read each section as follows: In the CHART, read line 1, then line 2, then vertical pairs across (A1–2, B1–2, etc.). Then read the SENTENCES.

		A	B	C	D
[sθ/θs]:	1.	Bess thought	Reece thanks	loose thinking	worse thumb
	2.	Beth sought	wreath sank	youth sinking	worth some

a) Miss Throop was less thorough.
b) They keep records of births and deaths.
c) Of course Thelma bought some nice things.
d) Plymouth's gone to great lengths.

		A	B	C	D
[s..θ/θ..s]:	1.	see-through	Scythia	Smith	Seth'll be
	2.	threesome	thickness	thistle	Thessaly

a) Samantha's sympathies were with the South.

b) Who wrote "Thoughts on Thanksgiving"?

c) Cynthia had something to do on the seventh.

d) It was thoughtless of Thurston to lose my thermos.

		A	B	C	D
[s..θs/θ..sθ]:	1.	Smith sings	Seth sue	Forsyth see	sloth's under
	2.	thinks things	Theseus threw	thrice three	thoughts thunder

a) The sleuth's following his trail.

b) Thewless thinks his threats threw me.

c) The Sabbath's almost over.

d) I read Thripp's thesis three times.

		A	B	C	D
[s..θsθ/s..sθs]:	1.	South's things	strength's thin	Seth's thanks	sleuth's theories
	2.	sixth singer	sixth sin	sixth sank	sixth series

a) Smith's thesis challenged Seth's theory.

b) The new baby is my sixth sister.

c) Forsyth's thinking of publishing Smith's third book.

d) She has a sixth sense.

Review Exercises

1. Spence threw three cents through the window.
2. Is Sixth Street a north-south street?
3. Forsyth sent for some theater tickets.
4. I dropped Ruth's thimble on Keith's thick rug.
5. Sam thinks Thelma lives on North Seneca Street.
6. The eighth Swiss athlete was a youth of strength.
7. Smith's thinking of Beth's third sonnet.
8. Whiskey comes in fifths, but not in sevenths or ninths.
9. Thurston's force withstood the fourth assault.
10. Three-sixths of sixty is thirty.

LESSON 38
[ð/θ] — *Initial, Medial, Final*

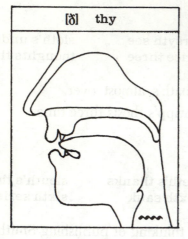

[ð] thy

To make [ð] and [θ], touch the tips of the upper teeth with the tip of the flattened tongue and force out a stream of air—voiced for [ð], voiceless for [θ].

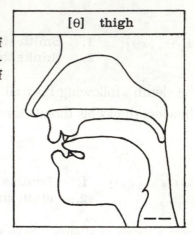

[θ] thigh

Contrast Chart

	A	B	C	D	E
1.	that	than	thy	though	those
2.	thatch	thank	thigh	Thoden	tholes
3.	then	thence	they	they'd	thee
4.	thenyl	thespian	thane	theta	thief
5.	thus	the	this	this'll	thou
6.	thud	thumb	thick	thistle	thousand
7.	leather	brethren	weather	tether	heather
8.	lethargy	breathy	ethic	method	Ethridge
9.	fathoms	gather	lather	worthy	further
10.	Athens	Kathy	Atherton	worthless	earthy
11.	hither	rhythmic	Smithers	another	pother
12.	Ithaca	arithmetic	mythic	anathema	apothecary
13.	sheathe	teethe	wreathe	seethe	clothe
14.	sheath	teeth	wreath	heath	cloth
15.	mouth [ð]	lithe	swathe	lathe	spathe
16.	mouth [θ]	Goliath	faith	wraith	path
17.	soothe	smooth	loathe	with [ð]	herewith [ð]
18.	forsooth	vermouth	oath	with [θ]	herewith [θ]

70

Contrast Exercises

A. *In the CHART on the opposite page, read the odd-numbered lines across (1, 3, 5, etc.). Then read the SENTENCES below.*

1. There's more than one of those.
2. Then this is the end.
3. That's the way the ball bounces.
4. I therefore prefer that they do it themselves.
5. Her mother and father left together.
6. Some others, Carruthers, would rather be rich.
7. I gather neither of you took a breather.
8. It was turned on a lathe and sanded smooth.
9. Swathe it in shadow, wreathe it in mist.
10. It's tax and tax, tithe and tithe, till a man can't breathe.

B. *In the CHART on the opposite page, read the even-numbered lines across (2, 4, 6, etc.). Then read the SENTENCES below.*

1. I think it's Thackeray's thermos bottle.
2. Theo threw it in a thicket.
3. He makes thirty-three thousand a year.
4. She threatened to thwart Thurman's plans.
5. Agatha's an authority on Gothic art.
6. Jonathan is Lutheran, not Catholic.
7. Timothy Hathaway believes in telepathy.
8. Keith left Plymouth on the seventh.
9. Garth has the strength of a mammoth.
10. Meredith never learned the truth about his birth.

Now read SENTENCES alternately from A and B above (A1,B1; A2,B2; A3,B3; etc.).

C. *In the CHART on the opposite page, read vertical pairs across (A1–2, B1–2, C1–2, etc.). Then read the SENTENCES below.*

1. Except for Thayer, they all approved.
2. All these theses proved false.
3. Their therapist is an able man.
4. Can't we use ether, either?
5. The bomb blew the smithy to smithereens.
6. He was wrathful rather than amused.
7. I don't know whether Ethel's here.
8. Your bath is hot; bathe now, before dinner.
9. He can't breathe; let him catch his breath.
10. I'm loath to say it, but I loathe rock music.

D. *In the CHART on the opposite page, read down each column. Then read the SENTENCES below.*

1. The thieves thought they'd been thorough.
2. Then Thea told them her theory.
3. They'll be through by this Thursday.
4. Smathers is the author of "Another Birthday."
5. Cynthia's father wasn't altogether truthful.
6. Nothing bothers Matthew's brother.
7. Heather's playthings are rather pathetic.
8. A little broth will soothe you, Ruth.
9. Smythe greeted them both with warmth.
10. "Lithe and Lovely," with Judith Blythe, just opened in Duluth.

LESSON 39

[ð/z] — *Initial, Medial, Final*

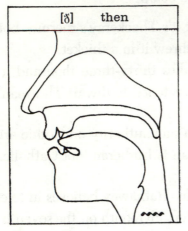

[ð]   then

To make [ð], touch the tips of the upper teeth with the tip of the flattened tongue and force out a voiced stream of air.

To make [z], place the tip of the tongue very close to the front part of the tooth-ridge, just behind (but not touching) the upper teeth. Groove the front of the tongue and force a voiced stream of air between tongue tip and tooth-ridge.

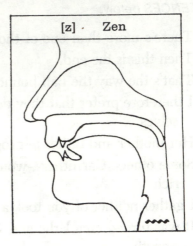

[z] ·   Zen

Contrast Chart

	A	B	C	D
1.	than	these	though	thou
2.	zander	Z's	zodiac	zowie
3.	they	that	them	this
4.	Zale	zap	zemmi	zip
5.	thee	thine	thence	those
6.	zee	Zion	Zennist	zoist
7.	prithee	withered	rhythm	blithered
8.	prison	wizard	risen	blizzard
9.	heather	leather	either	wreathing
10.	hesitate	Ezzard	easier	reason
11.	brother	another	hither	dither
12.	buzzer	nuzzle	lizard	dizzy
13.	bathe	lathe	spathe	swathe
14.	bays	lays	spays	sways
15.	tithe	writhe	lithe	blithe
16.	ties	rise	lies	Bly's
17.	loathe	scathe	teethe	sheathe
18.	lows	Kay's	tease	she's

72

Contrast Exercises

A. *In the CHART on the opposite page, read the odd-numbered lines across (1, 3, 5, etc.). Then read the SENTENCES below.*

1. There, there—that's all right.
2. This is the last chance they'll get.
3. He gave them the rest of the money.
4. Their chief was then fifty or thereabouts.
5. Another mother might have smothered him with kisses.
6. Heather's a Southerner, not a Northerner.
7. Neither course is altogether worthy of him.
8. Smythe won't breathe a word of it.
9. You bathe the baby, and I'll clothe him.
10. Blythe saw him writhe in agony.

B. *In the CHART on the opposite page, read the even-numbered lines across (2, 4, 6, etc.). Then read the SENTENCES below.*

1. Zimmerman has all the zeal of a zombie.
2. Zero Zinc is a New Zealand company.
3. Zander's zest for zoology is boundless.
4. Our Zurich zoo has a new zebra.
5. What are his reasons for resigning from the organization?
6. Her designs are positively amazing.
7. *Amazon* is an amusing magazine.
8. He knows I oppose his views.
9. I suppose Rose always agrees.
10. Does Hayes ever use his skis?

Now read SENTENCES alternately from A and B above (A1,B1; A2,B2; A3,B3; etc.).

C. *In the CHART on the opposite page, read vertical pairs across (A1–2, B1–2, C1–2, etc.). Then read the SENTENCES below.*

1. That Zachary's a bright boy.
2. This one's a zinnia.
3. Then she took up Zen.
4. Susan was soothing her weeping child.
5. He's closing the clothing store early tonight.
6. Why bother Boswell about it?
7. Don't get into a lather, Lazarus.
8. Why seethe with anger? Seize your revenge!
9. Thanks to the breeze, we can breathe again.
10. This scythe is the wrong size for me.

D. *In the CHART on the opposite page, read down each column. Then read the SENTENCES below.*

1. That's why Zena bought them a xylophone.
2. They must have made a zillion of these zippers.
3. Back then, Zeller was at the zenith of his fame.
4. I gather Rizzo's work is rather hazardous.
5. Father is visiting my brother in Brazil.
6. Find out whether Basil has further results to report.
7. I wouldn't invest a farthing in Frazer's leather business.
8. Bathe the boy's foot, and then swathe it in gauze.
9. You can soothe Ray's feelings with a little praise.
10. I loathe his sharp eyes and smooth lies.

LESSON 40

[ð̆/d] – *Initial, Medial, Final*

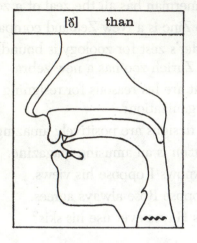

| [ð] | than |

To make [ð], touch the tips of the upper teeth with the tip of the flattened tongue and force out a voiced stream of air.

To make [d], stop the flow of air through the mouth by touching the tooth-ridge with the tip of the tongue. For initial [d], release the air with a voiced explosion; for medial [d] before a vowel, release less forcefully or make a flap sound; for final [d] and medial [d] before a consonant, do not release.

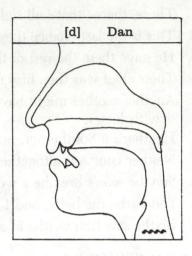

| [d] | Dan |

Contrast Chart

	A	B	C	D	E
1.	than	that	thence	them	this
2.	Dan	data	dense	demi-	disk
3.	these	then	thou	there	though
4.	Dee's	den	Dow	dare	dough
5.	those	thy	they've	thus	thine
6.	doze	die	Dave	dust	dine
7.	either	neither	wreathing	seething	heathen
8.	Edith	kneader	reading	seeding	heeding
9.	blather	gather	lather	hither	rhythm
10.	bladder	gadder	ladder	hidden	ridden
11.	heather	leather	weather	other	southern
12.	header	leaden	wedding	udder	sudden
13.	lathe	swathe	bathe	spathe	scathe
14.	laid	suede	bayed	spade	Cade
15.	sheathe	breathe	teethe	loathe	clothe
16.	she'd	breed	teed	load	code
17.	tithe	writhe	Smythe	soothe	smooth
18.	tide	ride	slide	sued	mood

74

Contrast Exercises

A. *In the CHART on the opposite page, read the odd-numbered lines across (1, 3, 5, etc.). Then read the SENTENCES below.*

1. Those are theirs and these are mine.
2. I like them even less than that.
3. They signed it then and there.
4. Smathers gathered them all together.
5. Without water, it'll wither within a week.
6. Heather'd rather have the leather one.
7. My other brother went further in school.
8. I won't soothe him—let him seethe!
9. He swung the scythe with smooth strokes.
10. Yes, I work at a lathe, and I loathe it.

B. *In the CHART on the opposite page, read the even-numbered lines across (2, 4, 6, etc.). Then read the SENTENCES below.*

1. Don't destroy Daley's diagram.
2. Doris didn't deny doing it.
3. She's Doctor Dower's daughter.
4. Eddie's ladder suddenly collapsed.
5. I've seldom seen a sadder muddle.
6. Nader solved the riddle of the hidden radio.
7. Buddy is already in Toledo.
8. We'd need a good guide to lead us.
9. Todd had played on her pride.
10. He tried to hide his bad mood.

Now read SENTENCES alternately from A and B above (A1,B1; A2,B2; A3,B3; etc.).

C. *In the CHART on the opposite page, read vertical pairs across (A1–2, B1–2, C1–2, etc.). Then read the SENTENCES below.*

1. I dare their experts to match these diesels.
2. One day they marched off on the double.
3. I like this district, though Dolan says it's dangerous.
4. Is Mrs. Withers a widow?
5. It's a feather in Fedder's cap.
6. He's a worthy man, but a wordy one.
7. You'll have to tether Tedder's horse.
8. Her lithe grace belied her age.
9. She'll just seethe if we succeed.
10. I put the scythe aside.

D. *In the CHART on the opposite page, read each column. Then read the SENTENCES below.*

1. Dennis will be there in December or thereabouts.
2. Let them discuss the details among themselves.
3. They decided that Denver was their best bet.
4. I doubt that Dan was there.
5. Madeleine's brother is a blithering idiot.
6. Neither candidate won Mother's confidence.
7. Order another soda for Dithers.
8. Isn't Fred with the Reed Lathe Company?
9. It's a broad, smooth road with little traffic.
10. Smythe lied with good grace.

LESSON 41
[ð̵ə/də] *and* [ð̵is/dis]

Be careful to pronounce initial [ð] and [d] distinctly before unstressed vowels. Make a sharp difference between *the* [ð̵ə] and *de-* [də], and between *this* [ð̵is] and *dis-* [dis].

Contrast Exercises

Read each section as follows: In the CHART, read vertical pairs across (A1–2, B1–2, etc.), then down each column. Then read the SENTENCES.

[ð̵ə/də]:

		A	B	C	D
	1.	the base	the bait	the claim	the fame
	2.	debase	debate	declaim	defame
	3.	the mean	the pleat	the feat	the meter
	4.	demean	deplete	defeat	Demeter
	5.	the vise	the fine	the side	the spies
	6.	devise	define	decide	despise

1. Deliver the liver.
2. The men are demented.
3. He won the seat by deceit.
4. The note denotes a change in policy.
5. Delaney crossed the lane.
6. The scribe described it.
7. That decree will please the Cree.
8. The man demands an answer.
9. I thought the Kleins declined.
10. The light delighted the baby.

___

[ð̵is/dis]:

		A	B	C	D
	1.	this favor	this claim	this place	this taste
	2.	disfavor	disclaim	displace	distaste
	3.	this comfort	this gust	this trust	this color
	4.	discomfort	disgust	distrust	discolor
	5.	this temper	this cent	this credit	this member
	6.	distemper	dissent	discredit	dismember

1. Don't dispel this spell I'm under.
2. This player displays talent.
3. Discard this card.
4. This tends to distend it.
5. I dislike this likeness.
6. This still distills whiskey.
7. Is this respect or disrespect?
8. I just discovered this cover is his.
9. I got this counter from a discounter.
10. This orderly is disorderly.

LESSON 42
Intonation: Tag Questions

A tag question consists of a statement phrase followed by a question phrase. Several different intonations may be used with tag questions. Two common patterns are shown here. The 232/2⌣ pattern indicates that the speaker is not sure that his statement is correct, and that he is seeking confirmation. The 231/31 pattern indicates that the speaker is merely making a comment and is inviting agreement. (In each section below, read down each column, then across each line. Example: A1-5, B1-5; then A1-B1, A2-B2, etc.)

A. *The 232/2⌣ pattern*

1. You don't belíeve him, dó you?
2. They haven't séen it, háve they?
3. It doesn't mátter, dóes it?
4. She wasn't réady, wás she?
5. He couldn't dó it, cóuld he?

6. It's going to ráin, ísn't it?
7. He wanted a lóan, dídn't he?
8. We should have stópped, shóuldn't we?
9. You were asléep, wéren't you?
10. They're pretty góod, áren't they?

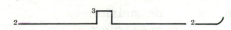

11. Martin isn't ángry about it, ís he?
12. You haven't seen my nótebook, háve you?
13. We could have retúrned it, cóuldn't we?
14. The mayor's in Flórida, ísn't he?
15. I shouldn't repórt it, shóuld I?
16. You don't mind tálking to him, dó you?
17. He makes a lot of móney, dóesn't he?
18. I'll have a sécretary, wón't I?
19. She hasn't divórced him, hás she?
20. They weren't too disórderly, wére they?

B. *The 231/31 pattern*

1. You don't belíeve him, dó you?
2. They haven't séen it, háve they?
3. It doesn't mátter, dóes it?
4. She wasn't réady, wás she?
5. He couldn't dó it, cóuld he?

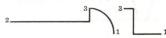

6. It's going to ráin, ísn't it?
7. He wanted a lóan, dídn't he?
8. We should have stópped, shóuldn't we?
9. You were asléep, wéren't you?
10. They're pretty góod, áren't they?

11. He isn't a very pléasant fellow, ís he?
12. You haven't learned your lésson, háve you?
13. We could have been ínjured, cóuldn't we?
14. His father's a búsinessman, ísn't he?
15. I shouldn't have sáid that, shóuld I?
16. You just don't trúst the fellow, dó you?
17. He takes a lot of chánces, dóesn't he?
18. I'll need a bábysitter, wón't I?
19. She hasn't been lúcky, hás she?
20. They weren't very práctical, wére they?

Note that the 232/2⌣ pattern is used both in tag questions and in statements with direct address. Read the following sentences across.

1. He won't téll them, wíll he?   He won't téll them, Wílly.
2. He isn't réady, ís he?   He isn't réady, Ízzy.
3. We don't néed it, dó we?   We don't néed it, Déwey.
4. He wouldn't séll it, wóuld he?   He wouldn't séll it, Wóody.
5. He can afford it, cán't he?   He can afford it, Cándy.

LESSON 43

[ʒ/dʒ] *in Medial Position*

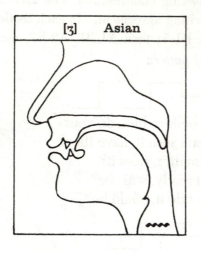

[ʒ]   Asian

To make [ʒ], curve the front of the tongue high, groove it, and bring it very close to the back part of the tooth-ridge. Keep the tongue tip turned down, and round the lips slightly. Force a voiced stream of air between the tongue and the back of the tooth-ridge.

To make [dʒ], start in [d] position, with the tip of the tongue touching the tooth-ridge; release the voiced air stream with the tongue in [ʒ] position.

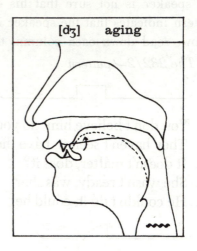

[dʒ]   aging

Contrast Chart

	A	**B**	**C**	**D**
1.	Asian	equation	abrasion	persuasion
2.	aging	waging	raging	assuaging
3.	Caucasian	Eurasia	aphasia	glazier
4.	contagion	courageous	aphagia	gauging
5.	derision	vision	precision	division
6.	rigid	vigil	pigeon	individual
7.	decision	elision	visionary	provisional
8.	deciduous	religion	vigilant	original
9.	lesion	seizure	Parisian	adhesion
10.	legion	procedure	region	Egypt
11.	version	Persian	excursion	immersion
12.	virgin	purging	scourging	emerging
13.	submersion	diversion	conversion	incursion
14.	submerging	diverging	converging	urging
15.	closure	erosion	casual	azure
16.	cogent	Trojan	cadging	agile
17.	Hoosier	fusion	measure	pleasure
18.	huger	fugitive	edger	pledger

78

Contrast Exercises

A. *In the CHART on the opposite page, read the odd-numbered lines across (1, 3, 5, etc.). Then read the SENTENCES below.*

1. Not all excursions are pleasurable occasions.
2. Frazier envisioned several subdivisions.
3. The glazier measured it with precision.
4. I'm visualizing a leisurely trip through Polynesia.
5. The treasurer usually makes such decisions.
6. Since the explosion, Lozier's had amnesia.
7. He's getting unusual television exposure.
8. She played the Parisian in "Casual Persuasion."
9. This provision for reversion has caused some confusion.
10. Several of the casualties required transfusions.

B. *In the CHART on the opposite page, read the even-numbered lines across (2, 4, 6, etc.). Then read the SENTENCES below.*

1. Angela's managing the regional office.
2. I imagine the legend will gradually grow.
3. He's a project engineer in Nigeria.
4. It's no mere conjecture, but a logical projection of the trend.
5. Can Marjorie adjust to so great a tragedy?
6. When will the major rejoin his regiment?
7. Imogene rejected their apology.
8. He's energetic and intelligent — and extremely dangerous.
9. Put the vegetables and tangerines in the refrigerator.
10. The fugitive is somewhere in Georgia or Virginia.

Now read SENTENCES alternately from A and B above (A1,B1; A2,B2; A3,B3; etc.).

C. *In the CHART on the opposite page, read vertical pairs across (A1–2, B1–2, C1–2, etc.). Then read the SENTENCES below.*

1. He's rather cagey on occasion.
2. Reggie treasures that picture.
3. They need rigid supervision.
4. Virgil's conversion was a shock.
5. Yes, we have several agents in Asia.
6. He resented Ridgeway's derision.
7. Her version verges on the ridiculous.
8. That ended Eugene's regime.
9. They're urging a diversion.
10. I didn't like Nugent's allusion to my past.

D. *In the CHART on the opposite page, read down each column. Then read the SENTENCES below.*

1. Benjamin casually rejected all of my revisions.
2. The sergeant's disclosures led us to a dangerous conclusion.
3. Anastasia is subject to delusions of grandeur.
4. I preferred the original version of "A Measure of Magic."
5. It was Dr. Hodges' decision to make the emergency incision.
6. His protégé's apology was unusually abject.
7. Sedgwick was disillusioned by Roger's exclusion from the club.
8. That's plagiarized from Frazier's "Strangers in Asia."
9. I'm enjoying the luxury of indulging my illusions.
10. In the collision Bridget suffered contusions and other injuries.

[dʒ] *in Final Position*

Make final [dʒ] like medial [dʒ] (practiced in the preceding lesson). Be careful not to add a vowel to final [dʒ]: *edge* is [edʒ], not [edʒi]. Instead, let the voiced [dʒ] fade into voiceless [ʃ].

Step-down Exercises

	A	B	C	D	E
1.	midget	rigid	bridging	frigid	cringing
2.	Midge	ridge	bridge	fridge	cringe
3.	aging	wager	paging	gauging	cagey
4.	age	wage	page	gauge	cage
5.	wedging	legend	hedging	edger	pledging
6.	wedge	ledge	hedge	edge	pledge
7.	grudging	drudgery	judging	budget	trudging
8.	grudge	drudge	judge	budge	trudge
9.	barging	margin	sergeant	larger	charging
10.	barge	Marge	sarge	large	charge
11.	urgent	surgeon	virgin	merging	perjury
12.	urge	surge	verge	merge	purge

A. *In the CHART above, read down each column. (In each word-pair, make the final* [dʒ] *of the second word sound like the medial* [dʒ] *of the first.) Then read the SENTENCES below.*

1. Who's staging "Backstage"?
2. It's logical for Lodge to complain.
3. It all seemed like magic to Madge.
4. They're enlarging a large number of them.
5. Yes, of course Bridget plays bridge.

6. The stranger has a strange way about him.
7. Do you know her agent's age?
8. Georgia's where George grew up.
9. A messenger brought the message to me.
10. The manager just can't manage.

B. *In the CHART above, read each two-line group as follows: vertical pairs across (A1–2, B1–2, C1–2, etc.), then the second line of the group. Then read the SENTENCES below.*

1. Dodge made a large mortgage payment.
2. We'll manage to salvage the wreckage.
3. At college Midge had a high average.
4. There's a huge gorge near the village.
5. It took courage to divulge the shortage.

6. I'll urge Marge to learn the language.
7. At this stage, that could damage my image.
8. Charge the postage to Brundage.
9. Encourage them to arrange the exchange.
10. "Savage Revenge" was a huge success.

LESSON 45
Intonation Contrast:
Direct Address/Name as Object

Two sentences may be worded the same yet have entirely different meanings, as in the exercises below. In column A we are speaking *to* the person named; in column B we are speaking *about* the person. Phrase, stress and intonation differences convey the difference in meaning. (In each section below, read down each column, then across each line. Example: A1-10, B1-10; then A1-B1, A2-B2, etc.)

A. *Name in Direct Address*

1. I don't understánd, Sám.
2. You'd better stóp, Jóhn.
3. We ought to méet, Mrs. Háll.
4. He never ásks, Miss Róss.
5. Make them páy, Bárbara.
6. They're going to fíre, Hénry!
7. This may húrt, Mrs. Gréen.
8. You didn't sáy, Proféssor.
9. Don't fíght, Alex.
10. She must have léft, Jáck.

11. Why are you sháking, Jóe?
12. How could he refúse, Máry?
13. Which one fíts, Tímmy?
14. What time shall I phóne, Pát?
15. How long have you knówn, Fránk?
16. Why bóther, Mr. Fínch?
17. When did he wríte, Tóm?
18. Where are you híding, Bílly?
19. How can we hélp, Alan?
20. What will you óffer, Míchael?

21. Don't you sée, Mr. Brówn?
22. Has he cálled, Hárriet?
23. Had she forgótten, Júlie?
24. Would they accépt, Mr. Ádams?
25. Did the teacher fáil, Nóra?
26. Does he remémber, Alice?
27. Will you dríve, Mrs. Mórris?
28. Hasn't she héard, Márk?
29. Couldn't they téll, Jáson?
30. Are you still téaching, Bért?

B. *Name in Object Position*

1. I don't understand Sám.
2. You'd better stop Jóhn.
3. We ought to meet Mrs. Háll.
4. He never asks Miss Róss.
5. Make them pay Bárbara.
6. They're going to fire Hénry.
7. This may hurt Mrs. Gréen.
8. You didn't say "Proféssor."
9. Don't fight Álex.
10. She must have left Jáck.

11. Why are you shaking Jóe?
12. How could he refuse Máry?
13. Which one fits Tímmy?
14. What time shall I phone Pát?
15. How long have you known Fránk?
16. Why bother Mr. Fínch?
17. When did he write Tóm?
18. Where are you hiding Bílly?
19. How can we help Álan?
20. What will you offer Míchael?

21. Don't you see Mr. Brówn?
22. Has he called Hárriet?
23. Had she forgotten Júlie?
24. Would they accept Mr. Ádams?
25. Did the teacher fail Nóra?
26. Does he remember Álice?
27. Will you drive Mrs. Mórris?
28. Hasn't she heard Márk?
29. Couldn't they tell Jáson?
30. Are you still teaching Bért?

LESSON 46
[d/dʒ] *before* [i iy ir uw]

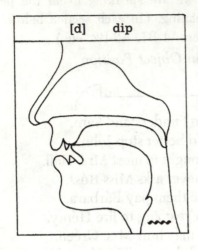

[d]   dip

Begin both [d] and [dʒ] by touching the tooth-ridge with the tip of the tongue. For [d], release the stopped air suddenly, with a voiced explosion. For [dʒ], release the voiced air stream more slowly by shifting to [ʒ] position, placing the grooved front of the tongue very close to the back part of the tooth-ridge.

(Note: Medial [d] before a stressed vowel is exploded less strongly than initial [d]; before an unstressed vowel it is usually *flapped* — see Lesson 14.)

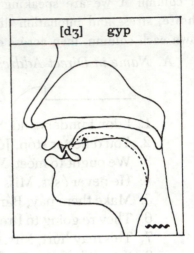

[dʒ]   gyp

Contrast Chart

	A	B	C	D
1.	dip	din	dill	dig
2.	gyp	gin	Jill	jig
3.	dib	ditto	dingle	dippy
4.	jib	jitters	jingle	gypsy
5.	digger	differ	distant	dinner
6.	jigger	jiffy	gist	Ginny
7.	Dee	dear	deep	deal
8.	gee	jeer	jeep	congeal
9.	Dino	demon	dean	diesel
10.	Gina	G-man	hygiene	gees
11.	deeper	gardenia	decent	endearing
12.	jeepers	genial	G-string	jeering
13.	deuce	dual	do	duke
14.	juice	jewel	Jew	juke
15.	dune	Doob	dude	dupe
16.	June	jubilant	judo	Jupiter
17.	duel	doodad	duty	dubious
18.	julep	Judah	jute	jubilee

Contrast Exercises

A. *In the CHART on the opposite page, read the odd-numbered lines across (1, 3, 5, etc.). Then read the SENTENCES below.*

1. Dixon's from a different district.
2. It was dictated under difficult conditions.
3. Didn't Dickerson use the dictionary?
4. Deacon took a detour through Aberdeen.
5. It was decent of Dietrich to redeem it.
6. Dietz is a mediator in Dearborn.
7. So much I deduced from Dugan's doodles.
8. Duval was dubious about duplicating it.
9. It's Dewey's duty to do it.
10. Duchin's due at Purdue in the spring.

B. *In the CHART on the opposite page, read the even-numbered lines across (2, 4, 6, etc.). Then read the SENTENCES below.*

1. The magician made Ginny a bit jittery.
2. Jill's jingle is just gibberish.
3. I suspect that Jim gyps at gin rummy.
4. Gee, Jean, you're a genius!
5. He took geography, geology, and geometry.
6. Eugene sold the jeep in Algeria.
7. Julian's a junior at the Juilliard School.
8. I'll bet Julia was jubilant at graduation.
9. June prefers juice to julienne soup.
10. Judy's the perfect juvenile to play Juliet.

Now read SENTENCES alternately from A and B above (A1,B1; A2,B2; A3,B3; etc.).

C. *In the CHART on the opposite page, read vertical pairs across (A1–2, B1–2, C1–2, etc.). Then read the SENTENCES below.*

1. Jill's diligence paid off.
2. It looks as if Dillon's jilted her.
3. Ginger's home is a dingy place.
4. The gym was dimly lit.
5. Dina is quite ingenious.
6. Jeeves is a devious fellow.
7. Dean wore jeans to the party.
8. Julie was duly nominated.
9. They produce tomato juice.
10. Miss Dooley's jewels are missing.

D. *In the CHART on the opposite page, read down each column. Then read the SENTENCES below.*

1. The Egyptian diplomat registered his disapproval.
2. Didn't Jibby dismiss the engineer?
3. Jillson has the dismal task of writing jingles for the *Dispatch*.
4. The last edition of the *Virginia Dissident* carried Jim's story.
5. The clergyman was deeply moved by the refugees' ordeal.
6. Deevers has a managerial job with Belvedere Hygiene Products.
7. So far, Gina's ideas haven't congealed into an ideology.
8. What the deuce is Jewett doing in Juneau?
9. DuPont has jury duty in June.
10. Can you induce Julius to introduce me to the adjutant?

LESSON 47

[t/tʃ] *before* [i iy ir uw]

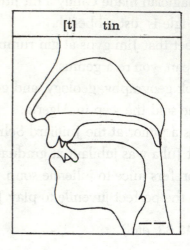

[t]	tin

Begin both [t] and [tʃ] by touching the tooth-ridge with the tongue tip. For [t], release the stopped air suddenly and completely. For [tʃ], release the air more slowly by shifting to [ʃ] position—placing the grooved front of the tongue very close to the back part of the tooth-ridge. Both [t] and [tʃ] are voiceless, and both are *aspirated*—released with a puff of air—in initial position and in medial position before a stressed vowel. (Medial [t] before an unstressed vowel is usually *flapped* — see Lesson 14.)

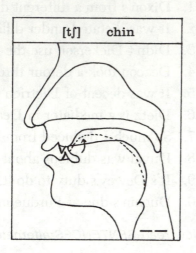

[tʃ]	chin

Contrast Chart

	A	B	C	D
1.	tin	Tim	till	tick
2.	chin	chimney	chill	chick
3.	tinsel	tickle	timpani	tipper
4.	chintz	chicle	chimp	chipper
5.	titter	tiller	ticker	tizzy
6.	chitter	chiller	chicory	chisel
7.	tepee	teen	tease	tier
8.	cheap	chino	cheese	cheer
9.	teak	Tiefer	teeter	teacher
10.	cheek	chief	cheater	chicha
11.	teasing	teary	teapot	TV
12.	Parcheesi	cheery	cheapen	Cheevey
13.	too	Tuesday	Tudor	tuba
14.	chew	choosy	chewed	chuba
15.	twofer	too-too	twos	Toohey
16.	chufa	choochoo	choose	chewy
17.	tattoo	her too	Bantu	Hess too
18.	statue	virtue	Manchu	eschew

84

Contrast Exercises

A. *In the CHART on the opposite page, read the odd-numbered lines across (1, 3, 5, etc.). Then read the SENTENCES below.*

1. Timmons is a typical politician.
2. He continued his egotistical behavior.
3. Tilson anticipated a large tip.
4. She's a statistician with the Tiffin Tinwear Company.
5. The team's tee shirts are teal blue.
6. Tina has fourteen teeth now.
7. That TV has a warranty and a guarantee.
8. The whole platoon got tattooed in Tombstone.
9. Toomey paid his tuition on Tuesday.
10. His tutor is touring Tunisia.

B. *In the CHART on the opposite page, read the even-numbered lines across (2, 4, 6, etc.). Then read the SENTENCES below.*

1. Chisholm used a chisel to chip it away.
2. Miss Chipman has a chinchilla coat.
3. Buy chicken, chicory, and fish chips.
4. Chilcott had studied the Chickasaw and Chippewa cultures.
5. Fritchie's cheating at Parcheesi again.
6. Cochise was an Apache chief.
7. Richie has an itchy cheek.
8. His constituents in Massachusetts understood the situation.
9. Their intellectuals are contemptuous of all ritual.
10. He eventually found sanctuary in Saskatchewan.

Now read SENTENCES alternately from A and B above (A1,B1; A2,B2; A3,B3; etc.).

C. *In the CHART on the opposite page, read vertical pairs across (A1–2, B1–2, C1–2, etc.). Then read the SENTENCES below.*

1. I haven't seen Tilden's children.
2. Mr. Chips tipped us off.
3. That really tickled Chickering.
4. He bought a cheap teapot.
5. I like Mr. Chee's goatee.
6. She's cheerful and tearful by turns.
7. I've met Mr. Chu, too.
8. He broke two statues.
9. These are the actual tools they used.
10. Am I too late to congratulate them?

D. *In the CHART on the opposite page, read down each column. Then read the SENTENCES below.*

1. Such tactics left Chipley inarticulate.
2. We'll stay in Chillicothe till Friday, then continue on to Wichita.
3. Chilton has a certificate of authenticity for his Chippendale chair.
4. He was teaching Christianity to the Comanches.
5. Teague had a cheeseburger, followed by tea and cheesecake.
6. "Tears and Cheers" is a dreary collection of cheap routines.
7. He got a toothache from chewing too much chewing gum.
8. "Tucson Choo-Choo" has a catchy tune but fatuous lyrics.
9. There's a good opportunity for a mature secretary at Tudor Mutual.
10. The two virtuosos made an impromptu trip to Portugal.

[d/z] *before* [i iy ir uw]

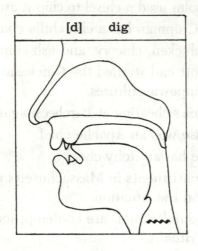

[d]   dig

To make [d], touch the tooth-ridge with the tip of the tongue; then release the stopped air with a voiced explosion.

To make [z], place the tip of the tongue very close to the front part of the tooth-ridge, just behind (but not touching) the upper teeth. Groove the front of the tongue and force a voiced stream of air between tongue tip and tooth-ridge.

(Note: Medial [d] before a stressed vowel is exploded less strongly than initial [d]; before an unstressed vowel it is usually *flapped* — see Lesson 14.)

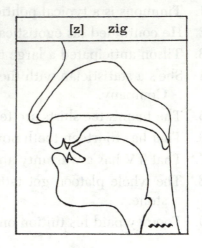

[z]   zig

Contrast Chart

	A	B	C	D
1.	dig	dink	ding	dip
2.	zig	zinc	zing	zip
3.	dinner	digger	distance	dibbing
4.	zinnia	ziggurat	existence	exhibit
5.	dither	Dillon	dipper	dinky
6.	zither	zillion	zipper	zinky
7.	demon	dean	deacon	dealing
8.	Zieman	Zena	Zeke	Zealand
9.	Dee	dear	Geraldine	per diem
10.	zee	zero	benzine	museum
11.	Dino	deeper	ideal	dearest
12.	Zeno	zebra	zeolite	Xerox
13.	do	doom	dues	dude
14.	zoo	zoom	zoos	exude
15.	deuce	duty	ado	reduce
16.	Zeus	zooty	kazoo	resume
17.	Paducah	Medusa	dooming	dual
18.	bazooka	Azusa	presuming	Zulu

86

Contrast Exercises

A. *In the CHART on the opposite page, read the odd-numbered lines across (1, 3, 5, etc.). Then read the SENTENCES below.*

1. What difference did his diploma make?
2. Dick's prediction is ridiculous.
3. Edith did the dishes, didn't she?
4. There's a defect in Dino's deep freezer.
5. Deaver's idealism endeared him to all.
6. "Demon or Deity" is Diebold's new book.
7. Diehl has the deed to the Pasadena property.
8. Our Dunes Club dues are overdue.
9. Duchin's redoing his duplex.
10. Can Dewey produce a due bill?

B. *In the CHART on the opposite page, read the even-numbered lines across (2, 4, 6, etc.). Then read the SENTENCES below.*

1. "Blazing Resistance" was filmed in Brazil.
2. My supposition is that the requisition exists.
3. Dr. Zimmer is the musician's physician.
4. Louisiana cuisine is Zeno's specialty.
5. Zieman caught the disease in New Zealand.
6. *Physique* is a sleazy magazine.
7. It's at the Ziegler Museum in New Jersey.
8. Zukor used a zoom lens.
9. Is there really a zoo in Kalamazoo?
10. Zulick's resumed casting "Montezuma."

Now read SENTENCES alternately from A and B above (A1,B1; A2,B2; A3,B3; etc.).

C. *In the CHART on the opposite page, read vertical pairs across (A1–2, B1–2, C1–2, etc.). Then read the SENTENCES below.*

1. Dillon's resilience is amazing.
2. He holds another position in addition to this one.
3. Zimmerman's dimming the lights.
4. It's easy for Edie to talk.
5. She has a great deal of zeal.
6. Dean was at the zenith of his career.
7. He brought Zena a gardenia.
8. They're dubious about Zubin's ability.
9. Dugan's bazooka exploded.
10. Zuma's plan was doomed to fail.

D. *In the CHART on the opposite page, read down each column. Then read the SENTENCES below.*

1. Dickens was visibly disappointed in the exposition.
2. We discussed his resignation and the difficult transition to follow.
3. Disraeli resisted prodigious Opposition pressure.
4. That's indicative of Zinsser's disposition.
5. Dietrich was uneasy about deviating from Zieffer's instructions.
6. Here comes nosy Andy, the neighborhood busybody.
7. McKenzie wrote "The Ordeal of Crazy Deer."
8. Dupré exuded confidence, but Zukerman was subdued.
9. I presume Dooley will resume his duties shortly.
10. Zuber's unduly exuberant about reducing the fare.

LESSON 49

The Suffixes $[s/z]$ *after Consonants*

The suffix *-s* is pronounced [s] after the voiceless consonants [f k p t θ]; it is pronounced [z] after the voiced consonants [v g b d ð l m n ŋ r]. Do not insert a vowel between these sounds and the suffix: *clothes* is [klowðz], not [klowðiz].

Contrast Exercises

Read each section as follows: In the CHART, read lines 1, 3, and 5; then lines 2, 4, and 6; then vertical pairs across (A1–2, B1–2, etc.). Then read the SENTENCES.

[fs/vz]:

	A	B	C	D	E
1.	waifs	safes	Rafe's	strafes	chafes
2.	waves	saves	raves	staves	shaves
3.	leafs	reefs	thief's	chiefs	griefs
4.	leaves	Reeves	thieves	achieves	grieves
5.	Duff's	luffs	wife's	life's	knife's
6.	doves	loves	wives	lives	knives

a) Those muffs and kerchiefs are cast-offs.

b) Reeves lives with his relatives.

c) These are Jeff's wife's galley-proofs.

d) She believes Steve's motives are good.

[ks/gz]:

	A	B	C	D	E
1.	bucks	tucks	ducks	Huck's	plucks
2.	bugs	tugs	Doug's	hugs	plugs
3.	picks	wicks	bricks	Dick's	Rick's
4.	pigs	wigs	brigs	digs	rigs
5.	hacks	racks	shacks	lacks	backs
6.	hags	rags	shags	lags	bags

a) Jack's folks won the sweepstakes.

b) Briggs brags about the bigwigs he knows.

c) Dix makes mistakes, too.

d) You'll find Craig's Rugs in our catalogues.

[ps/bz]:

	A	B	C	D	E
1.	caps	gaps	laps	taps	naps
2.	cabs	gabs	labs	tabs	nabs
3.	fops	mops	sops	cops	swaps
4.	fobs	mobs	sobs	cobs	swabs
5.	gyps	rips	nips	sips	Phipps
6.	jibs	ribs	nibs	sibs	fibs

a) Perhaps he keeps the envelopes in here.
b) Dobbs did it in dribs and drabs.

c) Chips hopes the grown-ups don't find out.
d) Did you hear the way Gibbs describes the suburbs?

[ts/dz]:

	A	B	C	D	E
1.	oats	boats	totes	moats	coats
2.	odes	bodes	toads	modes	codes
3.	heats	feats	beats	seats	meets
4.	heeds	feeds	beads	seeds	Meade's
5.	cots	knots	rots	tots	squats
6.	cods	nods	rods	Tod's	squads

a) Keats hates heights.
b) Rhodes needs better odds.

c) Bates gets into lots of fights.
d) Ed's kids love parades.

[θs/ðz]:

	A	B	C	D	E
1.	sheath's	wreath's	Keith's	heath's	breath's
2.	sheathes	wreathes	teethes	seethes	breathes
3.	mouth's	Ruth's	cloth's	lath's	bath's
4.	mouths	soothes	clothes	lathes	bathes

a) There are many myths about the earth's creation.
b) He just loathes Smythe's attitude.

c) She went to great lengths to get the youth's attention.
d) Every morning she smooths the bedclothes.

LESSON 50

The [iz] Suffix

The suffixes -es and -'s are pronounced [iz] after the consonants [s z ʃ ʒ tʃ dʒ].

Buildup Exercises

Follow this procedure in each section: In each two-line group of the CHART, read the first line, then vertical pairs across (A1–2, B1–2, etc.), then the second line. Then read the SENTENCES.

[z/ziz]:		A	B	C	D	E
	1.	laze	graze	daze	blaze	phase
	2.	lazes	grazes	dazes	blazes	phases
	3.	ease	tease	cheese	wheeze	appease
	4.	eases	teases	cheeses	wheezes	appeases
	5.	rise	size	prize	vise	surmise
	6.	rises	sizes	prizes	vises	surmises

a) Mays amazes me.

b) Guy's disguises don't fool anyone.

c) Ann despises Rose's compromises.

d) He uses pretty phrases, and this pleases her.

[s/siz]:		A	B	C	D	E
	1.	ace	lace	pace	base	case
	2.	aces	laces	paces	bases	cases
	3.	press	guess	bless	dress	Bess
	4.	presses	guesses	blesses	dresses	Bess's
	5.	bus	fuss	Gus	plus	muss
	6.	buses	fusses	Gus's	pluses	musses

a) Tell Guinness that the witnesses are ready.

b) Backus practices in New York.

c) Jess is Mrs. Moss's son.

d) There are lots of new faces in Mr. Rice's classes.

[ks/ksiz]:		A	B	C	D	E
	1.	mix	fix	Dix	coax	hoax
	2.	mixes	fixes	Dix's	coaxes	hoaxes
	3.	ax	sax	relax	pox	fox
	4.	axes	saxes	relaxes	poxes	foxes
	5.	hex	vex	sex	Rex	index
	6.	hexes	vexes	sexes	Rex's	indexes

a) Six sixes make thirty-six.

b) Put this box with the other boxes.

c) Alex's taxes are staggering.

d) I've never seen reflexes like Max's.

		A	**B**	**C**	**D**	**E**
[ʃ/ʃiz]:	1.	ash	gash	dash	sash	lash
	2.	ashes	gashes	dashes	sashes	lashes
	3.	gush	rush	hush	flush	crush
	4.	gushes	rushes	hushes	flushes	crushes
	5.	mash	stash	gnash	bash	smash
	6.	mashes	stashes	gnashes	bashes	smashes

a) Josh washes his own things.

b) Can't you cash Nash's check?

c) Give the Walshes our best wishes.

d) Then she finishes the dishes and polishes the silver.

		A	**B**	**C**	**D**	**E**
[tʃ/tʃiz]:	1.	batch	catch	latch	patch	match
	2.	batches	catches	latches	patches	matches
	3.	itch	ditch	hitch	niche	pitch
	4.	itches	ditches	hitches	niches	pitches
	5.	etch	wretch	ketch	fetch	sketch
	6.	etches	wretches	ketches	fetches	sketches

a) Which sandwiches are yours?

b) Watch for the stolen watches.

c) He preaches in one of the churches in Natchez.

d) I've heard only snatches of Fitch's speeches.

		A	**B**	**C**	**D**	**E**
[dʒ/dʒiz]:	1.	age	cage	page	rage	wage
	2.	ages	cages	pages	rages	wages
	3.	edge	hedge	ledge	wedge	pledge
	4.	edges	hedges	ledges	wedges	pledges
	5.	fudge	nudge	drudge	smudge	trudge
	6.	fudges	nudges	drudges	smudges	trudges

a) George judges everyone harshly.

b) Marge never budges, once her mind's made up.

c) Mr. Bridges bought some oranges and sausages.

d) Midge's mother manages her life.

LESSON 51
The Suffixes [t/d] *after Consonants*

The verb suffix *-ed* is pronounced [t] after the voiceless consonants [f k p s ʃ tʃ θ]; it is pronounced [d] after the voiced consonants [v g b z ʒ dʒ ð l m n ŋ r]. Do not insert a vowel between these sounds and the suffix: *saved* is [seyvd], not [seyvid]. The stops [p b k g] are unreleased before the suffix; the suffix itself is released, but with very little explosion.

Contrast Exercises

Read each section as follows: In the CHART, read lines 1, 3, and 5; then lines 2, 4, and 6; then vertical pairs across (A1–2, B1–2, etc.). Then read the SENTENCES.

[ft/vd]:

	A	B	C	D	E
1.	luffed	stuffed	gruffed	cliffed	stiffed
2.	loved	shoved	gloved	lived	sieved
3.	chafed	reffed	staffed	proofed	roofed
4.	shaved	revved	salved	proved	grooved
5.	reefed	leafed	sheafed	knifed	wifed
6.	bereaved	believed	sheaved	knived	wived

a) We all laughed when Raft goofed.
b) The half-starved man he saved, survived.
c) Luft photographed Hal as he golfed.
d) We believed he'd received an engraved announcement.

[kt/gd]:

	A	B	C	D	E
1.	backed	lacked	sacked	tacked	snacked
2.	bagged	lagged	sagged	tagged	snagged
3.	tucked	bucked	plucked	mucked	chucked
4.	tugged	bugged	plugged	mugged	chugged
5.	cocked	frocked	hocked	clocked	flocked
6.	cogged	frogged	hogged	clogged	flogged

a) As we walked home, we picked flowers and talked.
b) She only shrugged when he begged for help.
c) I looked for the checked hat you liked.
d) They drugged him, gagged him, and dragged him away.

92

[pt/bd]:

	A	B	C	D	E
1.	capped	napped	tapped	loped	roped
2.	cabbed	nabbed	tabbed	lobed	robed
3.	swapped	lopped	mopped	supped	cupped
4.	swabbed	lobbed	mobbed	subbed	cubbed
5.	ripped	gypped	nipped	clipped	flipped
6.	ribbed	jibbed	nibbed	cribbed	fibbed

a) She shopped for a striped coat.

b) As he described it, he'd been robbed and stabbed.

c) He stopped for the typed manuscript.

d) She was so absorbed in it that nothing disturbed her.

[st/zd]:

	A	B	C	D	E
1.	laced	faced	raced	graced	braced
2.	lazed	fazed	raised	grazed	braised
3.	priced	dosed	bussed	ceased	pieced
4.	prized	dozed	buzzed	seized	pleased
5.	doused	loused	noosed	crossed	bossed
6.	dowsed	housed	newsed	caused	paused

a) At first Helen was convinced she'd passed.

b) He was surprised, confused, and a little amused by it.

c) I guessed Pete had missed the last bus.

d) She was accused of having abused her authority.

[tʃt/dʒd]:

	A	B	C	D	E
1.	perched	searched	lurched	smirched	birched
2.	purged	surged	splurged	merged	urged
3.	cinched	inched	pinched	flinched	clinched
4.	singed	hinged	impinged	fringed	cringed
5.	lunched	punched	bunched	crunched	munched
6.	lunged	plunged	budged	grudged	nudged

a) She searched for the retouched photo.

b) He staged and managed it himself.

c) He was reproached for his detached manner.

d) They salvaged half of the damaged goods and charged off the rest.

In the CHART, read line 1, then line 2, then vertical pairs across. Then read the SENTENCES.

[θt/ðd]:

	A	B	C	D
1.	birthed	sleuthed	toothed	smithed
2.	bathed	soothed	teethed	smoothed

a) A saber-toothed cat was unearthed here.   c) Where's the ship berthed?

b) Though unscathed, he seethed with anger.   d) I mouthed a few words and soothed him a bit.

In the CHART below, read across each line, then down each column. Then read the SENTENCES.

[ʃt]:

	A	B	C	D	E
1.	bashed	cashed	dashed	gashed	hashed
2.	mushed	flushed	hushed	blushed	rushed
3.	dished	fished	sloshed	meshed	fleshed

a) He dashed for the door and vanished from sight.

b) I wished Carol hadn't rushed home.

c) By the time she finished cooking, he was famished.

d) He was punished for having pushed Cathy.

94

LESSON 52
[n] *in Final Position*

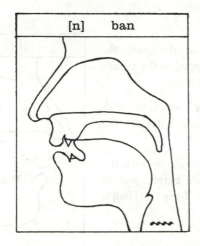

	[n]	ban

To make [n], stop the flow of air through the mouth by touching the tooth-ridge with the tip of the tongue; let the voiced air stream escape through the nose. Do not close the lips.

Step-down Exercises

	A	B	C	D	E	F
1.	banner	panel	tanner	honor	conifer	Ronald
2.	ban	pan	tan	on	con	Ron
3.	penny	benefit	henna	funny	gunner	punish
4.	pen	Ben	hen	fun	gun	pun
5.	inner	tinny	dinner	sooner	lunatic	crooner
6.	inn	tin	din	soon	loon	croon

A. *In the CHART above, read down each column. (In each word-pair, make the final [n] of the second word sound like the medial [n] of the first.) Then read the SENTENCES below.*

1. Muni's immune to her charms.
2. We'll meet you for tennis at ten.
3. Connally could con the Devil himself.
4. What manner of man is he?
5. This will just about finish Finn.
6. I've never met a mechanic that can.
7. Rooney's team wore maroon.
8. Many men have tried and failed.
9. Someday Lerner will learn what happened.
10. That would be a bonanza for Nan.

B. *In the CHART above, read each two-line group as follows: vertical pairs across (A1–2, B1–2, C1–2, etc.), then the second line of the group. Then read the SENTENCES below.*

1. Ben is known as a man of action.
2. One of the women had been uptown.
3. Dunn can, if anyone can.
4. We mean to turn in at nine.
5. When will Stan be in Oregon again?
6. It's none too soon to explain the plan.
7. Has Monahan gone on alone?
8. It was his son who'd taken the gun down.
9. Quinn has often blown his own horn.
10. They may listen in on our conversation.

LESSON 53

[n/ŋ] *in Final Position*

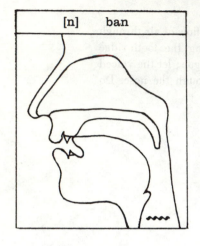

[n] ban

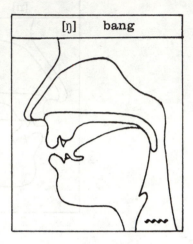

[ŋ] bang

Both [n] and [ŋ] are nasal sounds: the voiced air stream is stopped in the mouth but escapes through the nose.

To make [n], touch the tooth-ridge with the tip of the tongue; do not close the lips.

To make [ŋ], touch the velum with the back of the tongue. (Be careful not to add [g] to final [ŋ]: *bang* is [baŋ], not [baŋg].)

Contrast Chart

	A	B	C	D	E
1.	ban	fan	ran	tan	pan
2.	bang	fang	rang	tang	pang
3.	run	bun	ton	pun	stun
4.	rung	bung	tongue	pung	stung
5.	pin	kin	sin	been	win
6.	ping	king	sing	bing	wing
7.	clan	span	Chan	Ann	Dan
8.	clang	spang	Chang	hang	dang
9.	Hun	done	won	fun	spun
10.	hung	dung	swung	flung	sprung
11.	tin	thin	din	Lynn	chin
12.	ting	thing	ding	Ling	Ching
13.	basin	taken	Payson	chasten	bacon
14.	basing	taking	pacing	chasing	baking
15.	muffin	glutton	button	Mullen	Kullen
16.	muffing	glutting	butting	mulling	culling
17.	foeman	Bolen	open	Dolan	motor inn
18.	foaming	bowling	hoping	doling	motoring

Contrast Exercises

A. *In the CHART on the opposite page, read the odd-numbered lines across (1, 3, 5, etc.). Then read the SENTENCES below.*

1. John was born in San Juan.
2. None of the women had been in on it.
3. Does Shawn plan to live in Maine?
4. No more than ten men have been sworn in.
5. When will Owen arrive in Japan?
6. Then again, that joke's worn pretty thin.
7. Don ran on and on about the typhoon.
8. Call station-to-station, not person-to-person.
9. Ken gave him a rundown on it.
10. The cartoon was drawn especially for *Harpoon* magazine.

B. *In the CHART on the opposite page, read the even-numbered lines across (2, 4, 6, etc.). Then read the SENTENCES below.*

1. I'll string along with Lessing.
2. They shipped everything to Hong Kong.
3. She gave him a long tongue-lashing.
4. He speaks with a singsong twang.
5. I'm driving him to Corning this evening.
6. Lang is still playing Ping Pong.
7. They're doing nothing to prolong her life.
8. The young king is quite headstrong.
9. Strang is taking the wrong bus.
10. This morning she was wearing a sarong.

Now read SENTENCES alternately from A and B above (A1,B1; A2,B2; A3,B3; etc.).

C. *In the CHART on the opposite page, read vertical pairs across (A1–2, B1–2, C1–2, etc.). Then read the SENTENCES below.*

1. That doesn't belong on the lawn.
2. Moran rang for help.
3. Her son is an unsung hero.
4. There'll be no last fling for Flynn.
5. They began to gang up on him.
6. Couldn't Brynn bring himself to do it?
7. He just bought a tan Mustang.
8. A few of the women are swimming.
9. Isn't Mason an amazing fellow?
10. Last week she sang in San Diego.

D. *In the CHART on the opposite page, read down each column. Then read the SENTENCES below.*

1. Mr. Wong has gone to Spring Inn for the weekend.
2. "Swan Song" had a long run.
3. Gwen is baking a lemon meringue pie.
4. That's the one thing that can boomerang.
5. When he was young, Ron was a strong man.
6. Did anything else happen during the afternoon?
7. That song was written by Irving Berlin.
8. Lanning was wrong to pawn his ring.
9. The plane is coming in for a landing.
10. Whiting began calling at nine.

97

LESSON 54

[g/ŋ] *in Medial Position*

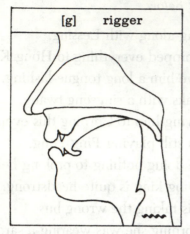

[g]   rigger

To make [g], keep the nasal passage closed and stop the flow of air through the mouth by touching the velum with the back of the tongue. For medial [g] before an unstressed vowel, release the stop with voice but without explosion; before most consonants, do not release at all.

To make [ŋ], touch the velum with the back of the tongue and let the voiced air stream escape through the nose.

[ŋ]   wringer

Contrast Exercises

	A	B	C	D	E
1.	stigma	rigger	digger	Sigmund	trigger
2.	stinger	wringer	dinghy	singer	stringer
3.	haggard	wagging	slaggy	bagging	gagging
4.	hanger	twanging	slangy	banging	ganging
5.	logging	Saugerties	augur	rigging	swigging
6.	longing	songster	wronger	ringing	swinging

A. *In the CHART above, read lines 1, 3, and 5. Then read the SENTENCES below.*

1. Hogan's ego staggers me.
2. I dreamed of dragons and ogres again.
3. Peggy was eager to meet the juggler.
4. I wrote "The Agony of Eggleston Tuggle."
5. *Regal* magazine figured in the scandal.

Now read SENTENCES alternately from A and B above (A1,B1; A2,B2; A3,B3; etc.).

B. *In the CHART above, read lines 2, 4, and 6. Then read the SENTENCES below.*

1. Springer's plane is in the hangar.
2. He owns the Swinger Club in Kingston.
3. Sanger left Shanghai yesterday.
4. We don't serve stingers to youngsters.
5. Longman is a real humdinger.

C. *In the CHART above, read vertical pairs across (A1–2, B1–2, etc.). Then read the SENTENCES below.*

1. These cigarettes are from Singapore.
2. He's a dead ringer for Wrigley.

3. It's the biggest house in Binghampton.
4. The sauce was too tangy for Taggert.
5. Relax — he's a gagster, not a gangster.

D. *In the CHART above, read down each column. Then read the SENTENCES below.*

1. Sanger's regular hangout is the Digger Cafe.
2. "The Singing Beggar" is a fairy tale about the kingdom of Agabar.
3. Egan's bringing his meager belongings.
4. "Swinging Wagon" is showing in Bigelow.
5. Langer is the *Eagle's* stringer in Vegas.

LESSON 55

[g/ŋg] *in Medial Position*

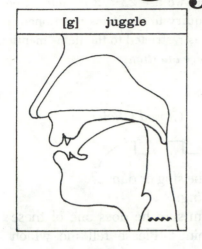

[g]	juggle	

Make [g] as practiced in the preceding lesson.

To make [ŋg], first make [ŋ] (practiced in the preceding lesson); then close the nasal passage to make [g], breaking the tongue-velum contact with a slight voiced explosion.

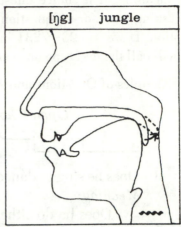

[ŋg]	jungle	

Contrast Exercises

	A	B	C	D	E
1.	baggy	ragged	waggle	dagger	lagger
2.	bangle	wrangle	wangle	dangle	languor
3.	hugger	juggle	buggy	boggle	coggle
4.	hunger	jungle	bungle	bongo	conga
5.	cigarette	digger	figure	jigger	bigger
6.	single	dingle	finger	jingo	bingo

A. *In the CHART above, read lines 1, 3, and 5. Then read the SENTENCES below.*

1. The figurine was smuggled in some time ago.
2. Tuggle's in the Michigan dugout.
3. He's bigger and more vigorous than Mulligan.
4. We made "The Legacy" on a meager budget.
5. *Vigor* magazine published "The Irregulars."

B. *In the CHART above, read lines 2, 4, and 6. Then read the SENTENCES below.*

1. Fingerman has the lingo down pat.
2. They flew from Angola to the Congo.
3. Angus was stronger than the Englishman.
4. We saw a kangaroo and three flamingos.
5. Engel didn't miss a single angle.

Now read SENTENCES alternately from A and B above (A1,B1; A2,B2; A3,B3; etc.).

C. *In the CHART above, read vertical pairs across (A1–2, B1–2, etc.). Then read the SENTENCES below.*

1. The loggers can't wait much longer.

2. I think Agatha's angry.
3. Have you read Hingle's "Igloo Life"?
4. The strangler had killed two stragglers.
5. The bells jingle when you jiggle the string.

D. *In the CHART above, read down each column. Then read the SENTENCES below.*

1. One linguist was eagerly studying the Tagalog language.
2. Inga Logan wrote "A Single Signal."
3. Regan's entangled in a legal wrangle.
4. Haggerty had a lingering, nagging hunger.
5. "Rangoon Dragon" is Stengel's biggest hit.

LESSON 56

Intonation: Choice Questions

The meaning of a choice question depends upon the intonation used. If we use 23⌐/23⌐ intonation, we are asking a yes-or-no question and are not necessarily limiting the inquiry to the items mentioned in the question. If we use 23⌐/231 intonation, we are offering a choice which is restricted to the items mentioned. We will call the first type *open-choice questions* and the second *closed-choice questions*.

A. Examples of Questions and Answers.

Open Choice

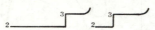

1. Does he síng or dánce?
   Meaning:
   > Does he do either of these things? If so, please tell me which one. If not, please tell me if he does anything else of this kind.

   Some possible answers:
   > Yes, he sings.
   > Yes, he does both.
   > No, he doesn't.
   > No, but he plays the piano.

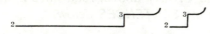

2. Would you like cóffee or téa?
   Meaning:
   > Would you like either of these things? If so, please tell me which one. If not, perhaps I can offer you something else.

   Some possible answers:
   > Yes, thanks, tea would be fine.
   > No, thanks.
   > (Note: to be polite, do not ask for something else until it is offered.)

Closed Choice

1. Does he síng or dánce?
   Meaning:
   > I'm sure he does one of these things. Please tell me which one.

   Some possible answers:
   > He sings.
   > He does both.
   > Neither one.

2. Would you like cóffee or téa?
   Meaning:
   > I'm sure you want something hot to drink. Only coffee and tea are available. Which do you want?

   Some possible answers:
   > Tea, please.
   > Nothing for me, thanks.

B. Note that open-choice questions can be asked in negative form:

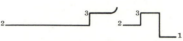

Doesn't he síng or dánce?   Wouldn't you like some cóffee. tea?

Closed-choice questions, however, cannot be asked in negative form.

C. Practice the following sentences, reading down each column (1-10), then across each line (1-1, 2-2, etc.). In each sentence, the second phrase begins with the word *or*.

<table>
<tr><td>*Open Choice*</td><td>*Closed Choice*</td></tr>
</table>

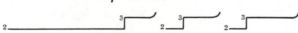

Open Choice	*Closed Choice*
1. Won't you have some cáke or some cóokies?	1. Do you take sóda or wáter?
2. Has he studied phýsics or chémistry?	2. Is that Bíll or Hárold?
3. Could you come on Mónday or Túesday?	3. Shall we swím or go físhing?
4. Is it too swéet or too spícy?	4. Are they in Tókyo or Ósaka?
5. Do you want to be a dóctor or a láwyer?	5. Were you glád or sórry?
6. Doesn't she play gólf or ténnis?	6. Is she cóming or nót?
7. Would you like a stéak or some lámb chops?	7. Are we éarly or láte?
8. Shall we invite the Smíths or the Mártins?	8. Do you want chócolate or vanílla?
9. Can he do the bréast stroke or the cráwl?	9. Is this yóur book or míne?
10. Didn't you bring a swéater or a jácket?	10. Are they Itálian or Spánish?

D. Each of the following questions presents three choices. For open choice the intonation pattern is 23⌐/(2)3⌐/23⌐; or closed choice it is 23⌐/(2)3⌐/231. (Note: in both types of question, the first two phrases are sometimes spoken without the final rise.) Read down each column, then across each line.

Open Choice	*Closed Choice*
1. Have you been to Páris, or Róme, or Móscow?	1. Is he a báss, a báritone, or a ténor?
2. Does he drínk, smóke, or gámble?	2. Are they tíred, síck, or just lázy?
3. Will we need bóots, glóves, or háts?	3. Do you take créam, súgar, or bóth?
4. Don't you like córn, or spínach, or cárrots?	4. Shall we have ríce, spaghétti, or béans?
5. Are they chípped, crácked, or bróken?	5. Will you go by bús, tráin, or pláne?
6. Do you have any níckels, dímes, or quárters?	6. Is that sátin, sílk, or ráyon?
7. Can she speak Frénch, or Gérman, or Itálian?	7. Do you want órange, lémon, or líme?
8. Have you asked Máry, or Álice, or Cárol?	8. Should I báke, bóil, or frý them?
9. Shall I buy some róses, or túlips, or lílacs?	9. Is it stríped, chécked, or pláid?
10. Do you play cárds, or chéckers, or chéss?	10. Was he pléased, ángry, or indífferent?

VOWELS

LESSON 57

The Vowels [iy/i]

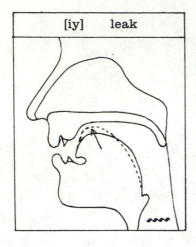

[iy]   leak

To make [iy], start with the tongue curved quite high in front, the jaws slightly open, and the lips slightly spread. Glide the tongue further up and forward while voicing the vowel.

Make [i] with the tongue curved rather high in front, the jaws slightly open, and the lips slightly spread. Do not glide the tongue while voicing the vowel.

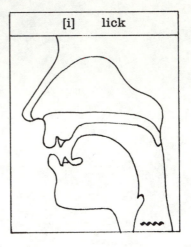

[i]   lick

Contrast Chart

	A	B	C	D	E	F
1.	leak	peak	weak	seek	teak	reek
2.	lick	pick	wick	sick	tick	Rick
3.	heal	meal	keel	feel	peal	deal
4.	hill	mill	kill	fill	pill	dill
5.	deep	heap	peep	leap	neap	keep
6.	dip	hip	pip	lip	nip	Kip
7.	bead	deed	heed	reed	lead	seed
8.	bid	did	hid	rid	lid	Sid
9.	team	ream	scheme	deem	theme	gleam
10.	Tim	rim	skim	dim	thimble	glimmer
11.	eat	beat	feet	heat	meet	neat
12.	it	bit	fit	hit	mitt	knit
13.	reach	each	beach	peach	feature	breach
14.	rich	itch	bitch	pitch	Fitch	britches
15.	Jean	keen	dean	bean	queen	mean
16.	gin	kin	din	bin	Quinn	Min
17.	wheeze	fees	lees	ease	he's	freeze
18.	whiz	fizz	Liz	is	his	frizz

Contrast Exercises

A. *In the CHART on the opposite page, read the odd-numbered lines across (1, 3, 5, etc.). Then read the SENTENCES below.*

1. They seem to be extremely pleased.
2. Deacon's reading the *Evening Eagle.*
3. He's agreed to meet me there.
4. Rita really needed the sleep.
5. At least the legal fee seems reasonable.
6. Gleason believes he succeeded.
7. He was released three weeks ago.
8. Meade's a real eager beaver.
9. We reached Cleveland that evening.
10. Even Jean's teacher was speechless.

B. *In the CHART on the opposite page, read the even-numbered lines across (2, 4, 6, etc.). Then read the SENTENCES below.*

1. Fix it this minute!
2. Phyllis is still in Ithaca.
3. Mix it with a swizzle-stick.
4. This is Miss Sylvia Miller.
5. They've been considering a similar exhibit.
6. Gibbons will stick to the original script.
7. Six editions have been printed.
8. William's sister lives in Midville.
9. If it isn't Liz!
10. I was in Michigan till mid-winter.

Now read SENTENCES alternately from A and B above (A1,B1; A2,B2; A3,B3; etc.).

C. *In the CHART on the opposite page, read vertical pairs across (A1–2, B1–2, C1–2, etc.). Then read the SENTENCES below.*

1. Timmy's team is called the Busy Bees.
2. It isn't easy for Kip to keep still.
3. Green grinned at the silly seals.
4. It seemed simple till Teale came.
5. Beaton's bitter about missing the meeting.
6. His sister ceased to wear widow's weeds.
7. Leavy lives near Cricket Creek.
8. Seaton's sitting in Citron's seat.
9. He'd hidden Wiener's winning ticket.
10. Hasn't Beane been seen since?

D. *In the CHART on the opposite page, read down each column. Then read the SENTENCES below.*

1. Steven is interested in the steamship business.
2. The Indian and Greek bridge teams will meet soon.
3. Bill teaches simple reading skills.
4. This Little Leaguer will be in the Big Leagues some day.
5. Bickford's niece is still in Egypt, isn't she?
6. On her recent visit the Queen was given the keys to the city.
7. Miss Keating's ill and won't be in this week.
8. She considers it extremely difficult to reason with him.
9. Winston believes in the dignity of each individual.
10. This year our Christmas tree was six feet tall.

LESSON 58

The Vowels [i/e]

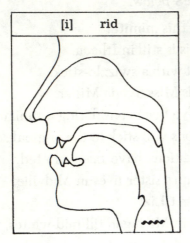

[i]	rid

Make [i] with the tongue curved rather high in front, the jaws slightly open, and the lips slightly spread.

Make [e] with the tongue curved about halfway up in front, the jaws half open, and the lips slightly spread.

Both [i] and [e] are short sounds.

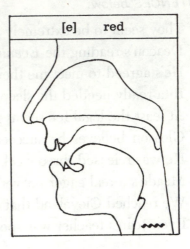

[e]	red

Contrast Chart

	A	B	C	D	E
1.	rid	bid	did	hid	lid
2.	red	bed	dead	head	led
3.	Dick	Nick	pick	Rick	chick
4.	deck	neck	peck	wreck	check
5.	Chris	miss	hiss	bliss	prissy
6.	cress	mess	Hess	bless	press
7.	bit	lit	mitt	pit	knit
8.	bet	let	met	pet	net
9.	pin	tin	bin	din	kin
10.	pen	ten	Ben	den	Ken
11.	Jill	hill	quill	sill	dill
12.	jell	hell	quell	sell	dell
13.	hicks	six	ticks	Vic's	flicks
14.	hex	sex	Tex	vex	flex
15.	tint	dint	lint	mint	winter
16.	tent	dent	lent	meant	went
17.	list	gist	wrist	tryst	fist
18.	lest	jest	wrest	tressed	fester

Contrast Exercises

A. *In the CHART on the opposite page, read the odd-numbered lines across (1, 3, 5, etc.). Then read the SENTENCES below.*

1. This is simply silly.
2. It isn't in his interest.
3. Kitty mixed it with milk.
4. His sister's pretty strict.
5. A little spilled on the window sill.
6. It's still within the six-minute limit.
7. Simpson's built sixty bridges.
8. Which picture did you give him?
9. This was filmed in Cincinnati.
10. The Dixons split fifty-fifty.

B. *In the CHART on the opposite page, read the even-numbered lines across (2, 4, 6, etc.). Then read the SENTENCES below.*

1. Jensen tested every element.
2. My friend sent the chess set.
3. Many guests left the reception.
4. Edward sells the best eggs.
5. Let's get together again.
6. Esther checked the regular entries.
7. Fetch the extra bedspread.
8. Edna's especially well dressed.
9. The men expected a better settlement.
10. Fletcher attended the special session.

Now read SENTENCES alternately from A and B above (A1,B1; A2,B2; A3,B3; etc.).

C. *In the CHART on the opposite page, read vertical pairs across (A1–2, B1–2, C1–2, etc.). Then read the SENTENCES below.*

1. Isn't Ezra listening to the lesson?
2. Sid said I should rest my wrist.
3. For years Ben's been selling silk.
4. Phil felt a bit better.
5. Minton's men dealt with Dillon.
6. Tell Tilson they went for the winter.
7. Stella still hid her head.
8. Send Cindy a bill for the belt.
9. Peck picked a winner Wednesday.
10. Desmond didn't enter into it.

D. *In the CHART on the opposite page, read down each column. Then read the SENTENCES below.*

1. I meant to give the Fentons a little extra.
2. Linton's best film was sent to the cinema festival in Italy.
3. The inventor insisted on inspecting it himself.
4. Jim will get this corrected within ten minutes.
5. Let's visit the Elwyns again next winter.
6. We've filled seventy prescriptions for sedatives since yesterday.
7. Lydia felt a little better by mid-September.
8. Professor Tilden dispensed with the regular physics test.
9. The critics selected "Sixes and Sevens" as the best picture.
10. Richard spent the interim getting the tickets ready.

Review of Vowels [iy/i/e]

Contrast Exercises

In each three-line group of the CHART, read across each line, then down each column (A1–2–3, B1–2–3, etc.). Next read down each full column. Then read the SENTENCES.

	A	B	C	D	E	F
1.	heel	Sheila	feel	meal	weal	kneel
2.	hill	shill	fill	mill	will	nil
3.	hell	shell	fell	Mel	well	Nell
4.	chick	Rick	hick	pick	Bick	sick
5.	check	wreck	heck	peck	beck	second
6.	cheek	reek	heak	peak	beak	seek
7.	bet	met	net	set	Chet	pet
8.	beat	meat	neat	seat	cheat	peat
9.	bit	mitt	knit	sit	chit	pit
10.	reed	bid	dead	hid	seed	led
11.	rid	bed	deed	head	Sid	lead
12.	red	bead	did	heed	said	lid
13.	din	ten	wean	ken	Min	bean
14.	dean	tin	wen	kin	mean	Ben
15.	den	teen	win	keen	men	bin

1. He's been exceptionally helpful this week.
2. Reid isn't getting any sleep.
3. This television set seems defective.
4. I think Philip tends to be a bit devious.
5. He's neither physically well nor mentally fit.
6. Ethan's been inventing things since he was seven.
7. She never gives me the benefit of the doubt.
8. He isn't dependent on Gleason's opinions anymore.
9. Better tell him to fix these wheels.
10. Incidentally, she still believes Wesley's guilty.

LESSON 60
Intonation: Listing

When several things, actions, or qualities are listed in a sentence, we ordinarily say each item as a separate phrase with its own primary stress. Two common intonation patterns are shown below.

A. *The end-rise pattern*: In each phrase except the last, the voice begins on pitch 2 and rises on the last syllable to a level slightly below pitch 3. Note that the rise occurs on the *last* syllable, whether that syllable is stressed or not. The final phrase has 231 intonation.

1. We need tomátoes, léttuce, and ónions.
2. I go on Móndays, Wédnesdays, and Frídays.
3. She likes knítting, séwing, and wéaving.
4. He has a féver, a rásh, and a héadache.
5. They went to Nára, Kyóto, and Kóbe.
6. She writes stóries, póems, and pláys.
7. I told Wílliam, Dávid, and Geórge.
8. She washed the wíndows, wálls, and flóors.
9. He plays sóccer, báseball, and gólf.
10. I bought cóffee, cócoa, and téa.

Use the same intonation with these longer sentences:

11. I'll need a hámmer, some náils, a wrénch, and a scréwdriver.
12. We've painted the kítchen, the háll, the stúdy, and the bédroom.
13. John plays the bánjo, the guitár, the accórdion, and the piáno.
14. He speaks Rússian, Pólish, Gérman, and Énglish.
15. Mr. Brown is hónest, intélligent, lóyal, and dédicated.

B. *The stress-rise pattern*: In each phrase except the last, the voice rises *at the stress* to pitch 3 and remains there until the end of the phrase. The final phrase has 231 intonation.

1. She bought a tápe recorder, a rádio, and a cámera.
2. He's climbed mountains in Aláska, Swítzerland, and Tibét.
3. I hate shópping, cóoking, and hóusework.
4. We've built brídges, dáms, and skýscrapers.
5. He's been a jóurnalist, a díplomat, and a spý.

C. In the exercise below, the stress-rise listing pattern is compared with the intonation used for closed-choice questions. The only difference is the rise from pitch 3 in the question pattern — and even this does not always occur. (Read across each line.)

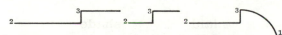 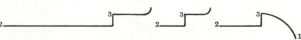

1. I read the *Tímes*, the *Póst*, and the *Néws*.
2. She wants a dóg, a cát, and a bírd.
3. It was réd, púrple, and pínk.
4. He got a bát, a báll, and a glóve.
5. I like sáusages, bácon, and hám.

Do you read the *Tímes*, the *Póst*, or the *Néws*?
Does she want a dóg, a cát, or a bírd?
Was it réd, púrple, or pínk?
Did he get a bát, a báll, or a glóve?
Would you like sáusages, bácon, or hám?

LESSON 61
The Vowels [ey/e]

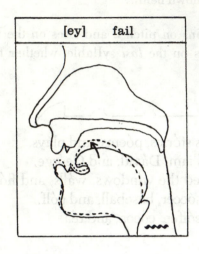

[ey]   fail

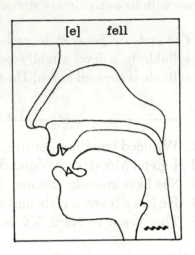

[e]   fell

To make [ey], start with the tongue curved about halfway up in front, the jaws half open, and the lips slightly spread. Glide the tongue up and forward while voicing the vowel.

Make [e] with the tongue curved about halfway up in front, the jaws half open, and the lips slightly spread. Do not glide the tongue while voicing the vowel.

Contrast Chart

	A	B	C	D	E
1.	ail	fail	bail	wail	dale
2.	el	fell	bell	well	dell
3.	stain	bane	cane	deign	mane
4.	sten	Ben	ken	den	men
5.	base	mace	lace	chase	trace
6.	Bess	mess	less	chess	tress
7.	mate	date	gate	bait	freight
8.	met	debt	get	bet	fret
9.	hail	jail	male	nail	stale
10.	hell	jell	Mel	knell	Stella
11.	Jane	lain	pain	feign	rain
12.	Jen	Len	pen	fen	wren
13.	aid	raid	fade	laid	shade
14.	Ed	red	fed	led	shed
15.	late	sate	Nate	pate	wait
16.	let	set	net	pet	wet
17.	sail	tail	Yale	shale	quail
18.	sell	tell	yell	shell	quell

110

Contrast Exercises

A. *In the CHART on the opposite page, read the odd-numbered lines across (1, 3, 5, etc.). Then read the SENTENCES below.*

1. The nation is facing a brain drain.
2. The trade name is Gay Blades.
3. Grayson's playing a dangerous game.
4. They say haste makes waste.
5. Avery baked a raisin cake.
6. The rains came late in May.
7. Bailey failed to gain weight.
8. The tailor made a rayon cape.
9. Mine is a Great Dane named James.
10. Is this the Great Lakes Naval Training Station?

B. *In the CHART on the opposite page, read the even-numbered lines across (2, 4, 6, etc.). Then read the SENTENCES below.*

1. Let's correct the rest of the text.
2. Helen settled for second best.
3. The regular session starts next September.
4. Bennett never expected any credit.
5. The red letters said "Exit."
6. Edson's friend gets the featherbed.
7. The general was very self-possessed.
8. Many of the men respect Keller.
9. Tell them I meant separate sentences.
10. The title was "Medical Ethics and Mental Health."

Now read SENTENCES alternately from A and B above (A1,B1; A2,B2; A3,B3; etc.).

C. *In the CHART on the opposite page, read vertical pairs across (A1–2, B1–2, C1–2, etc.). Then read the SENTENCES below.*

1. Let Mel mail the letter later.
2. Sadie said a lady led them.
3. Tell Taylor to sell the sailboat.
4. Fred's afraid he'll get the gate.
5. I'll bet Bates stayed instead.
6. Ted's taking the Trenton train.
7. We met Maitland at Wade's wedding.
8. Rader's ready to race the rest of them.
9. He saved several days to spend in Spain.
10. Wayne went to Ed's aid.

D. *In the CHART on the opposite page, read down each column. Then read the SENTENCES below.*

1. Tell the maid to get the plates and set the table.
2. Gail's debts were paid by the end of May.
3. The Hempstead train left at 8:07.
4. Betty was ashamed to mention her grades in French.
5. It rained heavily on Amy's wedding day.
6. Professor Rayburn set the date for the test.
7. Eight Senators waited for the President to make his entrance.
8. Ellen bakes the best cakes in seven states.
9. I'm tempted to remain at West Lake for the rest of my vacation.
10. Let Rachel get the baby ready today.

LESSON 62

The Vowels [ey/æ]

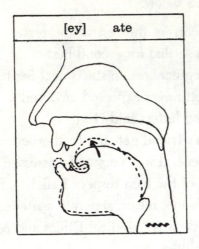

[ey]   ate

To make [ey], start with the tongue curved about halfway up in front, the jaws half open, and the lips slightly spread. Glide the tongue up and forward while voicing the vowel.

Make [æ] with the tongue low and slightly pushed forward, the jaws quite open, and the lips slightly spread.

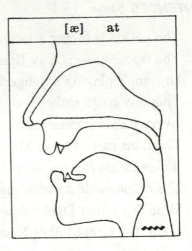

[æ]   at

Contrast Chart

	A	B	C	D	E
1.	ate	rate	bait	fate	skate
2.	at	rat	bat	fat	scat
3.	bake	sake	take	shake	lake
4.	back	sack	tack	shack	lack
5.	fade	bayed	paid	laid	made
6.	fad	bad	pad	lad	mad
7.	gape	nape	cape	tape	grape
8.	gap	nap	cap	tap	grapple
9.	aim	tame	lame	same	dame
10.	am	tam	lamb	Sam	dam
11.	cane	mane	rain	bane	vein
12.	can	man	ran	ban	van
13.	pace	lace	mace	grace	brace
14.	pass	lass	mass	grass	brass
15.	ale	gale	hail	vale	pale
16.	Al	gal	Hal	Val	pal
17.	hate	Kate	sate	mate	slate
18.	hat	cat	sat	mat	slat

112

Contrast Exercises

A. *In the CHART on the opposite page, read the odd-numbered lines across (1, 3, 5, etc.). Then read the SENTENCES below.*

1. Mason staked his claim today.
2. The waiter's taking the plates away.
3. Stacy made a grave mistake.
4. Maybe they'll be able to trade places.
5. Grady wagered away his wages.
6. The freight train came late.
7. Mavis became a famous lady.
8. I'm afraid they may stay the day.
9. Davis played the ace of spades.
10. Make arrangements to raise the rates.

B. *In the CHART on the opposite page, read the even-numbered lines across (2, 4, 6, etc.). Then read the SENTENCES below.*

1. The Ambassador is a tactful man.
2. Did that actually happen to Jackson?
3. The factory manager was catnapping.
4. Agnes had a bad accident.
5. I can't have passed the Latin exam.
6. Adam will have the last laugh.
7. Who commanded the cavalry at Nashville?
8. The fandango is a Spanish dance.
9. Gladys ran to catch the cab.
10. We manufacture plastic bags.

Now read SENTENCES alternately from A and B above (A1,B1; A2,B2; A3,B3; etc.).

C. *In the CHART on the opposite page, read vertical pairs across (A1–2, B1–2, C1–2, etc.). Then read the SENTENCES below.*

1. Atkins ate the candy cane.
2. Hasn't Hayes cabled Cabot?
3. Madden made his plans plain.
4. In January Jane's going back to the bakery.
5. Hattie hates taking taxis.
6. The *Salvador* sailed with Matson as mate.
7. Campbell came from a famous family.
8. Dade's dad ate a stack of steaks.
9. I'll pay Patrick to paint the panel.
10. Hazel has to face the facts.

D. *In the CHART on the opposite page, read down each column. Then read the SENTENCES below.*

1. The candidate explained the campaign strategy to his aides.
2. Elaine hadn't planned to stay after today.
3. They've practically finished laying the track from Maine to Alabama.
4. Frank's played his last game of blackjack.
5. The chaplain complained to the captain, who later complained to the admiral.
6. Danny traded his rabbit for a black snail.
7. Dad claims he's satisfied with Raymond's math grades.
8. Tracy asked the stationmaster to explain the fantastic delay.
9. The actor's agent had to wait backstage.
10. Janice made a batch of tasty pancakes.

113

LESSON 63
The Vowels [æ/e]

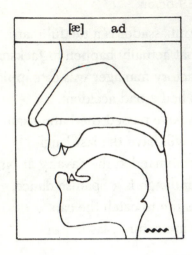

[æ]   ad

Make [æ] with the tongue low and slightly pushed forward, the jaws quite open, and the lips slightly spread.

Make [e] with the tongue curved about halfway up in front, the jaws half open, and the lips slightly spread.

Make [æ] a little longer than [e].

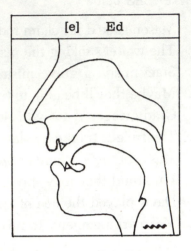

[e]   Ed

Contrast Chart

	A	B	C	D	E	F
1.	ad	fad	dad	had	bad	lad
2.	Ed	fed	dead	head	bed	led
3.	ran	tan	pan	than	Stan	Jan
4.	wren	ten	pen	then	sten	Jen
5.	pack	knack	rack	track	flack	back
6.	peck	neck	wreck	trek	fleck	Beck
7.	ham	jam	tamper	lamb	clam	am
8.	hem	gem	temper	Lem	Clem	em
9.	gnat	mat	sat	bat	pat	rat
10.	net	met	set	bet	pet	ret
11.	man	ban	can	Dan	fan	an
12.	men	Ben	ken	den	fen	en
13.	sad	brad	shad	pad	mad	tad
14.	said	bread	shed	peddle	meddle	Ted
15.	bass	gas	lass	mass	crass	ass
16.	Bess	guess	less	mess	cress	ess
17.	and	land	band	sand	Rand	bland
18.	end	lend	bend	send	rend	blend

114

Contrast Exercises

A. *In the CHART on the opposite page, read the odd-numbered lines across (1, 3, 5, etc.). Then read the SENTENCES below.*

1. The janitor's ladder collapsed.
2. Anderson's having a ham sandwich.
3. The acrobat is an added attraction.
4. Ralph ran faster than a jackrabbit.
5. It's his last chance to catch a nap.
6. Can't we have frank answers?
7. Aladdin had a magic lamp.
8. Perhaps the bank'll cash the draft.
9. That family has a Cadillac.
10. Banyon's pal is a back-slapper.

B. *In the CHART on the opposite page, read the even-numbered lines across (2, 4, 6, etc.). Then read the SENTENCES below.*

1. We sent seven delegates to the convention.
2. It's Professor Beckett's pet test.
3. A special election was held in September.
4. Elephants never forget.
5. Senator Devlin left on Wednesday.
6. The editor read every letter.
7. Chester wrestles exceptionally well.
8. The sentry'd better let them enter.
9. Reggie spent yesterday sledding.
10. The next step is to get them dressed.

Now read SENTENCES alternately from A and B above (A1,B1; A2,B2; A3,B3; etc.).

C. *In the CHART on the opposite page, read vertical pairs across (A1–2, B1–2, C1–2, etc.). Then read the SENTENCES below.*

1. The lad led Beck back home.
2. Hedda hadn't said it so sadly.
3. I think the man meant to panic Penny.
4. Send Sandra ten tan nets.
5. Never had Matt met a better batter.
6. Fran's friends left laughing.
7. The rancher wrenched it from Henderson's hands.
8. Dennis was dancing when his aunt entered.
9. He mentioned the mansion to Gantry again.
10. Kent can't have had a head start.

D. *In the CHART on the opposite page, read down each column. Then read the SENTENCES below.*

1. The President has regular staff sessions after ten.
2. Edgar passed several bad checks last Wednesday.
3. "Better have the extra apples ready," the manager said.
4. Natalie seldom has temper tantrums.
5. He practically begged the banker for venture capital.
6. Ken plans to sever his last connection with them.
7. With less haggling, we can get matters settled faster.
8. Ella's had several dancing lessons.
9. "Fellow actors," Leonard began, "let's act sensibly."
10. He never actually expected financial help.

Review of Vowels [ey/æ/e]

Contrast Exercises

In each three-line group of the CHART, read across each line, then down each column (A1–2–3, B1–2–3, etc.). Next read down each full column. Then read the SENTENCES.

	A	B	C	D	E	F
1.	hake	ache	bake	rake	flake	sake
2.	hack	act	back	rack	flack	sack
3.	heck	echo	beck	wreck	fleck	second
4.	ass	fast	lass	mass	bass	past
5.	ess	fess	less	mess	Bess	pest
6.	ace	face	lace	mace	base	paste
7.	em	Lem	gems	Clem	temper	phlegm
8.	aim	lame	James	claim	tame	flame
9.	am	lam	jams	clam	tam	flam
10.	cane	Dan	pen	fan	main	wren
11.	can	den	pain	fen	man	rain
12.	ken	Dane	pan	feign	men	ran
13.	bat	ret	sate	het	pat	mate
14.	bait	rat	set	hat	pate	met
15.	bet	rate	sat	hate	pet	mat

1. I mailed the letter yesterday afternoon on my way to the bank.
2. Della's planning to take the 7 a.m. plane from Akron.
3. You'll have to wait several days before they send the application.
4. David does backbends and stands on his head.
5. My friend spent her last vacation in France.
6. Ray can't take any of the credit.
7. They haven't any expensive habits, have they?
8. Jane practically never pays attention in class.
9. You'll have to tell the landlady that the rent'll be late again.
10. I can't blame Selma for getting angry.

LESSON 65
Intonation Contrast: Direct Address/Name in Apposition

Here again we contrast sentences worded the same but different in meaning. In column A, we are speaking *to* the person named; in column B, we are speaking *about* the person, identifying him first by relationship or position and then by name. In lines 1-10, the contrasted sentences differ in phrase division, stress, and intonation; in lines 11-20, intonation alone conveys the difference in meaning. (Read down, then across in each section. Example: A1-5, B1-5; then A1-B1, A2-B2, etc.).

A. *Name in Direct Address*

1. Where's your són, Jóe?
2. This is my niéce, Cárol.
3. How's her bróther, Jáck?
4. I like your fríend, Geórge.
5. That's his úncle, Fránk.

6. Have you seen my cóusin, Róy?
7. Is this your néphew, Tóm?
8. Do you know our dáughter, Jáne?
9. Was that her síster, Súe?
10. Have you met my áunt, Máry?

11. I'll phone my láwyer, Mr. Báker.
12. She's my assístant, Miss Pórter.
13. There's your néighbor, Mrs. Jónes.
14. He's the bóss, Mr. Thómpson.
15. We talked with his téacher, Miss Whíte.

16. Is that the new ówner, Mr. Múllins?
17. Do you know the président, Mr. Llóyd?
18. Is she the áuthor, Miss Dávis?
19. May I speak to the mánager, Mr. Dráke?
20. Have you told your pártner, Mr. Fíelds?

B. *Name in Apposition*

1. Where's your son Jóe?
2. This is my niece Cárol.
3. How's her brother Jáck?
4. I like your friend Geórge.
5. That's his uncle Fránk.

6. Have you seen my cousin Róy?
7. Is this your nephew Tóm?
8. Do you know our daughter Jáne?
9. Was that her sister Súe?
10. Have you met my aunt Máry?

11. I'll phone my láwyer, Mr. Báker.
12. She's my assístant, Miss Pórter.
13. There's your néighbor, Mrs. Jónes.
14. He's the bóss, Mr. Thómpson.
15. We talked with his téacher, Miss Whíte.

16. Is that the new ówner, Mr. Múllins?
17. Do you know the président, Mr. Llóyd?
18. Is she the áuthor, Miss Dávis?
19. May I speak to the mánager, Mr. Dráke?
20. Have you told your pártner, Mr. Fíelds?

LESSON 66

The Vowels [æ/a]

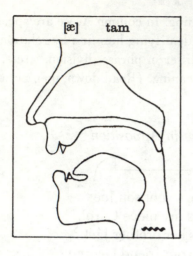

[æ] tam

Make [æ] with the tongue low and slightly pushed forward, the jaws quite open, and the lips slightly spread.

Make [a] with the tongue low, rather flat, and centered (farther back than for [æ]). The jaws should be fully open and the lips relaxed.

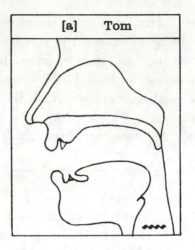

[a] Tom

Contrast Chart

	A	B	C	D	E
1.	tam	cam	pram	Sam	ma'am
2.	Tom	calm	prom	psalm	mom
3.	band	fanned	canned	panned	bland
4.	bond	fond	conned	pond	blond
5.	cab	blab	slab	nab	jab
6.	cob	blob	slob	knob	job
7.	map	pap	tap	chap	cap
8.	mop	pop	top	chop	cop
9.	sag	jag	bag	flag	tag
10.	sog	jog	bog	flog	tog
11.	at	sat	gnat	hat	rat
12.	Ott	sot	not	hot	rot
13.	pad	had	shad	ad	sad
14.	pod	hod	shod	odd	sod
15.	lack	tack	hack	back	knack
16.	lock	tock	hock	bock	knock
17.	valley	galley	dally	Calley	pally
18.	volley	golly	dolly	collie	Polly

118

Contrast Exercises

A. *In the CHART on the opposite page, read the odd-numbered lines across (1, 3, 5, etc.). Then read the SENTENCES below.*

1. I haven't had a chance to thank you.
2. Allan laughed at the tap dancer.
3. I can't imagine having to backtrack.
4. Janet has a fabulous appetite.
5. That last act was rather bad.
6. Bracken tackled the halfback.
7. We had to have the facts fast.
8. Can't Sally add and subtract?
9. The handyman plastered the crack.
10. After sanding the plaster, he shellacked it.

B. *In the CHART on the opposite page, read the even-numbered lines across (2, 4, 6, etc.). Then read the SENTENCES below.*

1. The stocks dropped to rock bottom.
2. Joshua's problems are common knowledge.
3. I've got lots of lollipops.
4. Bob's responsible for stopping the project.
5. The garage is opposite the hock shop.
6. I'm positive Block's a qualified psychologist.
7. He solemnly promised not to involve us.
8. Monica's fond of comic opera.
9. Stockton honestly wanted the job.
10. It's a logical consequence of modern technology.

Now read SENTENCES alternately from A and B above (A1,B1; A2,B2; A3,B3; etc.).

C. *In the CHART on the opposite page, read vertical pairs across (A1–2, B1–2, C1–2, etc.). Then read the SENTENCES below.*

1. Hackett hocked the last lot.
2. Connell can't possibly pass.
3. Robert's rabbit hopped happily along.
4. Lonigan's landing the captain's copter.
5. The panel pondered Ann's honors paper.
6. Gatti's got a lot of latitude in his job.
7. Fallon followed my logic, but not Natalie.
8. Have the stockboy stack the boxes in back.
9. Oscar asked Madeleine to model it.
10. Platte's plot was panned in Pond's review.

D. *In the CHART on the opposite page, read down each column. Then read the SENTENCES below.*

1. Her pots have odd brass and copper handles.
2. Add a bottle of black olives to the Saturday shopping list.
3. Johnston hasn't commented on that contract.
4. The occupants plan to stop the landlord's dishonest practices.
5. This is a snapshot of Grandma and Grandpa.
6. Scott's last novel had a saccharine plot.
7. Lots of laughing toddlers gather at the sandbox.
8. This brand is not advertised in popular magazines.
9. Stanley apologized for having involved his manager in the conflict.
10. Put the jack-in-the-box and the alphabet blocks back in the closet.

LESSON 67

The Vowels [æ/ʌ]

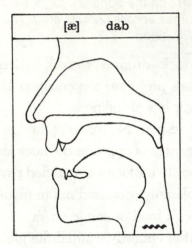

[æ]   dab

Make [æ] with the tongue low and slightly pushed forward, the jaws quite open, and the lips slightly spread.

Make [ʌ] with the tongue curved about halfway up in the center, the jaws half open, and the lips relaxed.

Make [æ] a little longer than [ʌ].

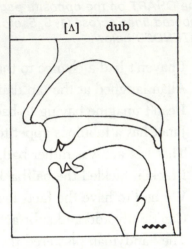

[ʌ]   dub

Contrast Chart

	A	B	C	D	E	F
1.	dab	nab	cab	tab	drab	stab
2.	dub	nub	cub	tub	drub	stub
3.	bad	mad	dad	had	cad	sadden
4.	bud	mud	dud	Hud	cud	sudden
5.	mat	cat	tat	bat	rat	hat
6.	Mutt	cut	tut	but	rut	hut
7.	sack	tack	lack	pack	back	Mac
8.	suck	tuck	luck	puck	buck	muck
9.	jag	rag	bag	lag	slag	tag
10.	jug	rug	bug	lug	slug	tug
11.	calf	gaff	graph	staff	half	laugh
12.	cuff	guff	gruff	stuff	huff	luff
13.	ran	fan	pan	Dan	tan	ban
14.	run	fun	pun	done	ton	bun
15.	ham	dam	ram	Sam	cram	swam
16.	hum	dumb	rum	sum	crumb	swum
17.	gash	lash	hash	rash	mash	crash
18.	gush	lush	hush	rush	mush	crush

120

Contrast Exercises

A. *In the CHART on the opposite page, read the odd-numbered lines across (1, 3, 5, etc.). Then read the SENTENCES below.*

1. It's the last map of Africa we have.
2. Grant had half an apple.
3. Bad language angers Dad.
4. Alex asked for Cracker Jacks.
5. Aunt Valerie is standing pat.
6. It's at Grand and Amsterdam Avenues.
7. We plan to practice till half past.
8. Abbott's answer can't be valid.
9. The camper packed his knapsack.
10. Is that his actual batting average?

B. *In the CHART on the opposite page, read the even-numbered lines across (2, 4, 6, etc.). Then read the SENTENCES below.*

1. The mother won custody of her young son.
2. Sullivan must be a glutton for punishment.
3. The discussion touched on other subjects.
4. The sudden influx of drugs puzzled me.
5. Rusty loves buttered buns.
6. My husband was among the ones consulted.
7. His company doesn't publish such stuff.
8. Hubbard plundered public funds.
9. Supper is just coming up.
10. We've discovered another structure under this one.

Now read SENTENCES alternately from A and B above (A1,B1; A2,B2; A3,B3; etc.).

C. *In the CHART on the opposite page, read vertical pairs across (A1–2, B1–2, C1–2, etc.). Then read the SENTENCES below.*

1. Masters must handle hundreds of them.
2. This summer Sam'll come to camp.
3. Hudson had to land in London.
4. Her uncle's ankle was crushed in the crash.
5. Andy's under Thackeray's thumb.
6. None of Nan's shutters were shattered.
7. Luft laughed and rubbed his rabbit's foot.
8. Don't ask us if Cameron's coming.
9. Muncie managed Amanda's money.
10. Give Kappit a couple of the rag rugs.

D. *In the CHART on the opposite page, read down each column. Then read the SENTENCES below.*

1. I understand that Uncle Sam is cutting taxes.
2. One of Stanton's companies is bankrupt.
3. Clancy conducts the band and doubles on the piano.
4. My son manages the Columbus branch of the National Trust Bank.
5. "Alice in Wonderland" is a classic for youngsters.
6. He suffered a fractured skull as a result of the accident.
7. Dudley's adequate on the trumpet but fantastic on the drums.
8. Last summer Baxter's son was at Camp Sumter.
9. Some of the class had trouble grasping the subject matter.
10. Maxwell summed up his plans for the company's expansion.

121

LESSON 68

The Vowels [ʌ/a]

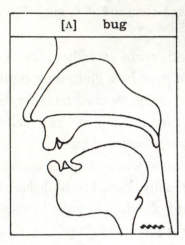

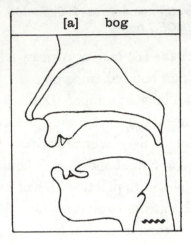

Make [ʌ] with the tongue curved about halfway up in the center, the jaws half open, and the lips relaxed.

Make [a] with the tongue lower than for [ʌ], centered, and rather flat. The jaws should be fully open, and the lips relaxed.

Make [a] longer than [ʌ].

Contrast Chart

	A	B	C	D	E
1.	bug	jug	slug	tug	smug
2.	bog	jog	slog	tog	smog
3.	cud	mud	dud	Rudd	Hud
4.	cod	mod	Dodd	rod	hod
5.	snub	cub	hub	nub	rub
6.	snob	cob	hob	knob	rob
7.	un-	run	none	done	won
8.	on	Ron	non-	don	wan
9.	dull	lull	mull	hull	gull
10.	doll	loll	moll	holly	golly
11.	sum	plumb	bum	mum	come
12.	psalm	aplomb	bomb	mom	calm
13.	pup	up	cup	sup	Muppet
14.	pop	opt	cop	sop	mop
15.	luck	Huck	puck	buck	duck
16.	lock	hock	pock	bock	dock
17.	hut	nut	rut	cut	jut
18.	hot	not	rot	cot	jot

of = /əv/

Contrast Exercises

A. *In the CHART on the opposite page, read the odd-numbered lines across (1, 3, 5, etc.). Then read the SENTENCES below.* iza

1. The other puzzle is a tough one.
2. Russell's an up-and-coming conductor.
3. My youngest son sucks his thumb.
4. Dutch is Ulman's mother tongue.   Duchess
5. The bulk of his money comes from construction.   bulʹkoviz money
6. Culver was unlucky in love.   wɑnavizʌnklez
7. One of his uncles is an instructor at Rutgers.
8. Buxton's pulse was a hundred and one. dwʌn
9. The Dunstans won a summary judgment.
10. The subsidy was a touchy subject for the Governor.

B. *In the CHART on the opposite page, read the even-numbered lines across (2, 4, 6, etc.). Then read the SENTENCES below.*

1. He's a topnotch stock operator.
2. Connery's squad did a competent job.
3. My colleagues scoff at his economic policies.   -nam
4. Rosalind has property in Holland.
5. The hollyhocks and pompons have blossomed.
6. Brodwin concocted a monstrous plot.
7. She's probably got a lot of problems.
8. Polly solemnly promised to stop.
9. He's not obligated beyond tomorrow.
10. Foxwell's novel is impossibly complicated.

Now read SENTENCES alternately from A and B above (A1,B1; A2,B2; A3,B3; etc.).

C. *In the CHART on the opposite page, read vertical pairs across (A1–2, B1–2, C1–2, etc.). Then read the SENTENCES below.*

1. Cully's collie has a colorful collar.
2. He wanted one of Potter's puppets.
3. Jocelyn just had a couple of cocktails.
4. Some psalms lull Lollie to sleep.
5. Comden's coming with Monty on Monday.
6. None of the nominees had enough knowledge.
7. Cotter's cutter was scuttled near Scotland.
8. Robin rubbed his lucky locket.
9. Wanda's won a copper cup.
10. Did Cummings comment on his son's sonnets?

D. *In the CHART on the opposite page, read down each column. Then read the SENTENCES below.*

1. Dutton's watch suddenly stopped functioning.
2. There's not enough profit in such an operation.
3. Buddy's father is coming on from Rockville.
4. A hundred dollars is just a drop in the bucket.
5. Judson operates a costume and button shop.
6. Mother wants them to stop jumping on the rocker.
7. Tommy's uncle got him a spotted puppy.
8. He's stuffing his pockets with a lot of junk.
9. Veronica once modeled summer pajamas.
10. Her brother got somewhat hot under the collar.

LESSON 69

The Vowels $[\Lambda/e]$

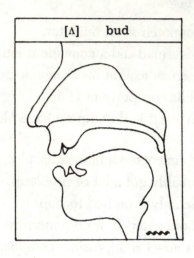

[ʌ]	bud

Make [ʌ] with the tongue curved about halfway up in the center, the jaws half open, and the lips relaxed.

Make [e] with the tongue curved about halfway up in front, the jaws half open, and the lips slightly spread.

Both [ʌ] and [e] are short sounds.

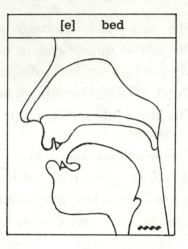

[e]	bed

Contrast Chart

	A	B	C	D	E
1.	bud	dud	flood	spud	stud
2.	bed	dead	fled	sped	stead
3.	muss	bus	Gus	truss	tussle
4.	mess	Bess	guess	tress	Tess
5.	gut	nut	putt	jut	butt
6.	get	net	pet	jet	bet
7.	pun	run	stun	ton	one
8.	pen	wren	sten	ten	wen
9.	truck	chuck	duck	buck	puck
10.	trek	check	deck	beck	peck
11.	dull	hull	Tully	mull	null
12.	dell	hell	tell	Mel	knell
13.	lug	mug	bug	pug	drugs
14.	leg	Meg	beg	peg	dregs
15.	fund	punned	Lund	sunned	trundle
16.	fend	pend	lend	send	trend
17.	just	lust	rust	crust	fussed
18.	jest	lest	rest	crest	festive

124

Contrast Exercises

A. *In the CHART on the opposite page, read the odd-numbered lines across (1, 3, 5, etc.). Then read the SENTENCES below.*

1. He was unaccustomed to such bluntness.
2. Justin consulted one of his brothers.
3. His cousin suffers from stomach ulcers.
4. The undertaking was utterly unproductive.
5. Huxley's just a struggling instructor.
6. Much injustice results from corruption.
7. None of the others come from the suburbs.
8. Duffy's suddenly run out of luck.
9. One of the adults interrupted the youngster.
10. The Hunters own a lovely bungalow in the country.

B. *In the CHART on the opposite page, read the even-numbered lines across (2, 4, 6, etc.). Then read the SENTENCES below.*

1. Many settlers headed west.
2. Bella's friend has endless energy.
3. Several tenants' rents went down.
4. Jeffrey spent every penny.
5. Her left leg's definitely better.
6. Edmond says it's set for Wednesday.
7. You'd better get plenty of rest.
8. Lester felt especially helpless.
9. Let's bet ten cents.
10. Messages are generally left with the receptionist.

Now read SENTENCES alternately from A and B above (A1,B1; A2,B2; A3,B3; etc.).

C. *In the CHART on the opposite page, read vertical pairs across (A1–2, B1–2, C1–2, etc.). Then read the SENTENCES below.*

1. Chuck's checking the best bus to take.
2. Rustin rested instead of studying.
3. I guess Gus thinks it's just a gesture.
4. Cutter kept some semblance of order in the class.
5. Trent's truck weighs ten tons.
6. The Senator's son was at Bundy's benefit.
7. Lufton left his desk at dusk.
8. There are many money-men among them.
9. Wendell wondered if Dennis had done it.
10. Tell Tully he's a dead duck.

D. *In the CHART on the opposite page, read down each column. Then read the SENTENCES below.*

1. Hutton says his brother intends to run for the Senate.
2. He expects to become president of the company, eventually.
3. Sutter gets upset when he's under pressure.
4. Some of us were affected by the cuts in Federal funds.
5. Gunther will send his mother extra money next month.
6. The discussion ended abruptly when Hull entered.
7. Lenny has trouble with chemistry but excels in Russian.
8. Many customers spend much less.
9. Jennie loves pretending to be someone else.
10. Is Benson's blood pressure up again?

LESSON 70

Review of Vowels [æ/a/ʌ/e/i]

Contrast Exercises

In each five-line group of the CHART, read across each line, then down each column (A1–2–3–4–5, B1–2–3–4–5, etc.). Next read each full column. Then read the SENTENCES.

	A	B	C	D	E	F
1.	pat	mat	gnat	sat	cat	rat
2.	pot	Mott	not	sot	cot	rot
3.	putt	mutt	nut	subtle	cut	rut
4.	pet	met	net	set	kettle	ret
5.	pit	mitt	knit	sit	kit	writ
6.	knack	pock	suck	beck	Rick	hack
7.	knuckle	pick	sock	back	wreck	huck
8.	knock	peck	sick	buck	rack	hock
9.	nick	pack	second	bock	ruck	hick
10.	neck	puck	sack	bicker	rock	heck
11.	id	hod	bud	dad	said	piddle
12.	Ed	hid	body	dud	sad	peddle
13.	udder	had	bed	did	sod	puddle
14.	odd	Hud	bad	dead	Sid	pod
15.	add	head	bid	Dodd	suds	pad

1. I wonder whether Roger has this edition.
2. Robert's cousin went to Alaska with him.
3. Some of the questions were not exactly simple.
4. Rodney sent his son to camp in Ithaca.
5. A couple of his friends dropped in last night.
6. Jonathan is becoming less difficult to handle.
7. I think I'd rather spend a month in the Tropics.
8. Dudley managed to finish the job just before the deadline.
9. It's natural for Edna's children to want what other children have.
10. Little Bobby plans to become President one day.

Intonation: Two-Phrase Statements (A)

Any statement may be spoken in two or more phrases, each with its own primary stress. This most often happens when the sentence is long, or when it contains balanced elements which seem to call for equal stress. The usual intonation pattern is (2)32/231. In the practice sentences below, phrase division is indicated by a comma (,) or a slash (/).

A. Simple sentences — even short ones — are often broken into two or more phrases for added emphasis.

1. Thís one / tastes térrible.
2. The gás tank / was émpty.
3. Óne mistake / is enóugh.
4. His lást film / was brílliant.
5. Móst of them / just láughed.

6. He spéaks / like a nátive.
7. Míne / cost a dóllar.
8. The fírst step / is the hárdest.
9. Óur car / is smáller.
10. The scénery / was beaútiful.

B. In comparison sentences, the two elements compared are often stressed. The boundary between the phrases may be variously placed, as indicated below.

1. The wórk / was more fun than the pláy.
2. Her húsband's / as old as her fáther.
3. The hát / cost more than the cóat.
4. She síngs / as well as she dánces.
5. He spéaks / even better than he wrítes.

6. Yóu know it / as well as Í do.
7. Shé's even braver / than hé is.
8. Théy need it / more than wé do.
9. The búll was as frightened /as Í was.
10. Her bróther talks faster / than shé does.

C. In compound sentences, the independent clauses may be spoken as separate phrases.

1. I knów him / and I respéct him.
2. We've chécked them / and they're okáy.
3. It was wíndy / and he was cóld.
4. She rang the béll, but no one ánswered.
5. I tried to líft it, but it was too héavy.

6. The radio didn't wórk, so he retúrned it.
7. I had no tícket, so I couldn't get ín.
8. Hurry úp / or you'll miss the tráin.
9. We'd better stúdy / or we'll fail the tést.
10. Write it dówn / or you'll forgét it.

D. In complex sentences, the main and subordinate clauses may be spoken as separate phrases.

1. She had léft / by the time we arríved.
2. I'll have some cóffee / while it's still hót.
3. Let's start nów, before it gets too dárk.
4. You can watch TV / after you've had dínner.
5. I'll wait in his óffice / until he gets báck.

6. I couldn't ópen it / because I'd lost my kéy.
7. We all felt háppier / when the ráin stopped.
8. I'll give you an ánswer / as soon as I cán.
9. They'd work fáster / if you páid them more.
10. We hadn't séen each other / since we gráduated.

The Vowels [ow/a]

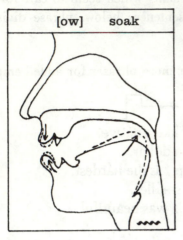

[ow]   soak

To make [ow], start with the tongue curved about halfway up in back, the jaws half open, and the lips rounded. Glide the tongue further up and back, and round the lips more closely, while voicing the vowel.

Make [a] with the tongue low, centered, and rather flat. The jaws should be fully open, and the lips relaxed.

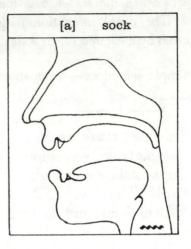

[a]   sock

Contrast Chart

	A	B	C	D	E
1.	soak	bloke	poke	cloak	croak
2.	sock	block	pock	clock	crock
3.	goad	code	ode	road	toad
4.	god	cod	odd	rod	Todd
5.	dole	mole	sole	pole	foal
6.	doll	moll	Sol	Polly	folly
7.	own	Joan	cone	known	lone
8.	on	John	con	non-	Lon
9.	folks	oaks	hoax	Doakes	coax
10.	fox	ox	hocks	docks	Cox
11.	cope	hope	lope	mope	pope
12.	cop	hop	lop	mop	pop
13.	note	goat	dote	coat	oat
14.	not	got	dot	cot	Ott
15.	hoed	node	mode	showed	soda
16.	hod	nod	mod	shod	sod
17.	choke	spoke	stoke	smoke	broke
18.	chock	Spock	stock	smock	Brock

Contrast Exercises

A. *In the CHART on the opposite page, read the odd-numbered lines across (1, 3, 5, etc.). Then read the SENTENCES below.*

1. It won't hold up Owen's promotion.
2. The cold froze me to the bone.
3. Grover donated his old clothes.
4. We're going to show it in slow motion.
5. Lois was supposed to postpone it.
6. The soldier told him the revolt was over.
7. Jody poked at the gopher hole.
8. We don't oppose Roland's proposal.
9. Those roses are grown locally.
10. Copeland stole the whole show.

B. *In the CHART on the opposite page, read the even-numbered lines across (2, 4, 6, etc.). Then read the SENTENCES below.*

1. He occupies a prominent spot on the roster.
2. I'm concentrating on economic geography.
3. He's got a lot of hot prospects.
4. Thomas solved a knotty problem.
5. His colleagues will probably respond.
6. There's a spot on Roger's pajama top.
7. Proctor's logic demolished the opposition.
8. They're watching Dr. Hopkins operate.
9. It's not possible to stop the contest.
10. The Congressman's confident of nomination.

Now read SENTENCES alternately from A and B above (A1,B1; A2,B2; A3,B3; etc.).

C. *In the CHART on the opposite page, read vertical pairs across (A1–2, B1–2, C1–2, etc.). Then read the SENTENCES below.*

1. Locke located Oliver's old records.
2. Cox coaxed the local locksmith into fixing it.
3. The note's not for Lon alone.
4. Tollifer told her their host seemed hostile.
5. Foley followed us on his own.
6. We were both bothered by Conan's conduct.
7. Goldie's got a cotton coat.
8. Spock spoke of his holiday in the Holy Land.
9. He won't want this nonsense known.
10. Rod rode in the bottom of the boat.

D. *In the CHART on the opposite page, read down each column. Then read the SENTENCES below.*

1. Popular Home Products won't sponsor the soap opera.
2. Joe's got a cold bottle of soda pop.
3. "The Pot of Gold" is not the only sonnet he wrote.
4. Boswell owns and operates a clothing shop.
5. I know he's not going to stop smoking on the job.
6. Joel's pockets overflowed with odd and broken objects.
7. The columnist had photocopies of most of the documents.
8. Father Robeson promised he'd only stop for a moment.
9. They want to go on with the Wyoming project.
10. O'Connor's disclosures shocked most of his followers.

LESSON 73

The Vowels [a/aw]

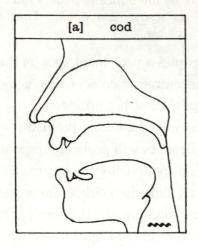

[a] cod

Make [a] with the tongue low, centered, and rather flat. The jaws should be quite open, and the lips relaxed.

To make [aw], start in [a] position. Glide the tongue up and back, and round the lips, while voicing the vowel.

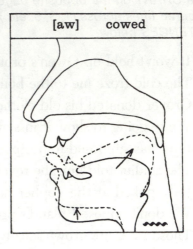

[aw] cowed

Contrast Chart

	A	B	C	D	E
1.	cod	hod	wad	plod	rod
2.	cowed	howdy	wowed	plowed	rowdy
3.	got	dot	not	lot	pot
4.	gout	doubt	knout	lout	pout
5.	Ollie	collie	folly	holly	jolly
6.	owl	cowl	fowl	howl	jowl
7.	rot	tot	shot	clot	trot
8.	rout	tout	shout	clout	trout
9.	donned	frond	Honda	tonic	chronic
10.	downed	frowned	hound	town	crown
11.	Scot	snot	spot	grotto	bottle
12.	scout	snout	spout	grout	bout
13.	volley	Polly	Tolliver	doll	Holling
14.	vowel	Powell	towel	dowel	howling
15.	bond	wand	pond	Rhonda	fond
16.	bound	wound	pound	round	found
17.	prod	bodkin	clod	vodka	Dodd
18.	proud	bowed	cloud	vowed	dowdy

Contrast Exercises

A. *In the CHART on the opposite page, read the odd-numbered lines across (1, 3, 5, etc.). Then read the SENTENCES below.*

1. The model's costume was positively shocking.
2. They wanted to drop in at the Trotters in Yonkers.
3. Thompson's shopping for a lobster pot.
4. He probably got to the top through politics.
5. Comstock is a prominent astronomer.
6. Honestly, Bob's not responsible.
7. Bonnie's playing hopscotch and potsy.
8. The bomb squad responded promptly.
9. Doctor Conti's in the hospital lobby.
10. John's stopping in Oshkosh tonight.

B. *In the CHART on the opposite page, read the even-numbered lines across (2, 4, 6, etc.). Then read the SENTENCES below.*

1. The Foundation was proud to announce the endowment.
2. Pound can vouch for the accountant's background.
3. Flowers were sprouting around the house.
4. Powers spent an hour downtown.
5. How about some brown trout?
6. Southby was the founder of our town.
7. He devoured a pound of flounder.
8. Strauss now has doubts about the outcome.
9. They're sounding Dow out now.
10. The hound's howling roused the house-keeper.

Now read SENTENCES alternately from A and B above (A1,B1; A2,B2; A3,B3; etc.).

C. *In the CHART on the opposite page, read vertical pairs across (A1–2, B1–2, C1–2, etc.). Then read the SENTENCES below.*

1. Knox announced Oster's ouster yesterday.
2. Housing is the hottest topic in town.
3. Ott is out, but Rhonda's around somewhere.
4. I doubt that Dot allowed him a lot of leeway.
5. Connie counted on her counsel's conscience.
6. Donley downed about a bottle.
7. They followed Fowler from the house to the hospital.
8. Potter was pouting then, but he's not now.
9. Doctor Dower's got the gout.
10. Fonda found contentment in the mountains of Montana.

D. *In the CHART on the opposite page, read down each column. Then read the SENTENCES below.*

1. Plow's not proud of being a college dropout.
2. Send Miss Cowell a box of flowers — compliments of the house.
3. The accountant was bothered about the problem of allowances.
4. The Browders stopped for an hour at the Rocky Mountain Lodge.
5. Downing College is outside Thomasville, opposite the foundry.
6. Kraus wanted to shout it from the housetops.
7. Stroud probably encountered a lot of powerful opposition.
8. His property is a block south of the Rockland County line.
9. The Bauers promised the Foundling Hospital a thousand dollars.
10. Johnson denounced their conduct in the House of Commons.

LESSON 74

The Vowels [ow/aw]

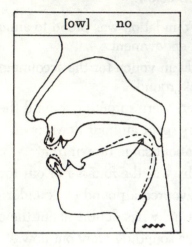

[ow]	no

To make [ow], start with the tongue curved about halfway up in back, the jaws half open, and the lips rounded. Glide the tongue further up and back, and round the lips more closely, while voicing the vowel.

To make [aw], start in [a] position, with the tongue low, centered, and rather flat, the jaws fully open, and the lips relaxed. Glide the tongue up and back, and round the lips, while voicing the vowel.

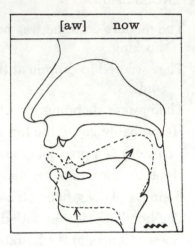

[aw]	now

Contrast Chart

	A	B	C	D	E
1.	oh	hoe	though	no	pro
2.	ow	how	thou	now	prow
3.	so	low	dough	co-	woe
4.	sow	allow	Dow	cow	wow
5.	coal	foal	hole	skoal	Joel
6.	cowl	foul	howl	scowl	jowl
7.	phoned	boned	groaned	honed	moaned
8.	found	bound	ground	hound	mound
9.	lode	crowed	code	road	bode
10.	loud	crowd	cowed	rowdy	bowed
11.	boat	dote	float	goat	rote
12.	bout	doubt	flout	gout	rout
13.	poach	grow	encroach	slow	coach
14.	pouch	grouch	crouch	slouch	couch
15.	role	toll	bowl	pole	dole
16.	rowel	towel	bowel	Powell	dowel
17.	crone	known	tone	drone	clone
18.	crown	noun	town	drown	clown

Contrast Exercises

A. *In the CHART on the opposite page, read the odd-numbered lines across (1, 3, 5, etc.). Then read the SENTENCES below.*

1. Rose drove them to Oklahoma.
2. He chose to go to the Gold Coast.
3. Coty knows the ropes in Hoboken.
4. The whole episode will blow over.
5. Hogan enclosed both notes.
6. His opponent polled most of the votes.
7. Tobin sold his motorboat.
8. The older hotels are going broke.
9. Coleman won't stay home alone.
10. The road show closed in November.

B. *In the CHART on the opposite page, read the even-numbered lines across (2, 4, 6, etc.). Then read the SENTENCES below.*

1. It amounts to about a thousand pounds.
2. Powell's down South now.
3. You're learning how to pronounce vowels.
4. Gower has clout in the town council.
5. The prowler scouted around the grounds.
6. Lowery's an out-and-out scoundrel.
7. They allowed the discount anyhow.
8. Crowell was hounded out of town.
9. I hear Dowling's about to bow out.
10. We counted on Browning's power in the House.

Now read SENTENCES alternately from A and B above (A1,B1; A2,B2; A3,B3; etc.).

C. *In the CHART on the opposite page, read vertical pairs across (A1–2, B1–2, C1–2, etc.). Then read the SENTENCES below.*

1. Tower told us never to boast about it.
2. Howe's home is outside Oakland.
3. Now I know a little about boats.
4. Cohn countered that Otis was out of it.
5. Foner found them roaming around town.
6. Hope's house is overcrowded.
7. I don't doubt that he'll hold out.
8. Townsend's tone astounded Stone.
9. Konig's counsel made no announcement today.
10. Howard's host showed him out.

D. *In the CHART on the opposite page, read down each column. Then read the SENTENCES below.*

1. Downes knows how to go about it.
2. The old houseboat went aground.
3. Bowker opened his mouth, but no sound came out.
4. We found him in a roadhouse on Old Town Road.
5. Dowd has donated thousands to the Dover Foundation.
6. Don't put that old brown bowl on the counter.
7. Howell owns a house in Overton, South Dakota.
8. Our pony outran Holden's brown colt.
9. Only Crowley knows how the gold was found.
10. The whole town is so proud of Homer's prowess.

LESSON 75

The Vowels [ow/ɔ]

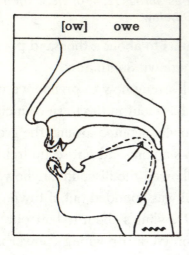

[ow]	owe

To make [ow], start with the tongue curved about halfway up in back, the jaws half open, and the lips rounded. Glide the tongue further up and back, and round the lips more closely, while voicing the vowel.

Make [ɔ] with the tongue low, pulled back, and higher in back than in front (but not as high as for [ow]). The jaws should be quite open, and the lips slightly rounded. Do not glide the tongue or round the lips further while voicing the vowel.

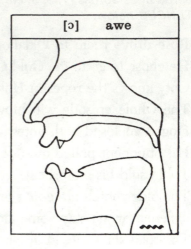

[ɔ]	awe

Contrast Chart

	A	B	C	D	E
1.	owe	low	show	row	flow
2.	awe	law	Shaw	raw	flaw
3.	slow	doe	Poe	so	crow
4.	slaw	daw	paw	saw	craw
5.	coke	woke	soak	choke	stoke
6.	calk	walk	Salk	chalk	stalk
7.	pole	goal	foal	stole	shoal
8.	pall	gall	fall	stall	shawl
9.	node	sewed	hoed	code	bode
10.	gnawed	sawed	hawed	cawed	bawd
11.	Holt	molt	bolt	dolt	Foley
12.	halt	malt	Balt	Dalton	falter
13.	phone	pone	drone	lone	own
14.	fawn	pawn	drawn	lawn	awn
15.	boast	coast	toast	most	roast
16.	bossed	cost	tossed	moss	Ross
17.	oat	boat	coat	note	tote
18.	ought	bought	caught	naught	taught

Contrast Exercises

A. *In the CHART on the opposite page, read the odd-numbered lines across (1, 3, 5, etc.). Then read the SENTENCES below.*

1. I don't suppose the custodian's home.
2. Joan spoke in low tones.
3. He's told that old joke over and over.
4. Olin chose to go it alone.
5. They sold most of the overcoats.
6. I know Toby will hold his own.
7. Both of them are going to quote Poe.
8. We hope to expose Joseph's motives.
9. He wrote whole tomes of poetry.
10. Logan disposed of his old boat.

B. *In the CHART on the opposite page, read the even-numbered lines across (2, 4, 6, etc.). Then read the SENTENCES below.*

1. I thought we ought to draw straws.
2. The Lawsons have fought all along.
3. Their brawling was audible across the hall.
4. Vaughn was recalled to the Austin office.
5. Talking to him is always awkward.
6. Frost was appalled at their awful losses.
7. The audience applauded all the songs.
8. The long walk exhausted Ball.
9. He often thought of auctioning it off.
10. Claudia bought some broadcloth.

Now read SENTENCES alternately from A and B above (A1,B1; A2,B2; A3,B3; etc.).

C. *In the CHART on the opposite page, read vertical pairs across (A1–2, B1–2, C1–2, etc.). Then read the SENTENCES below.*

1. Saul sold his whole haul.
2. Brophy brought his own auditor.
3. Show Shaw your new bowling ball.
4. Thoden thought his boss was boasting.
5. We saw Sophie alone on the launch.
6. Oakie auditioned for Rawlins' role.
7. Has Shawn shown you the boat he bought?
8. Cody caught a cold from Calder.
9. Tony's taunts don't daunt me.
10. Audrey owed it all to Olson.

D. *In the CHART on the opposite page, read down each column. Then read the SENTENCES below.*

1. The Coles often stroll along Stone Street.
2. Knowland ought to postpone the drawing till October.
3. The whole audience rose to applaud the soloist.
4. Jones and Roth co-authored "The Lonely Astronaut."
5. Bolen's daughter is always so soft-spoken.
6. Spaulding's going to call for toast and coffee.
7. He offered to hold off the opening till fall.
8. Rosen thought the posters ought to be bolder.
9. This ghost often goes haunting alone.
10. Pauling told him to talk it over with his parole officer.

LESSON 76

The Vowels [ɔ/a]

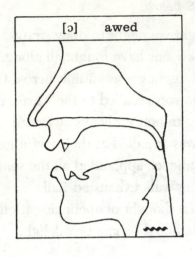

[ɔ]	awed

Make [ɔ] with the tongue low, pulled back, and higher in back than in front. The jaws should be quite open, and the lips slightly rounded. Do not glide the tongue or round the lips further while voicing the vowel.

Make [a] with the tongue low, centered, and rather flat. The jaws should be fully open, and the lips relaxed.

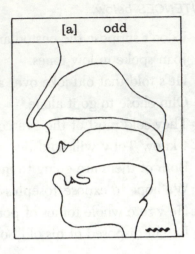

[a]	odd

Contrast Chart

	A	B	C	D	E
1.	awed	Maud	hawed	gnawed	cawed
2.	odd	mod	hod	nod	cod
3.	sought	wrought	nought	ought	bought
4.	sot	rot	not	Ott	bottle
5.	gall	hall	call	wall	vault
6.	golly	holly	collie	wallop	volley
7.	dawn	lawn	yawn	pawned	fawned
8.	don	Lon	yon	pond	fond
9.	pawed	sawed	Shaw'd	clawed	broad
10.	pod	sod	shod	clod	Brod
11.	stalk	chalk	balk	talk	hawk
12.	stock	chock	bock	tock	hock
13.	mall	fall	tall	stall	scald
14.	moll	follow	tolerant	stolid	scholar
15.	bawdy	gaudy	plaudit	dawdle	tawdry
16.	body	god	plod	Dodd	Todd
17.	caught	taught	daughter	haughty	Laughton
18.	cot	tot	dot	hot	lot

136

Contrast Exercises

A. *In the CHART on the opposite page, read the odd-numbered lines across (1, 3, 5, etc.). Then read the SENTENCES below.*

1. All in all, the cost was small.
2. McCauley's an officer of the law.
3. We saw a dog crossing the lawn.
4. Alden bought the shawl in Austria.
5. My daughter often paused to talk to him.
6. He was awed by Claude's audacity.
7. I bought a sausage and a malted at the Automat.
8. Wald was distraught when his belongings were lost.
9. The thought haunted him all autumn.
10. Crawford is almost always cautious.

B. *In the CHART on the opposite page, read the even-numbered lines across (2, 4, 6, etc.). Then read the SENTENCES below.*

1. Lock the top of the bottom box.
2. Tom's conscience stopped bothering him.
3. He was allotted a block of common stock.
4. Molly's polishing her copper pots.
5. We promised not to compromise on quality.
6. Hollis dropped his pocket watch.
7. They'll operate on Donald's tonsils tomorrow.
8. Bromley's confident they'll resolve the conflict.
9. He's probably got a responsible job.
10. Bronson's column is a lot of nonsense.

Now read SENTENCES alternately from A and B above (A1,B1; A2,B2; A3,B3; etc.).

C. *In the CHART on the opposite page, read vertical pairs across (A1–2, B1–2, C1–2, etc.). Then read the SENTENCES below.*

1. Collins called a halt to his holiday.
2. Totter taught them the Song of Solomon.
3. Bock balked at the cost of the costumes.
4. Olive almost lost her locket.
5. Ottinger ought to stop stalling.
6. Paul apologized to Doctor Dawson.
7. It dawned on Don that Ronald was wrong.
8. Cott caught it the following fall.
9. Brock brought Lonigan along.
10. Dot's daughter bought a bottle of milk.

D. *In the CHART on the opposite page, read down each column. Then read the SENTENCES below.*

1. They've probably lost confidence in all of his promises.
2. Crockett taught philosophy at a small college on Long Island.
3. We got the Albany property because Romney defaulted on it.
4. Rockwell always wanted a soft job.
5. I ought to stop off at the doctor's office tomorrow.
6. Frawley's prospects are not at all promising.
7. They resolved to launch the product this autumn.
8. Caulfield's conduct caused a lot of office gossip.
9. I bought the coffee pot at Slawson's shop.
10. He'd wanted to talk to his father all along.

137

LESSON 77

Review of Vowels [ow/ɔ/a/aw]

Contrast Exercises

In each four-line group of the CHART, read across each line, then down each column (A1–2–3–4, B1–2–3–4, etc.). Next read down each full column. Then read the SENTENCES.

	A	B	C	D	E	F
1.	oh	bode	code	hoed	load	Brody
2.	awe	bawd	cawed	hawed	laud	broad
3.	ah	body	cod	hod	lodge	Brod
4.	ow	bowed	cowed	how'd	loud	Browder
5.	non-	pond	don	fond	sonnet	monitor
6.	known	pone	Doan	phoned	sewn	moan
7.	noun	pound	down	found	sound	mound
8.	gnawn	pawned	dawn	fawned	sawn	Mauna
9.	hole	fall	Polly	vowel	coal	doll
10.	holly	foal	Powell	vault	cowl	dole
11.	haul	foul	pole	volley	call	dowel
12.	howl	follow	pall	vole	collie	dawdle
13.	ought	doubt	boat	rot	taught	knout
14.	out	dote	bottle	wrought	tot	note
15.	Ott	daughter	bout	wrote	tout	not
16.	oat	dot	bought	rout	tote	naught

1. You're not going to call for a slowdown, are you?
2. The Holdens have always wanted a house in some remote spot.
3. Father is fond of talking about how it was in the old days.
4. Potter's been awfully close-mouthed about the whole problem.
5. The following program is brought to you by the House and Lawn Products Company.
6. John showed us a small toad he'd found.
7. I don't know how often I've told them not to drop in without phoning.
8. Congressman Jones ought to be proud of his voting record.
9. Long ago they bought property on the outskirts of town.
10. It's only because of his powerful associates that Howell's gotten off so easily.

Intonation: Two-Phrase Statements (B)

Two-phrase statements often have the pattern (2)32⌐/(2)31, with a rise at the end of the first phrase. This is especially common when, because of grammatical structure or stress placement, the first phrase depends upon the second to complete its meaning — as in the examples below.

A. Compound statements of agreement, with the subject stressed in each clause.

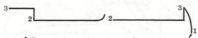
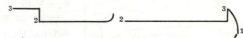

1. Téd was angry, and so was Í.
2. Míchael liked it, and so did Ánn.
3. My móney's gone, and so is my wátch.
4. Péars are in season, and so are ápples.
5. The hóuse is insured, and so is the cár.

6. Jáne isn't going, and neither am Í.
7. Wé didn't know it, and neither did théy.
8. His wífe isn't happy, and neither is hé.
9. Bíll can't dance, and neither can Fránk.
10. The kíds aren't tired, and neither are wé.

B. Contrasted positive and negative clauses connected by *but*, with the subject stressed in the first clause and the verb stressed in the second.

1. The néighbors don't care, but I dó.
2. Pául can't afford it, but Harry cán.
3. Advíce won't help me, but money wóuld.
4. The bánk's not open, but the market ís.
5. Í haven't read it, but he hás.

6. Shé wants to move, but he dóesn't.
7. Spéech may be free, but food ísn't.
8. Óthers may think so, but I dón't.
9. My áunt can drive, but my uncle cán't.
10. Álan agreed, but Jason dídn't.

C. Complex sentences with the subordinate clause first.

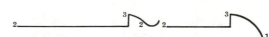

1. Before you rejéct the offer, think it óver.
2. Although he didn't sáy so, I think he's íll.
3. If thát's the case, nóthing will help.
4. When Í was in France, prices were lówer.
5. Since they can't dó anything, why wórry?

6. As long as you're hére, give me a hánd.
7. While you were óut, Mártin called.
8. Until we're súre, don't tell ányone.
9. By the time she retúrns, I'll be góne.
10. As soon as you knów, cáll me.

D. Compound sentences in which the second clause negates or casts doubt on the wish, opinion, or possibility stressed in the first.

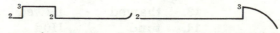

1. I hópe to attend, but I may not be áble to.
2. He tríed to explain, but he cóuldn't.
3. We wánted to go, but it cóst too much.
4. We'd líke to stay, but I'm afraid we cán't.
5. They sáy he's good, but I have my dóubts.

6. I guéss it's all right, but we'd better chéck.
7. I thínk it'll work, but who knóws?
8. They míght win, but it's not líkely.
9. That máy be true, but I'm not convínced.
10. She cóuld have married but didn't wánt to.

LESSON 79

The Vowels [ɔ/ʌ]

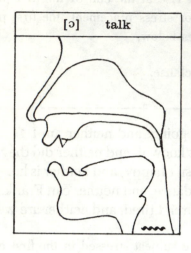

[ɔ] talk

Make [ɔ] with the tongue low, pulled back, and higher in back than in front. The jaws should be quite open, and the lips slightly rounded. Do not glide the tongue or round the lips further while voicing the vowel.

Make [ʌ] with the tongue curved about halfway up in the center, the jaws half open, and the lips relaxed.

Make [ɔ] a little longer than [ʌ].

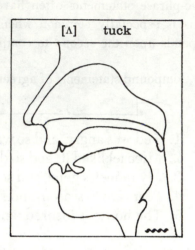

[ʌ] tuck

Contrast Chart

	A	B	C	D	E
1.	talk	chalk	balk	hawk	stalk
2.	tuck	chuck	buck	Huck	stuck
3.	call	gall	hall	maul	pall
4.	cull	gull	hull	mull	pulse
5.	dawn	pawn	faun	spawn	Shawn
6.	done	pun	fun	spun	shun
7.	mossed	cost	lost	crossed	bossed
8.	must	cussed	lust	crust	bust
9.	naught	bought	caught	wrought	taught
10.	nut	but	cut	rut	tut
11.	pause	maws	gauze	gnaws	cause
12.	puzzle	muzzle	guzzle	nuzzle	cousin
13.	thawed	hawed	Maud	cawed	sawed
14.	thud	Hud	mud	cud	suds
15.	haunch	launch	paunch	brawn	Mauna
16.	hunch	lunch	punch	brunch	munch
17.	song	strong	wrong	long	haunt
18.	sung	strung	rung	lung	hunt

140

Contrast Exercises

A. *In the CHART on the opposite page, read the odd-numbered lines across (1, 3, 5, etc.). Then read the SENTENCES below.*

1. The astronaut's talk was broadcast in August.
2. Halsey saw flaws in the law.
3. The sauce was altogether too salty.
4. He often brought his daughter to the office.
5. That costly bauble belongs in a vault.
6. The Ralstons waltzed till almost dawn.
7. Milwaukee to Austin is a long haul.
8. Paulson thought they ought to do an autopsy.
9. They all thought it was a lost cause.
10. Crosby bought a walkie-talkie.

B. *In the CHART on the opposite page, read the even-numbered lines across (2, 4, 6, etc.). Then read the SENTENCES below.*

1. Her husband runs the Summit Lumber Company.
2. Lovell was subject to sudden convulsions.
3. Youngsters love "The Ugly Duckling."
4. Wasn't Summers one of the front-runners?
5. Her brother cut up some of the onions.
6. A couple of my subjects were fun to study.
7. Rusk stubbornly stuck to his guns.
8. It's just another cover-up for government corruption.
9. The pun wasn't funny enough.
10. Jud trusts his mother's judgment.

Now read SENTENCES alternately from A and B above (A1,B1; A2,B2; A3,B3; etc.).

C. *In the CHART on the opposite page, read vertical pairs across (A1–2, B1–2, C1–2, etc.). Then read the SENTENCES below.*

1. Lunt longed for a cup of coffee.
2. Moss must be running the wrong tape.
3. Has Tucker talked to the other authors?
4. Cullin calls me often enough.
5. Dawes did a dozen somersaults.
6. Someone saw him give Mauna the money.
7. Cutter caught the Boston bus.
8. Saunders' son has an ulcer also.
9. My brother brought Douglas a dog.
10. Ulman almost cost Custer his job.

D. *In the CHART on the opposite page, read down each column. Then read the SENTENCES below.*

1. My son was appalled by the destruction he saw.
2. Something caused the judge to call an abrupt halt to the hearings.
3. Sutherland offered to cover the cost of subsequent lawsuits.
4. Mother always comes to Malden for the month of August.
5. One of the officers suddenly called his bluff.
6. His talk touched off another long discussion.
7. The bus ride from Baldwin left Dustin exhausted.
8. They've just bought a couple of small trucks.
9. My cousin belongs to the Huntington ball club.
10. Humphrey ought to study all summer.

141

LESSON 80
The Vowels [ʌ/u]

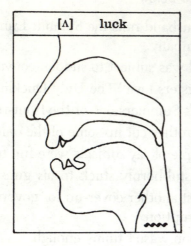

[ʌ] luck

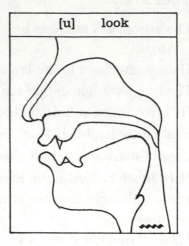

[u] look

Make [ʌ] with the tongue curved about halfway up in the center, the jaws half open, and the lips relaxed.

Make [u] with the tongue curved rather high in back, the jaws slightly open, and the lips rounded. Do not glide the tongue or round the lips further while voicing the vowel.

Both [ʌ] and [u] are short sounds.

Contrast Chart

	A	B	C	D
1.	luck	Huck	buck	cuckold
2.	look	hook	book	cook
3.	cud	stud	shudder	Hudson
4.	could	stood	should	hood
5.	shuck	tuck	suck	ruck
6.	shook	took	forsook	rook
7.	bulb	pulse	bulk	funnel
8.	bull	pull	bullock	full
9.	knuckle	Bruckner	ruckus	buckle
10.	nook	brook	rookery	bushel
11.	putter	Sutter	futtock	shutter
12.	put	soot	foot	sugar
13.	huckster	lux	crux	buxom
14.	hooks	looks	crooks	books
15.	gutter	butter	huddle	puddle
16.	good	butcher	hood'll	pudding
17.	but	huff	pus	gully
18.	Butch	hoof	puss	goodly

142

Contrast Exercises

A. *In the CHART on the opposite page, read the odd-numbered lines across (1, 3, 5, etc.). Then read the SENTENCES below.*

1. They discuss such dull subjects.
2. Wasn't Upton's uncle once a drummer?
3. There were just under a hundred at the luncheon.
4. Duncan is an understudy in the London production.
5. He's up to some skulduggery or other.
6. Some of the money was smuggled in.
7. Rudley's cousin is a tough customer.
8. It's nothing but a rusty pump.
9. She cut a dozen lovely buttercups.
10. Scully's been studying their customs for months.

B. *In the CHART on the opposite page, read the even-numbered lines across (2, 4, 6, etc.). Then read the SENTENCES below.*

1. That bully took my sugar cookies.
2. Hooker put his foot in it.
3. He reviews books for the *Brookfield Bulletin.*
4. Couldn't you get the yard goods at Woolworth's?
5. Bush mistook the butcher for a cook.
6. The woman wouldn't look at him.
7. Goodman played hooky in his childhood.
8. The bookstore's on Bushwick Boulevard.
9. You shouldn't put the pudding there.
10. Hood couldn't stop pussyfooting.

Now read SENTENCES alternately from A and B above (A1,B1; A2,B2; A3,B3; etc.).

C. *In the CHART on the opposite page, read vertical pairs across (A1–2, B1–2, C1–2, etc.). Then read the SENTENCES below.*

1. Cook's cousin couldn't come.
2. It stood in the study where Putnam had put it.
3. Little Gus is good at cooking custard.
4. He loves looking through Buckley's books.
5. I wonder — would Underwood do it?
6. Tucker took a trip to Bruckner's Brook.
7. That woman won a couple of cushions.
8. Puller's puppy is full of fun.
9. Wouldn't one of them make a good Governor?
10. Cummings couldn't put the puzzle together.

D. *In the CHART on the opposite page, read down each column. Then read the SENTENCES below.*

1. Brooks must be cooking up something good.
2. She understood someone would come to meet her.
3. Sonny couldn't even do one push-up.
4. The Cushman Company wouldn't publish my book.
5. One of the Goodwin youngsters is forever underfoot.
6. A truck pulled up in front of the bookstore.
7. Fuller just put out another bulletin.
8. He took the trouble to look up Bookman's number.
9. Woody's brother shouldn't suffer for it.
10. It wasn't good enough to put up.

LESSON 81

Review of Vowels [ɔ/ʌ/u]

Contrast Exercises

In each three-line group of the CHART, read across each line, then down each column (A1–2–3, B1–2–3, etc.). Next read down each full column. Then read the SENTENCES.

	A	B	C	D	E	F
1.	hawk	balk	law	gnaw	craw	Shaw
2.	huck	buck	luck	knuckle	crux	shuck
3.	hook	book	look	nook	crook	shook
4.	cud	shudder	stud	huddle	puddle	gutter
5.	could	should	stood	hood	pudding	good
6.	cawed	Shaw'd	stalk	hawed	pawed	gaudy
7.	soot	put	butch	cookie	foot	hoof
8.	sought	paw	bought	caught	fought	haw
9.	Sutter	putt	but	cut	fuss	huff
10.	talk	custard	hooker	suck	raucous	puss
11.	tuck	cook	hawker	forsook	ruckus	pause
12.	took	calk	huckster	Salk	rookie	pus
13.	bulb	goodly	pall	full	hulk	Balkan
14.	ball	gully	pull	funnel	hall	bullock
15.	bull	gall	pulse	fall	Hooke	bulk

1. Couldn't Audrey have looked up the auditor's number?
2. I thought Justin should have put his money in the vault.
3. The Hooker Awning Company is on Upton Boulevard in Raleigh.
4. She took one of Calder's law books from the study.
5. Woody taught his younger brother all he could.
6. None of us saw the Fulton-Culver football game.
7. Uncle Woodruff couldn't come because he'd caught a cold.
8. He offered to put them all up for one night.
9. Goodwin played the long-suffering brother in "Across the Footlights."
10. Rudley wouldn't be falling in love with the boss's daughter, would he?

144

LESSON 82

Intonation: Two-Phrase Statements (C)

We have seen that the first phrase of a two-phrase statement often ends in a rise: (2)32⌐/(2)31. In certain types of sentence, the pattern may be reversed: (2)31/(2)32⌐.

A. In conditional sentences, the *if* clause may end with a rise whether it precedes or follows the main clause. (Read down, then across.)

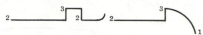 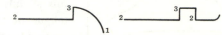

1. If you'll lét me, I can expláin.
2. If I had the móney, I'd búy one.
3. If it stops ráining, we'll play gólf.
4. If he ásked her, she'd márry him.
5. If I knéw, I'd téll you.

6. I can expláin / if you'll lét me.
7. I'd búy one / if I had the móney.
8. We'll play gólf / if it stops ráining.
9. She'd márry him / if he ásked her.
10. I'd téll you / if I knéw.

B. In negative-positive contrast sentences with no conjunction, the negative phrase usually ends with a rise, the positive phrase with a fall — regardless of which comes first. (In each of the following sections, read down, then across.)

The stress may be on contrasted predicate elements:

1. It wasn't mý fault; it was hís.
2. He's not a nóvelist; he's a póet.
3. She isn't thírteen; she's fóurteen.
4. He didn't bórrow it; he stóle it.
5. We haven't wón the case; we've lóst it.

6. It was hís fault, not míne.
7. He's a póet, not a nóvelist.
8. She's fóurteen, not thírteen.
9. He stóle it; he didn't bórrow it.
10. We've lóst the case, not wón it.

The subject of the negative phrase may be stressed when that phrase comes first:

11. Thát's not a house; it's a pálace.
12. Hé's no hero; he's a críminal.
13. Todáy's not Tuesday; it's Wédnesday.
14. Ál's not a wrestler; he's a bóxer.
15. Thís isn't a diamond; it's gláss.

16. That's a pálace, not a hóuse.
17. He's a críminal, not a héro.
18. Today's Wédnesday, not Túesday.
19. Al's a bóxer, not a wréstler.
20. This is gláss, not a díamond.

Contrasted subjects may be stressed:

 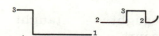

21. Sálly's not sick; Álice is.
22. Jánet shouldn't stay; Bétty should.
23. Yóu're not to blame; Í am.
24. Jóhn didn't break it; Geórge did.
25. Hárris isn't going; Jónes is.

26. Álice is sick, not Sálly.
27. Bétty should stay, not Jánet.
28. Í'm to blame, not yóu.
29. Geórge broke it, not Jóhn.
30. Jónes is going, not Hárris.

LESSON 83

The Vowels [ɔ/or]

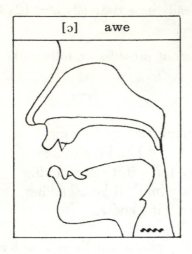

| [ɔ] | awe |

Make [ɔ] with the tongue low, pulled back, and higher in back than in front. The jaws should be quite open, and the lips slightly rounded. Do not glide the tongue or round the lips further while voicing the vowel.

To make [or], start with the tongue curved about halfway up in back, the jaws half open, and the lips rounded. Curl the tip of the tongue back to [r] position while voicing the vowel.

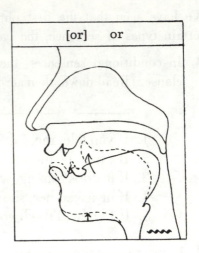

| [or] | or |

Contrast Chart

	A	B	C	D	E
1.	awe	maw	caw	law	saw
2.	or	more	core	lore	sore
3.	yaw	raw	haw	Shaw	chaw
4.	yore	roar	hoar	shore	chore
5.	thaw	paw	flaw	draw	jaw
6.	Thor	pore	floor	drawer	Jory
7.	moss	sauce	toss	caustic	faucet
8.	Morse	source	torso	course	force
9.	pawed	hawed	awed	bawd	cawed
10.	poured	hoard	oared	board	cord
11.	lawn	Shawn	Mauna	tawny	dawn
12.	lorn	shorn	mourn	torn	adorn
13.	caught	taught	sought	fought	haughty
14.	court	tort	sort	fort	Horton
15.	gauze	cause	daws	awes	pause
16.	gores	cores	doors	ores	pores
17.	sawed	laud	gnawed	jawed	Maud
18.	sword	lord	Nordic	Jordan	mordant

146

Contrast Exercises

A. *In the CHART on the opposite page, read the odd-numbered lines across (1, 3, 5, etc.). Then read the SENTENCES below.*

1. She often fought with her daughter-in-law.
2. Waldo has an awful cough.
3. They recalled almost all the faulty ones.
4. Aubrey defaulted on the August installment.
5. An automobile was stalled in the crosswalk.
6. Maude is awkward at small talk.
7. They offered Moss an audition in Fallsburg.
8. Hawkins taught law in St. Paul.
9. We've called off the softball game.
10. The Maltbys ought to water their lawn.

B. *In the CHART on the opposite page, read the even-numbered lines across (2, 4, 6, etc.). Then read the SENTENCES below.*

1. Judge Morse restored order in the court.
2. He was born the morning before the storm.
3. Gloria's porch floor is warped.
4. It's the fourth performance of the "Jordan Quartet."
5. Can he afford the organ he ordered?
6. Loring's divorce will be forthcoming shortly.
7. The storm forced them ashore on Corsica.
8. Warden's exploring the North Gorge.
9. Fortunately, the portrait can be restored.
10. We import the porcelain porpoises from Portugal.

Now read SENTENCES alternately from A and B above (A1,B1; A2,B2; A3,B3; etc.).

C. *In the CHART on the opposite page, read vertical pairs across (A1–2, B1–2, C1–2, etc.). Then read the SENTENCES below.*

1. All the orchids belong to Laura.
2. Foster was forced to pay court costs.
3. In the morning Mauna has a chorus call.
4. Borman bought the organ in August.
5. He fought with Foreman because of Cora.
6. Borden's boss ordered an audit.
7. According to Caldwell, she was born in the Balkans.
8. Dora's daughter offered the orphan a home.
9. It was sort of salty, Thornton thought.
10. Faulkner forged all four of them.

D. *In the CHART on the opposite page, read down each column. Then read the SENTENCES below.*

1. Falk swore the officer's story was false.
2. Of course they ought to perform an autopsy.
3. Unfortunately, Cross ignored all my warnings.
4. George sauntered back and forth along the boardwalk.
5. Port Clawson needs more law enforcement officers.
6. The recorder was bought in a store on Hawthorne Street.
7. Gordon and Long formerly had offices at the Broadmore.
8. He saw more false reports that autumn.
9. Morgan made the longshoremen an across-the-board offer.
10. Porter called before dawn to forestall the auction.

LESSON 84

The Vowels [ɔ/ər]

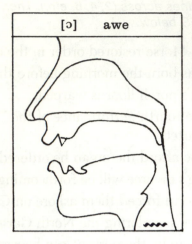

[ɔ]   awe

Make [ɔ] with the tongue low, pulled back, and higher in back than in front. The jaws should be quite open, and the lips slightly rounded. Do not glide the tongue or round the lips further while voicing the vowel.

Make [ər] with the tip of the tongue curled back in [r] position, the jaws slightly open, and the lips slightly rounded.

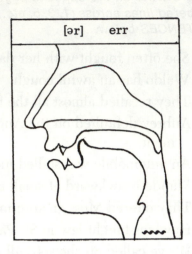

[ər]   err

Contrast Chart

	A	B	C	D	E
1.	awe	paw	saw	haw	Shaw
2.	err	per	sir	her	shirr
3.	all	fall	hall	pall	ball
4.	earl	furl	hurl	pearl	burl
5.	walk	talk	chalk	balk	caulk
6.	work	Turk	chirk	Burke	Kirk
7.	caught	haughty	bought	daughter	fought
8.	curt	hurt	Bert	dirt	fertile
9.	toss	boss	paucity	moss	naught
10.	terse	bursa	purse	Mercer	nurture
11.	spawn	lawn	yawn	fawn	awn
12.	spurn	learn	yearn	fern	earn
13.	hawed	thawed	Maud	bawd	pawed
14.	heard	third	murder	bird	purred
15.	gall	Saul	call	shawl	maul
16.	girl	Searle	curl	Shirley	Merle
17.	bossed	cost	foster	Austin	soft
18.	burst	cursed	first	erstwhile	surfed

148

Contrast Exercises

A. *In the CHART on the opposite page, read the odd-numbered lines across (1, 3, 5, etc.). Then read the SENTENCES below.*

1. We always walk along Broadway.
2. They auctioned off Laughton's autograph.
3. She thought Santa Claus brought the automobile.
4. The small dog belongs to Audrey.
5. I saw him take an awful fall.
6. Walsh had almost withdrawn from the race.
7. He'd been drawn to Pauline all along.
8. The auditing office is across the hall.
9. All of Dalton's caution was for naught.
10. He ought to have a long talk with his son.

B. *In the CHART on the opposite page, read the even-numbered lines across (2, 4, 6, etc.). Then read the SENTENCES below.*

1. We urged her to return the purse.
2. Jervis learned to do perfect impersonations.
3. It's certain to be affirmed by the Third Circuit.
4. Stern served a sherbet dessert.
5. Her first concern is to preserve the birds.
6. Myrtle yearned to work as a nurse.
7. They were disturbed by the hurricane alert.
8. Gert's in her early thirties.
9. The colonel emerged as a person of courage.
10. Dirkson's clerk is certainly courteous.

Now read SENTENCES alternately from A and B above (A1,B1; A2,B2; A3,B3; etc.).

C. *In the CHART on the opposite page, read vertical pairs across (A1–2, B1–2, C1–2, etc.). Then read the SENTENCES below.*

1. Walker's workers walk to work.
2. Bertha's the author of "This Awful Earth."
3. It's the first faucet Walter's worked on.
4. Bert bought that ball in Berlin.
5. Thurston had thought the surface was softer.
6. Dirk's daughters were all early risers.
7. First Foss ought to learn the law.
8. One of the servants saw Earl off.
9. Walton works at the waterworks.
10. Berkley balked at taking Lerner along.

D. *In the CHART on the opposite page, read down each column. Then read the SENTENCES below.*

1. A Red Cross worker brought them a thermos of coffee.
2. Hall's attorney got an urgent call to return home.
3. You referred to a tall girl with auburn hair.
4. Burnett thought he could purchase the flawed merchandise at cost.
5. The merger caused concern among the office workers.
6. Audie was worried about his dog's burned paw.
7. The author didn't deserve the applause and curtain calls.
8. The Burkes oughtn't to work at cross-purposes.
9. Next Thursday, August third, is Paula's birthday.
10. Longley is currently with a law firm in Waltham.

149

LESSON 85

The Vowels [ər/or]

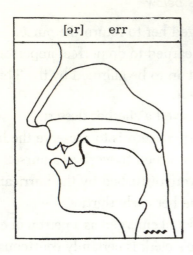

[ər] err

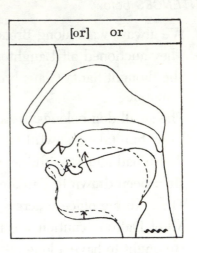

[or] or

Make [ər] with the tip of the tongue curled back in [r] position, the jaws slightly open, and the lips slightly rounded.

To make [or], start with the tongue curved halfway up in back, the jaws half open, and the lips rounded. Curl the tip of the tongue back to [r] position while voicing the vowel.

Contrast Chart

	A	B	C	D	E
1.	err	burr	cur	fir	her
2.	or	bore	core	for	hoar
3.	purr	sir	were	shirr	stir
4.	pore	sore	wore	shore	store
5.	heard	gird	bird	surd	curd
6.	hoard	gored	board	sword	cord
7.	shirt	pert	spurt	curt	Bert
8.	short	port	sport	court	abort
9.	certain	turtle	hurt	Myrtle	fertile
10.	sort	tort	Horton	Morton	fort
11.	firm	worm	derma	Burma	murmur
12.	form	warm	dorm	Borman	Mormon
13.	burn	kernel	turn	hernia	Werner
14.	born	corn	torn	horn	worn
15.	curse	hearse	immerse	nurse	terse
16.	course	horse	Morse	Norse	torso
17.	word	furred	sturdy	erred	purred
18.	ward	ford	stored	oared	poured

150

Contrast Exercises

A. *In the CHART on the opposite page, read the odd-numbered lines across (1, 3, 5, etc.). Then read the SENTENCES below.*

1. A nervous murmur was heard in the room.
2. Irwin works at 1313 McBurney Road.
3. The terms of the merger were disturbing.
4. Pearl's the first person he turns to.
5. The girl learned some Serbian words.
6. Kirsten's a clergyman in an urban church.
7. What do German workers earn?
8. On Thursday Herbert turned thirty.
9. The merchant should certainly reimburse her.
10. Jurgen's deferment was confirmed.

B. *In the CHART on the opposite page, read the even-numbered lines across (2, 4, 6, etc.). Then read the SENTENCES below.*

1. Norton bored us with his coarse stories.
2. I'll do the post-mortem before morning.
3. Dorian had more than a quart of port.
4. The court ordered a short moratorium.
5. This morning's editorial deplored the war.
6. Lord Corwin was born in York.
7. The store is at 444 Fourth Avenue.
8. Victoria wore an orchid corsage.
9. The source of his fortune is the Gorman Corset Company.
10. He was forced to conform to a more normal routine.

Now read SENTENCES alternately from A and B above (A1,B1; A2,B2; A3,B3; etc.).

C. *In the CHART on the opposite page, read vertical pairs across (A1–2, B1–2, C1–2, etc.). Then read the SENTENCES below.*

1. Curt's court case stirred up a storm.
2. Lorna learned what the furs were for.
3. Was Burns born in Burma or Borneo?
4. Forman's firm won its first four bids.
5. According to Kirk they weren't warm enough.
6. Burdick is bored with his current courses.
7. She entered her horse in the Dorset Derby.
8. Werner wore his new shirt ashore.
9. Report to Purdy before the first.
10. Horner heard her words of warning.

D. *In the CHART on the opposite page, read down each column. Then read the SENTENCES below.*

1. The firm Ward works for is on the thirteenth floor.
2. The order clerk was more courteous before.
3. Morley personally escorted the colonel to the performance.
4. The foreman was disturbed by reports of further shortages.
5. Norman attended the early morning service at the Fourth Street Church.
6. The third story concerned a notorious murderer.
7. I've heard Ordway's working for a recording firm.
8. He should certainly explore their terms more thoroughly.
9. Irma ordered thirty-four sterling forks.
10. Worse tortures were in store for Turner.

LESSON 86

Review of Vowels [ɔ/or/ər]

Contrast Exercises

In each three-line group of the CHART, read across each line, then down each column (A1–2–3, B1–2–3, etc.). Next read down each full column. Then read the SENTENCES.

	A	B	C	D	E	F
1.	awe	saw	caw	bawl	paw	Shaw
2.	ore	sore	core	bore	pore	shore
3.	err	sir	cur	burr	per	shirr
4.	lorn	adorn	horn	ornament	mourn	yore
5.	learn	dirndle	hernia	earning	Myrna	yearn
6.	lawn	dawn	haw	awning	Mauna	yawn
7.	bird	heard	purred	surd	erred	curd
8.	bawd	hawed	pawed	sawed	awed	cawed
9.	board	hoard	poured	sword	oared	cord
10.	toss	Orson	immerse	course	faucet	purse
11.	torso	Ursula	moss	curse	forced	paucity
12.	terse	awesome	Morse	caustic	first	porous
13.	court	turtle	fought	hurt	abort	sought
14.	caught	tort	fertile	Horton	bought	certain
15.	curt	taught	fort	haughty	Bert	sort

1. The Halden Corporation has offices at 1340 McBurney Street.
2. I've heard reports that Morgan offered to call it off.
3. Lerner audited his first course in August.
4. By Thursday morning they were all worn out.
5. Calder worked as a porter to earn money for law school.
6. Vernon ought to warn her to be more cautious.
7. The thought of Norman's turning against her was more than Audrey could bear.
8. The story was also covered by a reporter for *The Rawlins Journal*.
9. Dolores first called on the third or fourth of August.
10. He bought Pearl an orchid for her 40th birthday.

Intonation: One-Phrase Statements with Final Rise

The 232⌣ intonation pattern is not restricted to two-phrase sentences. In a single-phrase sentence, it often conveys uncertainty, hesitancy, or indecision on the part of the speaker.

A. The paired sentences below differ in stress and intonation. Those on the left are simple statements of opinion, wish, or possibility. Those on the right emphasize the speaker's unspoken doubts (as indicated in the parentheses). Read down, then across.

1. I think she was pléased.	10. I thínk she was pleased.
2. I suppose they'll agrée.	11. I suppóse they'll agree.
3. I guess they're cóming.	12. I guéss they're coming.
4. I hope to márry her.	13. I hópe to marry her.
5. I want to méet him.	14. I wánt to meet him.
6. I'd like to gó there.	15. I'd líke to go there.
7. I may have been wróng.	16. I máy have been wrong.
8. That might be hélpful.	17. That míght be helpful.
9. You could be ríght.	18. You cóuld be right.

(but I'm not sure.)

(but I may not succeed.)

(but I rather doubt it.)

B. Each question below is followed by two different short answers. In the first, the speaker is reasonably firm in his opinion. In the second, he is less sure. (Read across each line.)

1. Did you pass the tést?	I think só.	I thínk so.
2. Is he feeling bétter?	I guess só.	I guéss so.
3. Will she be thére?	I imagine só.	I imágine so.
4. Can it do any hárm?	I suppose nót.	I suppóse not.
5. Is it bróken?	I guess nót.	I guéss not.

C. In the following exercise, the contrasted short answers have the same stress but different intonation. The first answer is a definite affirmative reply. The second implies that the speaker has reservations, as if he were going to add "but . . ." (Read across each line.)

1. Can't you hélp him?	Yés, I cán.	I cán.
2. Shouldn't you téll her?	Yés, I shóuld.	I shóuld.
3. Couldn't you refúse?	Yés, I cóuld.	I cóuld.
4. Will we have tróuble?	Yés, we máy.	We máy.
5. Do you think he'd enjóy it?	Yés, he míght.	He míght.

LESSON 88

The Vowels [a/ar]

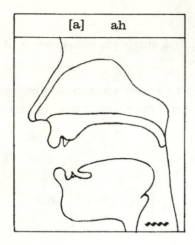

[a]   ah

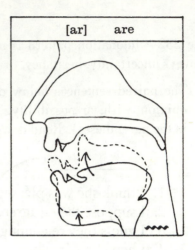

[ar]   are

Make [a] with the tongue low, centered, and rather flat. The jaws should be fully open, and the lips relaxed.

To make [ar], start in [a] position; curl the tip of the tongue back to [r] position while voicing the vowel.

Contrast Chart

	A	B	C	D	E
1.	ah	bah	spa	ma	pa
2.	are	bar	spar	mar	par
3.	hot	cot	dot	Ott	Mott
4.	heart	cart	dart	art	mart
5.	Spock	mock	hock	stock	dock
6.	spark	mark	hark	stark	dark
7.	cod	sod	mod	God	Todd
8.	card	sard	marred	guard	tarred
9.	shop	hop	top	cop	scop
10.	sharp	harp	tarp	carp	scarp
11.	don	yon	fond	bond	con
12.	darn	yarn	Farnum	barn	carnal
13.	moll	doll	collie	folly	holly
14.	marlin	darling	Karlin	Farley	Harley
15.	tot	pot	bot	spot	got
16.	tart	part	Bart	Sparta	garter
17.	box	lox	pox	shocks	clocks
18.	barks	larks	parks	sharks	Clark's

154

Contrast Exercises

A. *In the CHART on the opposite page, read the odd-numbered lines across (1, 3, 5, etc.). Then read the SENTENCES below.*

1. Jonathan promised to contact me.
2. This nonsense has positively got to stop.
3. Yvonne was not responding properly.
4. His shop stocks top-quality vodka.
5. Tompkins had a modest knowledge of electronics.
6. The sponsor wants some shocking copy.
7. Conrad's on the tom-tom.
8. She's probably not a competent stenographer.
9. Godwin got a job in Providence.
10. There's a bottle of Scotch in the bottom of the closet.

B. *In the CHART on the opposite page, read the even-numbered lines across (2, 4, 6, etc.). Then read the SENTENCES below.*

1. Farley starred in "The Art of Larceny."
2. Arnold was the target of their sarcasm.
3. A large part of the army is starving.
4. Charlie could hardly park his car.
5. They're enlarging the pharmacy on Farmingdale Boulevard.
6. Carla's remark started an argument.
7. Marcy's in charge of the garden party.
8. The parson was startled by Stark's harshness.
9. The architect lives in Harmon Park.
10. Marlow's partner is hard-hearted.

Now read SENTENCES alternately from A and B above (A1,B1; A2,B2; A3,B3; etc.).

C. *In the CHART on the opposite page, read vertical pairs across (A1–2, B1–2, C1–2, etc.). Then read the SENTENCES below.*

1. Donna darned the pockets of my parka.
2. His constant carping didn't bother Barbara.
3. Larsen's logic is beyond Yarney's understanding.
4. This pottery's part of the cargo for Chicago.
5. Barton's a botanist at Carlton College.
6. Fox is far from fond of Farnum.
7. Possibly Parsons can attend the Carnegie concert.
8. Mott's Market operates on a modest markup.
9. He got the cigars from Larkin's locker.
10. Carney has confidence in Arnold's honesty.

D. *In the CHART on the opposite page, read down each column. Then read the SENTENCES below.*

1. Harlow wants to start a cooperative farm.
2. The problem goes far beyond Mark's involvement.
3. Carl mixed lots of martinis for the cocktail party.
4. The contents of these jars and bottles aren't toxic.
5. Martin's father is partial to modern art.
6. The prosecutor charged Dodge with armed robbery.
7. Carstairs has a modest apartment opposite a parking lot.
8. It's hard not to argue with Dominick's far-out politics.
9. Doctor Barnes was honored for his remarkable accomplishments.
10. A squad car stopped Darby in Prospect Park.

LESSON 89

The Vowels [ar/ər]

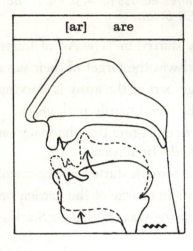

[ar]	are

To make [ar], start in [a] position, with the tongue low, centered, and rather flat, the jaws fully open, and the lips relaxed. Curl the tip of the tongue back to [r] position while voicing the vowel.

Make [ər] with the tip of the tongue curled back in [r] position, the jaws slightly open, and the lips slightly rounded.

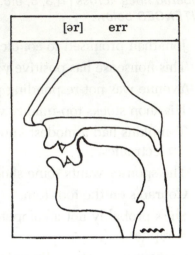

[ər]	err

Contrast Chart

	A	B	C	D	E
1.	are	far	car	par	bar
2.	err	fur	cur	per	burr
3.	mar	star	spar	harp	sharp
4.	myrrh	stir	spur	her	shirr
5.	guard	shard	bard	card	hard
6.	gird	shirred	bird	curd	heard
7.	Farley	Harley	garlic	barley	parley
8.	furl	hurl	girl	burl	pearl
9.	barn	yarn	Arnold	tarnish	varnish
10.	burn	yearn	earn	turn	Verna
11.	arc	park	lark	dark	mark
12.	irk	perk	lurk	dirk	murk
13.	cart	Bart	part	heart	dart
14.	curt	Bert	pert	hurt	dirt
15.	parse	varsity	farce	Garson	Carson
16.	purse	verse	first	Gerson	curse
17.	darby	carbon	harbor	Farber	arbor
18.	derby	Kirby	Herbert	Ferber	urban

Contrast Exercises

A. *In the CHART on the opposite page, read the odd-numbered lines across (1, 3, 5, etc.). Then read the SENTENCES below.*

1. Marvin's charm is disarming.
2. They have a garden apartment on Barkley Parkway.
3. The Art Department was the target of his barbs.
4. Garson's made a marvelous star chart.
5. There aren't any cartridges for the carbines.
6. Marlene's card was postmarked Scarsdale.
7. The farmhands started to harvest the rhubarb.
8. Harkins discarded a heart.
9. They aren't charging Jarvis with arson.
10. Barney's on guard at the arsenal.

B. *In the CHART on the opposite page, read the even-numbered lines across (2, 4, 6, etc.). Then read the SENTENCES below.*

1. It's Herman's first term at the University.
2. *Workaday World* is a journal for urban workers.
3. Perkins is an intern at the Worth Street Infirmary.
4. You certainly were thirsty!
5. Shirley learned the third verse.
6. Birds chirp and worms squirm.
7. She purchased her ermine at Sherman Furriers.
8. We splurged on convertible furniture.
9. Myrna's nervous about perjuring herself.
10. It works out to thirty cents per serving.

Now read SENTENCES alternately from A and B above (A1,B1; A2,B2; A3,B3; etc.).

C. *In the CHART on the opposite page, read vertical pairs across (A1–2, B1–2, C1–2, etc.). Then read the SENTENCES below.*

1. How Carson cursed when his barn burned!
2. At first the farce irked Arkin.
3. Kermit carpeted the parlor perfectly.
4. The sergeant searched Kirby's car.
5. Ferguson's farmland is far from fertile.
6. The parson's purpose was to get Purdy a pardon.
7. Clark's a clerk in Murphy's Market.
8. That's the pertinent part of Erna's argument.
9. Arnold's words were hardly heard.
10. He purchased part of the merchandise in March.

D. *In the CHART on the opposite page, read down each column. Then read the SENTENCES below.*

1. Marshall was termed "the party of the first part."
2. Charlotte's version of the yarn was certainly startling.
3. Aren't the conservatives starting a third party?
4. Hardy's first apartment had purple carpeting.
5. Carver works hard as a commercial artist.
6. Urban parks are deserted by dark.
7. Carmen's worst marks were in art.
8. The Gerbers are starting on their third safari.
9. After his Army service Harley returned to Arkansas.
10. Martha purchased some garments at the church bazaar.

LESSON 90

Review of Vowels [a/ar/ər]

Contrast Exercises

In each three-line group of the CHART, read across each line, then down each column (A1–2–3, B1–2–3, etc.). Next read down each full column. Then read the SENTENCES.

	A	B	C	D	E	F
1.	pock	ox	shock	mock	clock	stock
2.	park	arks	shark	mark	Clark	stark
3.	perk	irks	shirk	murk	clerk	stir
4.	dart	cart	tart	part	heart	Bart
5.	dirt	curt	turtle	pert	hurt	Bert
6.	dot	cot	tot	pot	hot	bot
7.	furl	hurl	curl	early	girl	Merle
8.	folly	holly	collie	Ollie	golly	Molly
9.	Farley	Harley	Carlin	Arlen	garland	marlin
10.	lock	dark	Burke	hark	tock	Kirk
11.	lark	dirk	bock	her	tar	cock
12.	lurk	dock	bark	hock	turkey	carcass
13.	bard	gird	hod	curd	shard	pod
14.	body	guard	heard	card	shod	Purdy
15.	bird	god	hard	cod	shirred	pardon

1. Margaret is certainly not responsible for her partner's purchases.
2. I want a hardtop convertible for my birthday.
3. Harley worked a lot harder on his first job.
4. She got her start as Birdie in "The Doll Market."
5. It's Doctor Arnold's first heart operation.
6. He turned out to be a smart operator in the stock market.
7. Barker promised we'd attend the first concert in the park.
8. That part turned out to be far beyond her competence.
9. Ma Parker's Furniture Mart is on Wadsworth Turnpike.
10. It's hard for Lerner to start a conversation.

LESSON 91

General Review of Vowels

Contrast Exercises

In the CHART below, read across each line, then down each column. Then read the SENTENCES.

	A	B	C	D	E
1.	pale	peel	pile	pole	pool
2.	pule	pall	Powell	poi	pal
3.	pelt	pill	Polly	pulse	pull
4.	bode	booed	imbued	bawdy	bowed
5.	Boyd	bad	bed	bid	body
6.	bud	book	bayed	bead	bide
7.	heal	highly	hole	who'll	Hugh'll
8.	hall	howl	Hoyle	Hal	hell
9.	hill	holly	hull	hook	hail
10.	noose	Ute	naught	knout	annoy
11.	gnat	net	knit	not	nut
12.	nook	Nate	neat	night	note
13.	Kiley	coal	cool	cue'll	call
14.	cowl	coil	Cal	Kelly	kill
15.	collie	cull	cook	kale	keel

1. Phil Foy found that he'd foolishly failed to file a full factory fuel report. Phil felt, and feels now, that the awful fuss that followed was Foreman Foley's fault.

2. As Sawyer sat sipping his soup, he sighted a flying saucer settling down to the south. Sawyer's son Solomon had seen the same sight. So had Sandy Silverman.

3. Kate Keats' cat "Kettle" has a cute coy kitten. It caught my cousin Connie's kite in the cow pasture, and Kate couldn't coax the kooky kitten to let go.

4. "Big Ben Bailey," by Buckley Bolen, is about Bolen's own boyhood. Banning of the book in Boston has boosted its sales beyond belief.

5. How Holly hates Hawkins! He's the one who high-hatted her in the "Head Hunters Bar" at Hooker's Hotel in Hickory.

REDUCED FORMS

LESSON 92

Reduced Forms: The Vowel [ə]

In normally rapid, rhythmic speech, parts of a sentence are often speeded up by reduction and compression. Certain words — particularly pronouns, auxiliary and modal verbs, prepositions, and conjunctions — are reduced in stress and combined with adjacent words, so that two or three words are spoken as one. The reduced word may lose a consonant or a whole syllable, and usually has its vowel changed (most often to [ə]).

It should be emphasized that reduced forms occur in fairly rapid speech. You should not use them when you are speaking slowly or hesitantly.

This lesson and those that follow provide practice in the most common reduced forms. The exercises are designed to increase your speaking speed and command of rhythm, and to improve your comprehension of everyday spoken English.

THE NEUTRAL VOWEL *SCHWA* [ə]

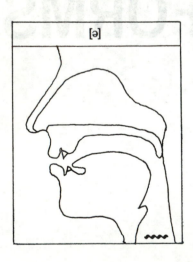

Make [ə] with the jaws slightly open, the lips relaxed, and the tongue curved about halfway up in the center (slightly higher and farther forward than for [ʌ]).

In reduced forms, [ə] is a very short sound.

When the following words are unstressed, the vowel is reduced to [ə]: *and, as, at, had, would, will, are, or, for, have, of, can, than, that, some, to, was.* (Note that *of* is pronounced [əv] before a vowel, but usually [ə] before a consonant.)

In each six-line section below, read across, then down.

		A	B	C
1.	[ən]	by and lárge	each and évery	ham and éggs
2.	[əz]	cold as íce	sweet as súgar	hálf as many
3.	[ət]	feel at éase	Look at thát.	hold at báy
4.	[əd]	Jane had léft.	The sun had sét.	Tom had lóst it.
5.	[əd]	That would be níce.	Jóhn would do it.	Steve would be glád.
6.	[əl]	Sam will be láte.	It will take tíme.	Máry will want one.

		A	B	C
7.	[ər]	These are bróken.	Mine are bétter.	Hers are stále.
8.	[ər]	two or thrée	sing or dánce.	one or the óther
9.	[fər]	Wait for mé.	Go for bróke.	Stay for dínner.
10.	[əv]	None have spóiled.	Some have retíred.	Times have chánged.
11.	[əv]	bag of óranges	badge of hónor	pound of ápples
12.	[ə]	cup of cóffee	one of thóse	box of cráckers

		A	B	C
13.	[kən]	We can gó.	I can téll.	It can wáit.
14.	[ðən]	less than thís	rather than páy	more than enóugh
15.	[ðət]	See that they dó.	now that we knów	not that I'd cáre
16.	[səm]	Get some fóod.	Have some fún.	Do some góod.
17.	[tə]	close to hóme	back to wórk	stands to réason
18.	[wəz]	That was thát.	He was óut.	She was ríght.

LESSON 93

Reduced Forms: Personal Pronouns

A. When the pronoun is unstressed, the following changes may occur: [h] may be dropped from *he*, *his*, *him*, and *her*; [ð] may be dropped from *them*; the vowel may change to [ə]. (In the word *our*, [aw] changes to [a].)

In each five-line section below, read across, then down.

1.	[iy]	Yes, he wíll.	How he láughed!	So he sáid.
2.	[iz]	Ask his náme.	Get his bóoks.	Bring his hát.
3.	[im]	Show him hów.	Deal him ín.	Help him alóng.
4.	[ər]	Send her hóme.	Leave her alóne.	Put her thére.
5.	[ðəm]	Shake them úp.	Throw them óut.	Have them óver.

6.	[əm]	Make them stóp.	Gíve them some.	Cut them óff.
7.	[yə]	See you sóon.	Serves you ríght.	No, you cán't.
8.	[yər]	Do your bést.	Take your tíme.	Open your éyes.
9.	[ar]	Be our guést.	Meet our fríends.	Call our láwyer.
10.	[əs]	Pay us nów.	Drop us óff.	Drive us báck.

B. The [y] of *you* may combine with a preceding [d] to form [dʒuw] or [dʒə]; it may combine with a preceding [t] to form [tʃuw] or [tʃə]. Similarly, the [y] of *your* may combine with a preceding [d] to form [dʒər], or with a preceding [t] to form [tʃər].

In each five-line section below, read across, then down.

1.	[dʒuw]	Would you allów it?	Did you inspéct it?	Could you expláin?
2.	[dʒuw]	He sold you óut.	Who said you ówed it?	What held you úp?
3.	[dʒə]	Could you téll?	Would you mínd?	Did you míss me?
4.	[dʒə]	I tóld you so.	He had you thére.	They páid you well.
5.	[dʒər]	Mend your wáys.	Hold your hórses.	Hide your héad.

6.	[tʃuw]	Shouldn't you ásk?	Weren't you upsét?	Can't you understánd?
7.	[tʃuw]	Who got you úp?	I bét you are!	We'd fit you ín.
8.	[tʃə]	Didn't you réad it?	Won't you cóme?	Wouldn't you knów it?
9.	[tʃə]	Who sént you here?	What got you stárted?	I'd méet you there.
10.	[tʃər]	Bite your tóngue.	Wait your túrn.	Suit yoursélf.

164

C. In contraction with *will*, a pronoun may have its vowel changed from a glide vowel to a simple vowel. Thus [iy] may change to [i], [uw] to [u], [ay] to [a], and [ey] to [e]. Similarly, when a pronoun contracts with *are*, its [y]- or [w]-glide is lost. (Note that *you're* is commonly pronounced [yur] when stressed, [yər] when unstressed.)

In each five-line section below, read across, then down.

1. [al]	I'll take a chánce.	I'll buy one móre.	I'll go by bús.
2. [hil]	He'll need anóther.	He'll fall óff.	Hé'll play ball.
3. [ʃil]	She'll remémber it.	She'll bake a píe.	Shé'll be there.
4. [wil]	We'll stay ín.	We'll get éven.	We'll ride aróund.
5. [yul]	Yóu'll be sorry.	Yóu'll find out.	You'll catch cóld.

6. [ðel]	They'll never knów.	They'll be láte.	They'll forgét.
7. [wir]	We're afráid.	We're losing gróund.	We're from Máine.
8. [yur]	Yóu're not hurt.	So yóu're the one!	I hope yóu're coming.
9. [yər]	You're doing fíne.	You're just in tíme.	You're looking wéll.
10. [ðer]	They're over hére.	They're only jóking.	They're turning báck.

165

LESSON 94

Reduced Forms: Question-Word Phrases

The sequence *question word* + *auxiliary* + *pronoun* may be uttered rapidly as a single word. When this is done, the following reductions commonly occur.

  a) The *question word* remains unchanged, except that the final [t] of *what* may be dropped before the reduced form of *did*: *What did* [hwʌd] *she say?* (Note that before a vowel the [t] of *what* is a voiced flap sound.)

  b) The *auxiliary* is reduced as follows:

> *is* becomes [s] after *what*, [z] elsewhere
> *are* becomes [ər]
> *am* becomes [əm]
> *will* becomes [əl] (syllabic [l] after *what* and *when*)
> *do* becomes [ə] after *what*, [də] elsewhere
> *does* becomes [əz] or [s] after *what*, [dəz] or [z] elsewhere
> *has* becomes [əz] or [s] after *what*, [əz] or [z] elsewhere
> *have* becomes [əv]
> *had* becomes [əd]
> *did* becomes [əd] or [d] after *what*, [d] elsewhere

  c) The *pronoun* is reduced to the forms practiced in the preceding lesson, and combines with the reduced auxiliary: *is he* [siy] or [ziy]; *are her* [ərər]; *have you* [əvyə].

Above each group of sentences in the following exercises, the reduced *auxiliary* + *pronoun* to be practiced is written in phonemic symbols. In each sentence, combine this form with the question word: *what* + [siy] = [hwʌtsiy]; *when* + [ərər]=[hwenərər]; *where* + [əvyə] =[hwerəvyə]; etc. Where two reduced forms are shown above a sentence group, the first form is used only after *what*.

In each of the following sections, read down, then across.

A	B	C
[siy] [ziy]	[siz] [ziz]	[sər] [zər]
1. What is he áfter?	What is his áddress?	What is her náme?
2. When is he léaving?	When is his tíme up?	When is her bírthday?
3. Where is he góing?	Where is his cár?	Where is her hát?
4. Why is he so láte?	Why is his dóor open?	Why is her són here?
5. How is he táking it?	How is his móther?	How is her týping?
6. Who is he wíth?	Who is his dóctor?	Who is her déntist?

A

[sit] [zit]
7. What is it abóut?
8. When is it arríving?
9. Where is it léaking?
10. Why is it clósed?
11. How is it cóming?
12. Who is it fróm?

[əryə]
13. What are you próving?
14. When are you móving?
15. Where are you stáying?
16. Why are you crýing?
17. How are you féeling?
18. Who are you cálling?

[əmay]
19. What am I sáying?
20. When am I expécted?
21. Where am I héaded?
22. How am I dóing?
23. Who am I kídding?

[əyə] [dəyə]
24. What do you thínk?
25. Where do you wórk?
26. Why do you kéep it?
27. How do you dó?
28. Who do you méan?

[əziy] [dəziy]
29. What does he wánt?
30. When does he stúdy?
31. Where does he éat?
32. Why does he smóke?
33. How does he stánd it?
34. Who does he líke?

B

[əriz]
What are his réasons?
When are his fínals?
Where are his glásses?
Why are his shóes off?
How are his fólks?
Who are his báckers?

[əryər]
What are your rátes?
When are your exáms?
Where are your bóots?
Why are your hánds dirty?
How are your párents?
Who are your clíents?

[əlyə]
What will you háve?
When will you fínish?
Where will you bé?
How will you gét there?
Who will you híre?

[əvyə]
What have you decíded?
Where have you lóoked?
Why have you stópped?
How have you mánaged?
Who have you chósen?

[ədʒə]
What had you úsed?
When had you lóst it?
Where had you mét?
Why had you léft?
How had you dóne it?
Who had you séen?

C

[ərər]
What are her próspects?
When are her kíds home?
Where are her tóys?
Why are her éyes red?
How are her grádes?
Who are her téachers?

[ərar]
What are our chánces?
When are our pápers due?
Where are our thíngs?
Why are our líghts on?
How are our fríends?
Who are our láwyers?

[əliy]
What will he chárge?
When will he decíde?
Where will he pút it?
How will he knów?
Who will he sénd?

[əziy]
What has he léarned?
Where has he táught?
Why has he retúrned?
How has he béen?
Who has he tóld?

[ədiy]
What had he fóund?
When had he máiled it?
Where had he góne?
Why had he páid it?
How had he knówn?
Who had he tálked to?

A
[ədit] [dit]
35. What did it mátter?
36. When did it begín?
37. Where did it háppen?
38. Why did it fáil?
39. How did it bréak?
40. Who did it húrt?

B
[dʒə]*
What did you forgét?
When did you stárt?
Where did you sléep?
Why did you refúse?
How did you guéss?
Who did you bríng?

C
[ədiy] [diy]
What did he búy?
When did he get ín?
Where did he applý?
Why did he belíeve it?
How did he find óut?
Who did he ásk for?

[ədər] [dər]
41. What did her jacket cóst?
42. When did her uncle díe?
43. Where did her class méet?
44. Why did her maid quít?
45. How did her pie táste?
46. Who did her brother téll?

[dʒər]*
What did your wífe say?
When did your térm end?
Where did your aunt líve?
Why did your marks dróp?
How did your team wín?
Who did your boss bláme?

[ədiz] [diz]
What did his fáther do?
When did his shíp come in?
Where did his móney go?
Why did his fámily leave?
How did his bóok sell?
Who did his síster marry?

*In these reductions, the final [t] is dropped from *what*.

LESSON 95

Reduced Forms: Modal Expressions

In each section below, read the sentences down, then across.

A. *Have* may be reduced to [əv] or [ə] and combine with a preceding modal verb: *could have* [kudəv], [kudə].

Modal + [əv]	*Modal* + [ə]
1. You could have refúsed.	6. He could have sáid so.
2. We should have léft.	7. I should have knówn.
3. Tom would have láughed.	8. Jean would have líked it.
4. She might have díed.	9. That might have wórked.
5. It must have ráined.	10. He must have been crázy.

B. A negative expression such as *couldn't have* may be spoken as one word, with *have* reduced to [əv] or [ə] : [kudəntəv], [kudəntə]. The [t] is sometimes dropped : [kudənəv], [kudənə].

Modal + [əntəv] or [ənəv]	*Modal* + [əntə] or [ənə]
1. It couldn't have lásted.	5. I couldn't have cared léss.
2. He shouldn't have ásked.	6. You shouldn't have cóme.
3. They wouldn't have dáred.	7. That wouldn't have máttered.
4. It mightn't have háppened.	8. They mightn't have dóne it.

C. The sequence *pronoun* + *would* + *have* may be spoken as a single word. In this case, the pronoun is unchanged, *would* is reduced to [d], and *have* is reduced to [əv] or [ə]. (Example: *I would have* [aydəv] , [aydə].)

Pronoun + [dəv]	*Pronoun* + [də]
1. I would have been glád to.	7. I would have háted to.
2. She would have árgued.	8. She would have wrítten.
3. He would have líed.	9. He would have been sórry.
4. We would have hélped.	10. We would have been láte.
5. You would have enjóyed it.	11. You would have lost the bét.
6. They would have cálled.	12. They would have tóld me.

169

Reduced Forms: Certain Verbs

A. In the sequence *verb + to + second verb*, *to* may be reduced to [tə] or [ə] and combine with the first verb, which itself may undergo changes. In reading the following exercises, note that *want to* may be reduced to [wantə] or [wanə] and that, in the expression *have got to*, *have* may be reduced to [v̩] or may be dropped.

In each five-line section below, read across, then down.

1. [hæftə]	I have to rún.	You have to éat.	We have to léave.
2. [hæstə]	She has to léarn.	It has to stóp.	He has to chóose.
3. [hædə]	We had to rést.	I had to húrry.	They had to stúdy.
4. [gatə]	It's gót to work.	They've gót to go.	She's got to prómise.
5. (drop [v])	I've got to knów.	You've got to trý.	We've got to híde it.

6. [ɔtə]	We ought to splít.	You ought to práctice.	Thát ought to do.
7. [wantə]	They want to séll.	We want to begín.	I want to gét one.
8. [wanə]	We want to pláy.	I want to be alóne.	They want to sée it.
9. [gownə]	I'm going to crý.	It's going to snów.	They're going to lóve it.
10. [yuwstə]	You úsed to care.	He used to drínk.	It úsed to fit.

B. Each of the following expressions is often spoken as a single word: *don't know, don't want to, give me, let me, come on*. The *-ing* verb suffix is frequently pronounced [in] rather than [iŋ].

Read across, then down.

1. [downow]	I don't knów.	We don't knów her.	They don't knów about it.
2. [dowanə]	I don't wánt to.	They don't want to gó.	We don't want to dó it.
3. [gimiy]	Give me a hánd.	Give me a chánce.	Give me a bréak.
4. [lemiy]	Let me gó.	Let me át it.	Let me sée.
5. [kəman]	Come on óver.	Come on dówn.	Come on ín.
6. [in]	Nothing dóing.	He's making tróuble.	I'm playing fáir.

Reduced Forms: Review and Rhythm Exercises

In the following sentences, primary stresses are marked ʹ. To maintain sentence rhythm, lightly stress the words marked with a dot (·). Use reduced forms wherever possible.

1. Whåt are you gòing to give him to dó?

2. I don't wånt to have to tèll her what he díd.

3. Whère are her fríends, nòw that she néeds them?

4. It lòoks as if they're plàying for kéeps.

5. Whÿ did you åsk them to còme at eléven?

6. She hås to gìve me an ánswer befòre the ènd of the mónth.

7. Còuldn't he have sènt for some còffee and cáke?

8. Let me sée — I guèss I ought to tåke twò or thrée of them.

9. Whåt did he såy he had to gèt at the stóre?

10. They must have knówn it was from bóth of us.

11. Dòn't you wånt to hèar hòw we ùsed to dó it?

12. Whère will he gó and whåt will he dó?

13. Things are looking úp for óur side.

14. Shòuldn't you have tòld him I was gòing to be thére?

15. I don't knòw if I can cárry more than this.

16. Whåt is his náme, whÿ is he hére, and whò does he wånt to sée?

17. Come ón, nòw, what do you réally think of it?

18. Whère have you been kéeping yoursèlf?

19. We've gòt to sèe her as sòon as póssible.

20. Whò can tèll whát he wòuld have dòne?

ADDITIONAL
CHART EXERCISES

LESSON 98

[w/hw] *in Initial Position*

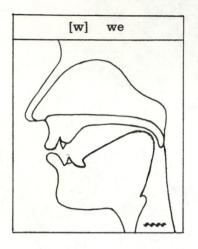

[w] we

Make [w] and [hw] with the lips tightly rounded and the back of the tongue high in the mouth. [w] is voiced. For [hw], blow out a voiceless stream of air before gliding into the following vowel.

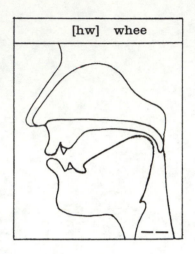

[hw] whee

1) *Read the odd-numbered lines across (1, 3, 5, etc.).*
2) *Read the even-numbered lines across (2, 4, 6, etc.).*
3) *Read vertical pairs across (A1–2, B1–2, etc.).*
4) *Read down each column.*

	A	B	C	D
1.	we	weal	weed	weasel
2.	whee	wheel	wheedle	wheeze
3.	wen	wet	weather	welkin
4.	when	whet	whether	whelk
5.	wetter	went	Wellman	wacky
6.	whetter	whence	whelm	whack
7.	wile	Y	wight	wine
8.	while	why	white	whine
9.	witch	wist	wig	wizard
10.	which	whist	Whig	whizzer
11.	wither	wicker	Winnie	wimple
12.	whither	whicker	whinny	whimper
13.	women	wish	wisp	wit
14.	whim	whish	whisper	whit
15.	were	world	war	warlike
16.	whir	whirled	wharf	whorl
17.	woops	win	wail	way
18.	whoops	whin	whale	whey

174

LESSON 99

[v/w] *in Initial Position*

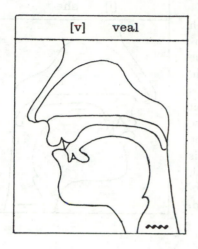

[v]   veal

To make [v], touch the tips of the upper teeth with the lower lip and force out a voiced stream of air. Be sure that the upper and lower lips are not in contact.

To make [w], raise the back of the tongue high in the mouth, round the lips tightly, and make a voiced sound. Be sure that the lower lip does not touch the upper teeth.

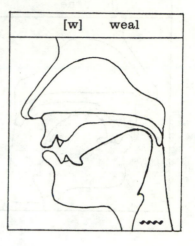

[w]   weal

1) Read the odd-numbered lines across (1, 3, 5, etc.).
2) Read the even-numbered lines across (2, 4, 6, etc.).
3) Read vertical pairs across (A1–2, B1–2, etc.).
4) Read down each column.

	A	B	C	D
1.	veal	veep	venal	visa
2.	weal	weep	wean	weasel
3.	Vic	villa	vista	vim
4.	wick	will	wistful	women
5.	vied	vise	vile	vine
6.	wide	wise	wile	wine
7.	vent	vest	vet	veldt
8.	went	west	wet	welt
9.	verse	vernal	vermin	verdant
10.	worse	Werner	worm	word
11.	vale	vacant	vein	vase
12.	wail	waken	wane	ways
13.	vigor	vicious	vicar	Vince
14.	wigger	wishes	wicker	wince
15.	vegetable	vend	venture	vex
16.	wedge	wend	wench	Wexley
17.	vaccinate	vag	vowed	vault
18.	waxen	wag	wowed	Walt

[h/ʃ] *before* [iy] *and* [i]

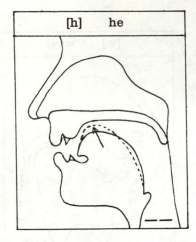

[h]	he

Before [iy] and [i], both [h] and [ʃ] are made with the tongue curved high in front—but there are important differences. For [hiy] and [hi], the tongue tips touch the back of the lower teeth, the jaws are slightly open, and the lips are slightly spread. For [ʃ], the front of the tongue is grooved and very close to the back part of the tooth-ridge; the tongue tip, although turned down, is higher than for [hiy] and does not touch the lower teeth; the jaws are closer together; and the lips are slightly rounded.

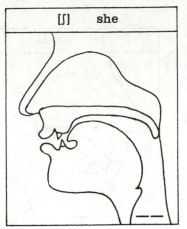

[ʃ]	she

1) *Read the odd-numbered lines across (1, 3, 5, etc.).*
2) *Read the even-numbered lines across (2, 4, 6, etc.).*
3) *Read vertical pairs across (A1–2, B1–2, etc.).*
4) *Read down each column.*

	A	B	C	D
1.	he	he'd	heat	he's
2.	she	she'd	sheet	she's
3.	heak	heap	heave	heath
4.	sheik	sheep	sheave	sheath
5.	healed	Hebrew	heathen	helium
6.	shield	Sheba	sheathe	Sheila
7.	he-men	Healey	heed	heated
8.	she meant	Sheeley	Sheed	sheeted
9.	hip	him	hill	Hingle
10.	ship	shim	shill	shingle
11.	hissed	hickory	hint	hippy
12.	schist	Shickle	shin	shipper
13.	Hindi	Hilary	hick	hilled
14.	shindig	shilling	Schick	shilled

LESSON 101

[t/θ] *in Initial Position*

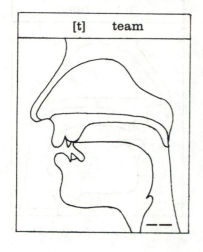

[t]   team

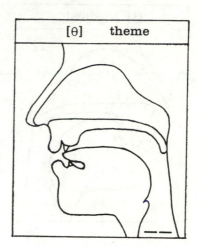

[θ]   theme

To make initial [t], stop the flow of air through the mouth by touching the tooth-ridge with the tip of the tongue; then release the stop with a voiceless puff of air (aspiration).

To make [θ], touch the tips of the upper teeth with the tip of the flattened tongue and force out a voiceless stream of air.

1) Read the odd-numbered lines across (1, 3, 5, etc.).
2) Read the even-numbered lines across (2, 4, 6, etc.).
3) Read vertical pairs across (A1–2, B1–2, etc.).
4) Read down each column.

	A	B	C	D
1.	team	TV	tea	tree
2.	theme	thief	Thea	three
3.	tick	tin	ticket	trill
4.	thick	thin	thicket	thrill
5.	tug	tummy	ton	trust
6.	thug	thumb	thunder	thrust
7.	turbid	terse	term	Tom
8.	Thurber	thirst	thermos	thrombus
9.	tank	tacker	tad	trash
10.	thank	Thackeray	Thad	thrash
11.	tell	Teflon	tie	trice
12.	Thelma	theft	thigh	thrice
13.	teeter	teed	tease	trees
14.	theater	Theda	theism	threes
15.	ting	Tim	tinker	trip
16.	thing	thimble	thinker	Thripp
17.	taught	taller	tore	torn
18.	thought	Thaller	Thor	thorn

LESSON 102

[ʃ/θ] *in Initial Position*

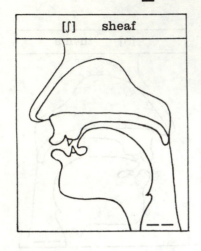

[ʃ] sheaf

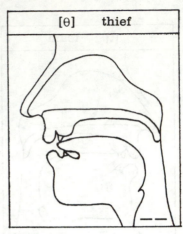

[θ] thief

To make [ʃ], curve the front of the tongue high in the mouth, groove it, and bring it very close to the back part of the tooth-ridge. Keep the tongue tip turned down, and round the lips slightly. Force a voiceless stream of air between the tongue and the back of the tooth-ridge.

To make [θ], touch the tips of the upper teeth with the tip of the flattened tongue and force out a voiceless stream of air.

1) *Read the odd-numbered lines across (1, 3, 5, etc.).*
2) *Read the even-numbered lines across (2, 4, 6, etc.).*
3) *Read vertical pairs across (A1–2, B1–2, etc.).*
4) *Read down each column.*

	A	B	C	D
1.	she	Sheed	sheaves	sheaf
2.	Thea	Theda	thieves	thief
3.	shore	shorn	short	Schwartz
4.	Thor	thorn	Thornton	thwarts
5.	shad	shall	shank	shack
6.	Thad	thallic	thank	Thackeray
7.	Schick	shin	shrift	shill
8.	thick	thin	thrift	thill
9.	Shaw	show	shoal	shrove
10.	thaw	Thoden	thole	throve
11.	Sherman	sherbet	shirt	shirred
12.	Thurman	Thurber	thirty	third
13.	shell	chef	shred	Shetland
14.	Thelma	theft	thread	threaten
15.	shy	shrive	shrill	shrink
16.	thigh	thrive	thrill	think
17.	shrug	shudder	Shane	Shay
18.	thug	thud	thane	Thayer

178

LESSON 103

[ʃ/ʒ] *in Medial Position*

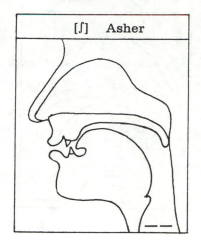

[ʃ] Asher

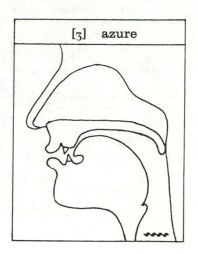

[ʒ] azure

To make [ʃ] and [ʒ], curve the front of the tongue high in the mouth, groove it, and bring it very close to the back part of the tooth-ridge. Keep the tongue tip turned down, and round the lips slightly. Force a stream of air—voiceless for [ʃ], voiced for [ʒ]—between the tongue and the back of the tooth-ridge.

1) Read the odd-numbered lines across (1, 3, 5, etc.).
2) Read the even-numbered lines across (2, 4, 6, etc.).
3) Read vertical pairs across (A1–2, B1–2, etc.).
4) Read down each column.

	A	B	C	D
1.	erasure	glacier	innovation	Haitian
2.	Eurasia	glazier	invasion	Asian
3.	Lucian	fuchsia	ablution	crucial
4.	illusion	fusion	occlusion	usual
5.	Tahitian	Grecian	seashore	Alicia
6.	cohesion	Parisian	seizure	leisure
7.	lotion	kosher	potion	ocean
8.	explosion	closure	exposure	erosion
9.	racial	nation	vocation	station
10.	abrasion	equation	occasion	Anastasia
11.	mesher	pressure	flesher	vicious
12.	measure	treasure	pleasure	visual
13.	Asher	cashing	Confucian	Aleutian
14.	azure	casual	confusion	allusion

[z/ʒ] *in Medial and Final Positions*

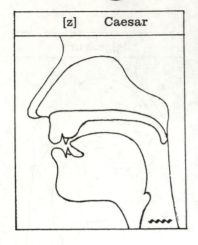

[z]　Caesar

To make [z], place the tip of the tongue very close to the front part of the tooth-ridge, just behind (but not touching) the upper teeth. Groove the front of the tongue and force a voiced stream of air between tongue tip and tooth-ridge.

To make [ʒ], curve the front of the tongue high in the mouth, groove it, and bring it very close to the back part of the tooth-ridge. Keep the tongue tip turned down, and round the lips slightly. Force a voiced stream of air between the tongue and the back of the tooth-ridge.

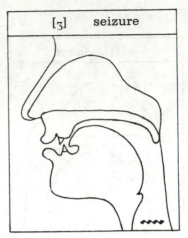

[ʒ]　seizure

1) *Read the odd-numbered lines across (1, 3, 5, etc.).*
2) *Read the even-numbered lines across (2, 4, 6, etc.).*
3) *Read vertical pairs across (A1–2, B1–2, etc.).*
4) *Read down each column.*

	A	B	C	D
1.	reason	pleasing	Caesar	easer
2.	Parisian	lesion	seizure	leisure
3.	phase	vase	hazing	raisin
4.	aphasia	invasion	Asian	Eurasian
5.	whose	ruse	losing	oozing
6.	Hoosier	rouge	illusion	contusion
7.	closing	poser	Rosen	hosing
8.	closure	exposure	erosion	hosiery
9.	purrs	curs	avers	incurs
10.	Persian	excursion	aversion	incursion
11.	using	fusing	user	diffusing
12.	usual	fusion	usury	diffusion
13.	lazy	brazen	gazer	razor
14.	Malaysia	abrasion	glazier	Frazier
15.	visit	scissors	risen	lizard
16.	vision	incision	derision	collision
17.	pleasant	resin	mezzanine	cruising
18.	pleasure	treasure	measuring	inclusion

[kit/kt] *in Final Position*

In pronouncing final [kt], do not insert a vowel between [k] and [t]. *Packed* [pækt] has the [k] unreleased, the [t] released. Contrast this with *pack it* [pækit] which has the [k] released, the [t] unreleased.

1) *Read the odd-numbered lines across (1, 3, 5, etc.).*
2) *Read the even-numbered lines across (2, 4, 6, etc.).*
3) *Read vertical pairs across (A1–2, B1–2, etc.).*
4) *Read down each column.*

	A	B	C	D
1.	flick it	ticket	trick it	picket
2.	afflict	ticked	strict	depict
3.	track it	packet	bracket	tack it
4.	tract	pact	bract	tact
5.	bucket	struck it	tuck it	ducat
6.	bucked	instruct	tucked	duct
7.	poke it	choke it	soak it	smoke it
8.	poked	choked	soaked	smoked
9.	hock it	dock it	mock it	knock it
10.	hocked	docked	mocked	knocked
11.	stake it	rake it	fake it	bake it
12.	staked	raked	faked	baked
13.	eke it	sneak it	tweak it	leak it
14.	eked	sneaked	tweaked	leaked
15.	like it	hike it	bike it	spike it
16.	liked	hiked	biked	spiked
17.	peck it	fleck it	check it	wreck it
18.	respect	deflect	checked	wrecked

[tʃ/dʒ] *in Initial Position*

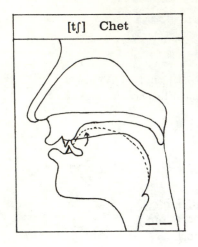

[tʃ] Chet

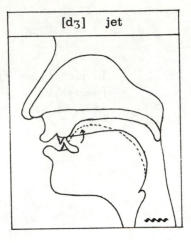

[dʒ] jet

To make [tʃ] and [dʒ], first touch the tooth-ridge with the tip of the tongue. Then release the stopped air by shifting to [ʃ/ʒ] position—curving the front of the tongue high in the mouth, grooving it, and bringing it very close to the back part of the tooth-ridge. The air stream is voiceless for [tʃ], voiced for [dʒ].

1) *Read the odd-numbered lines across (1, 3, 5, etc.).*
2) *Read the even-numbered lines across (2, 4, 6, etc.).*
3) *Read vertical pairs across (A1–2, B1–2, etc.).*
4) *Read down each column.*

	A	B	C	D
1.	Chet	chess	cheddar	chest
2.	jet	Jess	Jed	jest
3.	chin	chip	chigger	chill
4.	gin	gyp	jigger	Jill
5.	chap	chaff	Chan	champ
6.	jab	Jaffee	Jan	jam
7.	cheese	cheater	cheap	chino
8.	G's	Jeeter	jeep	Jean
9.	chase	chain	chambers	chafe
10.	Jason	Jane	James	jay
11.	chug	chump	chunk	chutney
12.	jug	jump	junk	jut
13.	chew	chuba	choosy	chewed
14.	Jew	jubilee	juicy	judo
15.	choke	chose	chaw	Chauncey
16.	joke	Joe's	jaw	jaunt
17.	chive	child	churning	chirk
18.	jive	Giles	journey	jerk

[tʃ/dʒ] *in Final Position*

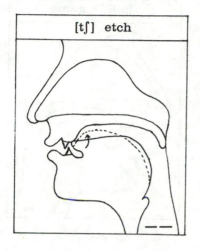

[tʃ] etch

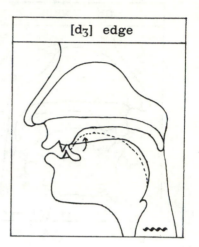

[dʒ] edge

Make [tʃ] and [dʒ] as practiced on the preceding page. Be careful not to add a vowel to final [dʒ]: *edge* is [edʒ], not [edʒi]. Instead, let the voiced [dʒ] fade into voiceless [ʃ].

1) *Read the odd-numbered lines across (1, 3, 5, etc.).*
2) *Read the even-numbered lines across (2, 4, 6, etc.).*
3) *Read vertical pairs across (A1–2, B1–2, etc.).*
4) *Read down each column.*

	A	**B**	**C**	**D**
1.	etch	ketch	letch	fletch
2.	edge	kedge	ledge	fledge
3.	perch	search	smirch	birch
4.	purge	surge	merge	urge
5.	Mitch	rich	twitch	pinch
6.	Midge	ridge	twinge	impinge
7.	lunch	punch	crutch	much
8.	lunge	plunge	grudge	smudge
9.	catch	match	batch	H
10.	cadge	Madge	badge	age
11.	starch	larch	march	blotch
12.	sarge	large	Marge	lodge
13.	hitch	bitch	cinch	inch
14.	hinge	binge	singe	tinge
15.	wench	touch	Dutch	such
16.	wedge	trudge	drudge	sludge

LESSON 108

[n/m] *in Final Position*

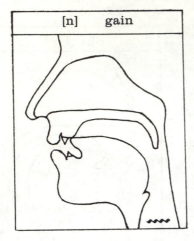

[n] gain

Both [n] and [m] are nasal sounds: the voiced air stream is stopped in the mouth but escapes through the nose.

To make [n], touch the tooth-ridge with the tip of the tongue; do not close the lips.

To make [m], touch the lips together.

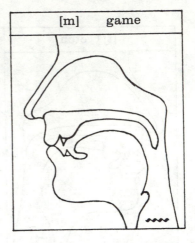

[m] game

1) Read the odd-numbered lines across (1, 3, 5, etc.).
2) Read the even-numbered lines across (2, 4, 6, etc.).
3) Read vertical pairs across (A1–2, B1–2, etc.).
4) Read down each column.

	A	B	C	D	E
1.	gain	Shane	sane	cane	feign
2.	game	shame	same	came	fame
3.	bean	seen	dean	teen	glean
4.	beam	seem	deem	team	gleam
5.	line	dine	Klein	Rhine	tine
6.	lime	dime	climb	rhyme	time
7.	own	cone	phone	lone	hone
8.	ohm	comb	foam	loam	home
9.	rune	loon	boon	soon	dune
10.	room	loom	boom	assume	doom
11.	din	grin	tin	gin	skin
12.	dim	grim	Tim	Jim	skim
13.	en	then	hen	sten	Jen
14.	em	them	hem	stem	gem
15.	son	bun	gun	done	run
16.	some	bum	gum	dumb	rum
17.	fern	turn	spurn	warn	adorn
18.	firm	term	sperm	warm	dorm

LESSON 109

[g/ŋ] *in Final Position*

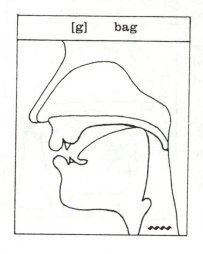

[g]   bag

To make final [g], keep the nasal passage closed and stop the flow of air through the mouth by touching the velum with the back of the tongue. The contact must be voiced. Do not release the stop—end the sound before breaking the contact.

To make [ŋ], touch the velum with the back of the tongue and let the voiced air stream escape through the open nasal passage. Be careful not to add [g] to final [ŋ]: *tongue* is [tʌŋ], not [tʌŋg].

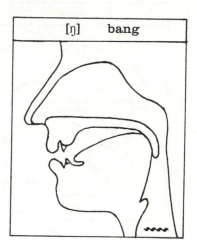

[ŋ]   bang

1) *Read the odd-numbered lines across (1, 3, 5, etc.).*
2) *Read the even-numbered lines across (2, 4, 6, etc.).*
3) *Read vertical pairs across (A1–2, B1–2, etc.).*
4) *Read down each column.*

	A	B	C	D
1.	bag	gag	lag	sag
2.	bang	gang	Lang	sang
3.	wig	sprig	rig	pig
4.	wing	spring	ring	ping
5.	rug	dug	bug	lug
6.	rung	dung	bung	lung
7.	slag	hag	tag	rag
8.	slang	hang	tang	rang
9.	dig	big	swig	zig
10.	ding	bing	swing	zing
11.	hug	slug	mug	tug
12.	hung	slung	among	tongue
13.	brig	trig	fag	stag
14.	bring	string	fang	mustang
15.	cog	fog	agog	bog
16.	Kong	Fong	gong	bong

185

LESSON 110

[ŋ/ŋg] *in Medial Position*

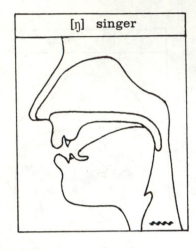

[ŋ] singer

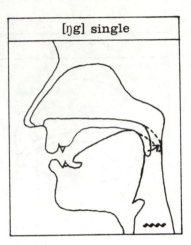

[ŋg] single

To make [ŋ], touch the velum with the back of the tongue and let the voiced air stream escape through the open nasal passage.

To make [ŋg], first make [ŋ]; then close the nasal passage to make [g], breaking the tongue-velum contact with a slight voiced explosion.

1) Read the odd-numbered lines across (1, 3, 5, etc.).
2) Read the even-numbered lines across (2, 4, 6, etc.).
3) Read vertical pairs across (A1–2, B1–2, etc.).
4) Read down each column.

	A	B	C	D	E
1.	flinger	singer	clinger	stinger	bringer
2.	finger	single	linger	tingle	bingo
3.	banger	Sanger	tangy	clangor	angstrom
4.	bangle	anger	tangle	kangaroo	angle
5.	Longacre	wronger	dinghy	tungsten	youngish
6.	longer	stronger	dingle	hunger	younger

[ŋ] before the [iŋ] Suffix

Read across each line, then down each column.
(Be careful not to pronounce a [g] before the [iŋ] ending.)

1.	stringing	ringing	pinging	springing
2.	clanging	panging	ganging	banging
3.	winging	clinging	stinging	flinging
4.	hanging	twanging	longing	wronging
5.	singing	slinging	bringing	swinging

186

Final [s/z] *after Vowels*

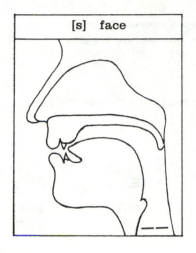

[s] face

To make [s] and [z], place the tip of the tongue very close to the front part of the tooth-ridge, just behind (but not touching) the upper teeth. Groove the front of the tongue and force a stream of air—voiceless for [s], voiced for [z] —between tongue tip and tooth-ridge.

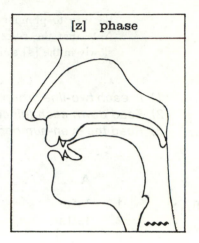

[z] phase

1) Read the odd-numbered lines across (1, 3, 5, etc.).
2) Read the even-numbered lines across (2, 4, 6, etc.).
3) Read vertical pairs across (A1–2, B1–2, etc.).
4) Read down each column.

	A	B	C	D
1.	face	lace	mace	race
2.	phase	laze	maize	raise
3.	lease	cease	peace	niece
4.	lees	seize	peas	knees
5.	ice	rice	lice	dice
6.	eyes	rise	lies	dies
7.	deuce	juice	Bruce	loose
8.	dues	Jews	bruise	lose
9.	base	space	case	pace
10.	bays	spays	cays	pays
11.	gross	dose	fuss	bus
12.	grows	doze	fuzz	buzz
13.	moss	cross	loss	sauce
14.	maws	craws	laws	saws
15.	entice	Weiss	vice	mice
16.	ties	wise	vise	demise
17.	place	brace	trace	grace
18.	plays	braise	trays	graze

187

The [s] Suffix in Final Clusters

Be sure to pronounce [s] when it appears as a suffix following a consonant cluster. Note that the voiceless stops [k p t] are not exploded before [s], but are released slowly in the [s] sound itself.

1) In each two-line group, read vertical pairs across (A1–2, B1–2, etc.), then the second line.
2) Read down each full column.
3) Read the even-numbered lines (2, 4, 6, etc.).

		A	B	C	D	E	F
[ft/fts]:	1.	left	heft	cleft	rift	sift	gift
	2.	lefts	hefts	clefts	rifts	sifts	gifts
	3.	shaft	craft	draft	Luft	tuft	loft
	4.	shafts	crafts	drafts	Luft's	tufts	lofts
[kt/kts]:	5.	act	fact	tract	sect	expect	effect
	6.	acts	facts	tracts	sects	expects	effects
	7.	duct	instruct	conduct	evict	inflict	depict
	8.	ducts	instructs	conducts	evicts	inflicts	depicts
[st/sts]:	9.	cast	last	mast	best	guest	rest
	10.	casts	lasts	masts	bests	guests	rests
	11.	fist	wrist	gist	dust	trust	cost
	12.	fists	wrists	gists	dusts	trusts	costs
[sk/sks]:	13.	ask	bask	mask	disc	risk	whisk
	14.	asks	basks	masks	discs	risks	whisks
	15.	husk	tusk	Rusk	mosque	desk	grotesque
	16.	husks	tusks	Rusk's	mosques	desks	grotesques
[sp/sps]:	17.	asp	grasp	clasp	lisp	wisp	crisp
	18.	asps	grasps	clasps	lisps	wisps	crisps
	19.	cusp	wasp	rasp	hasp	gasp	unclasp
	20.	cusps	wasps	rasps	hasps	gasps	unclasps